Native American Folklore, Activities, and Foods

A collection from Cobblestone publications of
histories and introductions;
stories, legends, poems, word lore, and folktales;
projects; activities and games;
and recipes of Native American peoples

edited by E. Barrie Kavasch

Cobblestone Publishing, Inc. 7 School Street Peterborough, NH 03458

Dedicated to all children

Copy-edited by Barbara Jatkola
Index by Anne Harbour
Design and page layout by C. Porter Designs, Fitzwilliam, New Hampshire
Cover illustration by Beth Krommes
Interior illustrations:
Part I and Part IV by Chris Wold Dyrud
Part II by Tim Foley
Part III and Part V by Joyce Audy Zarins
Map by Coni Porter
Icons from *North American Indian Designs*
by Madeleine Orban-Szontagh (Dover Publications, 1993) and
American Indian Design & Decoration by LeRoy H. Appleton (Dover Publications, 1971)
Copy input by Jane Gallagher Hooper
Printing and binding by Quebecor Printing Book Group

Manufactured in the United States of America
ISBN 0-942389-09-3

Earthmaker,
help us to cherish these gifts that surround us
and to share our blessings with our brothers and our sisters
so that our world is continually blessed.

*E*arthmaker's Lodge symbolically embraces North America in the relaxed, informative ways traditional to our tribal storytelling. American Indians, Eskimos, Aleuts, and Hawaiians each have distinctive origination stories (legends of how they began). Stories are valuable links between our surroundings, our imaginations, and our creative understandings. Earthmaker, the Creator of earth and sky and of all the inhabitants of our world as we know it, comes from the Winnebago, Osage, Cherokee, and Pima Indian traditions. Some native peoples recall, through their stories, how they were originally made by Earthmaker. Others recall the Creator as Spider Woman (Hopi), the Great Medicine (Cheyenne), the Creator and Changer (Snohomish), Tabaldak (Abenaki), Gitchee Manitou/Great Spirit (Anishinabé), Ha-Wen-Neyu/Creator (Iroquois), or Wakan Tanka/Tunka-Shila/Creator (Lakota Sioux).

The lodge is where we are right now, and also the earth and sky. The stories inform our caring and sharing of nature, the creative arts, writing, social studies, the sciences, and our own sensory awareness, as this book is designed to do for ages eight and up. A great portion of the material is from *COBBLESTONE* and *FACES* magazines and some of it from *ODYSSEY* magazine. Our interdisciplinary approach is enriched with the emphasis on Native American cultures and their awareness of everything that makes up our natural and spiritual worlds.

Stories, Dreams, and Spiritual Objects

Dreams are a central theme of this book, as they are in much of Native American life. We all dream, yet how many of us have made a dream catcher or kept a dream journal? Here we can do this together, easily. Everyone loves stories, and now you can make your own story bag and learn about the Eskimo story knife, which fathers or uncles made for their young daughters or nieces.

Storytelling and dreams interweave the spiritual realm with our everyday world and broaden us in many special ways. The Iroquois Husk Face Society had a special Dream Guessing Mask and rites devoted to guessing members' dreams. Dream amulets (good-luck objects), dream catchers, and dreamtime were important parts of many tribes' ways of life and some of their ceremonial practices. Many aspects of the Native American spiritual world are closed to outsiders. Sensitive to this, we appreciate what can be shared openly.

People, Places, and Legends

We go deeply into North American regions to visit many native peoples and listen to their legends and histories. The few select Native American stories included here explore the concepts of ancient times and how people, plants, and animals came to be. These stories also test relationships and understandings

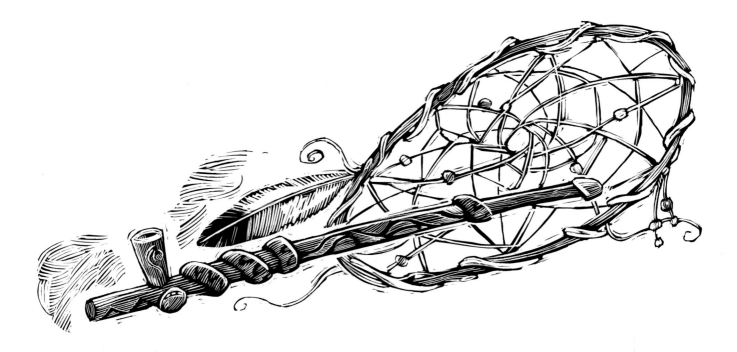

between people and animals, right and wrong, and fun and duty/responsibilities. Stories have always been powerful, beautiful teaching tools.

Native American words and place names fill the English language. We regularly use Native American words adapted from countless tribal dialects. Half of our U.S. states and many of our rivers have Indian names. The Word Lore features will give you some idea of how many Native American words we use every day.

Projects and Crafts

Enjoy the quiet creativity of making an Akwesasne star, Cherokee place mats, or cornhusk dolls. Design your own story beads or beadwork rosette. "Reaching for Your Roots" is a special activity designed to help you interview your family and relatives and find out more about your background and personal history. You also can make an Eskimo drum, a Plains Indian parfleche, Pueblo clay storyteller dolls, or a Navajo sand painting.

Puzzles and Games

Games of chance and skill have always challenged Native Americans. The Iroquois sacred bowl game and the Cherokee basket game remind us that most Native Americans have long had a love of gaming. Imagination and resourcefulness are keys to Native American games. The ancient game of Chunkey, Plains Indian corncob darts, and the Northwest Coast frog race help to expand our understanding of Indian cultures.

Recipes

The recipes in this book are contemporary selections from different regions of North America. They include "soul foods," ceremonial foods, trail foods, seasonal offerings, and farm and garden fare. Foods are fun. They also are vital cultural threads that tie us together. Food is our common language — a delicious teaching tool, nurturing our bodies, minds, and spirits. Many native peoples give thanks for food every day, and especially at important ceremonial times of thanksgiving. Some make a small "spirit plate," filled first from the table before everyone eats together. Many Native American peoples create an altar containing their most respected foods and fine objects in the room where their food is served and eaten. This altar is a way of thanking the Creator (Earthmaker), who has provided the food. Our modern Thanksgiving Day has evolved from these traditions, which are still actively honored.

> ### *"God told me to come back and tell my people they must be good and love one another, and not fight, or steal, or lie. He gave me this dance to give my people."*
>
> *Wovoka, Paiute medicine man,*
> *after his ghost dance vision during a solar eclipse in 1889*

Bows and arrows, war paint, and tomahawks have dominated most people's impressions of American Indians, even in contemporary times. Often movies, television, and books have shaped these stereotypes of the cultures and customs of American Indians. Unfortunately, these stereotypes have very little to do with what the culture is. As a member of the Southern Cheyenne tribe, I know the beautiful stories, beliefs, foods, and crafts that make up part of our many cultures — cultures that have survived for centuries. These living cultures have been passed down from grandparent to grandchild for many thousands of years. Some of these cultures are included in the pages that follow. As a contemporary member of one of these living cultures, it is my great honor and pleasure to introduce you to the ways of my people.

Stories make up a large part of American Indian traditions. They have been passed on orally for generations. Stories provide answers to questions about creation. They offer an entertaining way to pass on beliefs and values to children, educating them about their culture and people. They record historical events to be shared with grandchildren and great-grandchildren. *Earthmaker's Lodge* presents the many stories important to a variety of tribes and allows the reader to share in the lessons these stories try to teach.

History comprises a chain of events that unite to mold today and construct tomorrow. The history of American Indians is a building block not only for contemporary Native Americans but for all Americans. This book details the history of the many tribes to help you understand "Indian Country" as it is today, as well as its role within the United States.

The crafts, games, and foods presented here are physical evidence of the customs and cultures of American Indians that have been passed down and exist for us today. They provide a way for everyone to share in the gifts that have been left to us by our many generations of elders. As you participate in the activities in this book, know that you are sharing in the experiences of American Indian children of centuries past and present.

The cultures of American Indians are rich in variety, spanning the entire spectrum of art and culture as defined by European thinking. This book provides an extensive sample of the stories, crafts, foods, and games that are known and shared among the different tribes. It draws on the variety of the tribes and allows for comparison among them. At the same time, this book shows the interrelationship of all tribes and exhibits their similarities. *Earthmaker's Lodge* allows the reader to share in the beliefs and practices of American Indians and demonstrates how these beliefs and practices relate to everyone's life today.

Earthmaker's Lodge is an excellent means for sharing the vibrant customs and cultures of American Indians with all people. By presenting the history, stories, and many foods and crafts of American Indians, this book shares the gifts of Indian peoples and opens the doors to their worlds. I ask that you read this book with an open mind, remembering that American Indian cultures are living cultures with a dynamic past, an active present, and a promising future.

W. Richard West, Jr.
Director, National Museum of the American Indian,
Smithsonian Institution

Contents

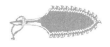

Part III   Projects and Crafts

Part IV   Puzzles and Games

Part V Recipes

Native American Tribes

by E. Barrie Kavasch

There are more than five hundred federally recognized tribes in the United States, including some two hundred Alaskan native villages and groups and Hawaiian Islanders, located on approximately three hundred federal Indian reservations. Many additional tribes, groups, and reservations, most of them east of the Mississippi River, do not have federal recognition.

An Indian reservation is an area of land specifically reserved for Indian use. The term comes from the early period of Indian settlement history in North America, when tribes relinquished land through various treaties, reserving a portion for their specific use.

Originally, the term "tribe" referred to a body of people bound together by blood relationships, occupying a definite territory, and speaking a common language or dialect. A tribe also is socially, religiously, and politically linked together. Through time, "tribe" has come to have additional meanings. Today the term can mean a distinct group within a village, series of communities, or tribal nation, as well as a widely scattered group of people, villages, or communities with a common heritage, and possibly a common language, but not necessarily a tribal government.

Native American men and women were the first leaders on this continent. Some of their leadership concepts helped shape the foundations of the U.S. and Canadian governments. In most tribes, women are equal to men. Among the Iroquois, for example, women choose the men who will be the leaders and chiefs. In many tribes, women own the dwellings, many family possessions, and the fields and gardens. Children often trace their descent through their mother's clan. Many women are tribal leaders. They have historically been referred to as "squaw sachems" and "sunksquaws," terms of great respect.

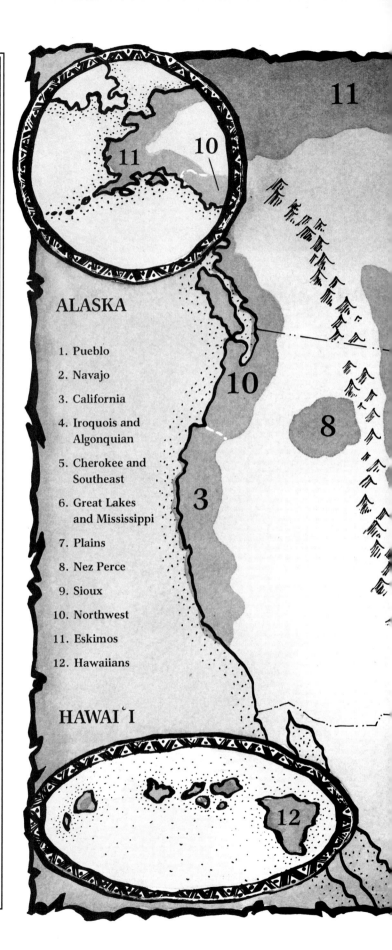

ALASKA

1. Pueblo
2. Navajo
3. California
4. Iroquois and Algonquian
5. Cherokee and Southeast
6. Great Lakes and Mississippi
7. Plains
8. Nez Perce
9. Sioux
10. Northwest
11. Eskimos
12. Hawaiians

HAWAI‘I

11

This map looks at
tribal/cultural group
placement in the early
1800s to present.
Although everything has
changed, many native
descendants still live in or
near their origin points.
These groups frequently
overlapped and still do.
Placement of the broad,
general cultural areas —
well spoken to in this
book — allows easy refer-
ence. Refer to National
Geographic and
Smithsonian Institution
Native American maps
for the latest details.

less-strict dividing lines where
people crossed in many ways

Missouri R.

Mississippi R.

Ohio R.

Stories, Dreams,

Stories, dreams, and spiritual objects enlarge our understanding of the spiritual realms of Native American life. These are very important areas, each with its own vital energies, and they add great dimension to the practical, everyday world of countless peoples. A sense of fun is usually woven into the serious side of life, and dreams often show us this in fantastic ways. Share these wonderful ways of learning; stories, dreams, and spiritual objects are avenues of understanding more about ourselves.

STORYTELLING

by E. Barrie Kavasch

One of the oldest forms of human teaching and entertainment is storytelling. Stories recall an ancient past brought close to us at the point of telling, and later when we remember and retell the stories. Each time a story is told, it changes through the unique abilities of the storyteller. That way, it never gets stale. Stories are gathered together in a story bag or basket or in a storyteller's memory. Some native storytellers have special story aids that can trick the story out.

Think about the most important stories in your life. Each of us has favorites. Who are your favorite storytellers? My grandmother, mother, and some of my aunts and uncles top my list of special storytellers. I can still hear their wonderful voices, the tone and emphasis of certain words, as they held my attention with bizarre tales of hunting for snipe in Tennessee pastures, listening for bears in Ohio caverns, or chasing ghosts through the lush hills and cotton fields of Alabama. My cousin Verlon Ferguson, age eighty-five, is our family historian and storyteller.

Stories weave us together. They

and *S*piritual *O*bjects

are the spiritual glue of our culture and the collective consciousness of our people. The best stories blend history, imagination, and values into memorable forms.

Storytelling cycles and epic traditions strengthen our Native American traditions. Some center on long-standing social and political conflicts, our beginnings, and the world as we know it. Origination stories are central to American Indian wisdom, and most tribes have their own distinctive versions. Many stories begin like this: "The world did not always exist as we know it today..." or "In a time much earlier...."

Stories come out of the earth, and animals, plants, mountains, and rivers are woven through stories into the human realm. Stories flow with rhythms of the natural and supernatural worlds, spun richly with human form and imagination. "Indian time" shapes these mysteries into practical forms. Oral traditions continue to be the magnetic reference points for new generations of Native American storytellers. As storytellers give some of these precious gifts to listeners and readers, each person takes the gifts and in turn becomes a storyteller.

Native American stories vary with our country's changing geography, climate, ways of life, and foods. Each culture has a different feel for itself, and each, having traveled and traded, relates many interesting cultural exchanges in its stories.

White Buffalo Woman is the holy woman (first a sacred white buffalo, then White Buffalo Woman, and

"We Indians live in a world of symbols where the spiritual and the commonplace are one."

John Lame Deer, Miniconjou Sioux

---

eventually a white buffalo again) who brought the sacred pipe to the Sioux. After this event, the Sioux learned how to live and develop their traditions. The Iroquois relate the story of Sky Woman, who fell down through a hole in the Sky World into the unformed watery world below. She was saved from drowning by the water birds, and Turtle and the other animals hurried to help. They created Turtle Island, which became North America as we know it. Some Northwest Coast peoples tell of descending to earth through a smoke hole in the sky. Others believe that they were created by Raven, and some say that they emerged from a giant clamshell.

Some Pueblo peoples of the Southwest recall that their earliest ancestors emerged from the underworld at the point called Cipapu. Four worlds, each different in colors, elements, and problems, were stacked upon each other. The people climbed a plant stalk through a hole in each world, escaping one dying world to be born fresh in the next. The Hopi believe that they are currently living in their fourth world.

Human creation stories reflect native peoples' close attachment to the natural world. The Cherokee and some Great Lakes tribes recall their creation by the Great Sun; the Sioux and Ojibway credit the Great Mystery with giving their people early form. Glooscap is the creative power in countless Algonquian stories. He shaped the landscape, tamed the wind, found water and food for the people, and settled disputes among the animals and people. Earthmaker is the creator of everything in the world for other tribes.

Pueblo Corn Maidens brought the knowledge of corn (maize) and early planting ceremonies to the people, inventing basketry and pottery in close association with gardening. Changing Woman, Turquoise Woman, and White Shell Woman are legendary Navajo heroines associated with many life needs. Little Sister called the buffalo and fed the Cheyenne.

The Little People brought sacred ceremonies and healing to the Iroquois and taught them annual rites that are carried on from generation to generation. Many Native

Make a Story Bag

by E. Barrie Kavasch

Many Native American story-tellers have their own story baskets or bags. Baskets can take many different forms, from traditional curly baskets made from black ash splints among the northeastern tribes, to brightly colored plaited cane southeastern Indian baskets, to simple woven pack baskets trimmed in special tribal styles. Most are decorated according to the taste of a particular storyteller, with feathers, shells, leather ties, and bits of animal fur to jog his or her memories about special tales and stories.

Story bags also are artistic creations. Some are made of buckskin or calico to match the storyteller's attire.

The most fascinating part of any story basket or bag is the contents. A basket or bag may contain any number of items, such as shells, wild mushrooms, a feather, plant roots, a storyteller doll wrapped in red flannel, a pottery bear wrapped in a rabbit skin, or a tiny strawberry or alligator basket. The contents are limited only by the storyteller's imagination and the size of the container.

To make a story bag, take a large brown paper bag and draw pictures, symbols, and designs on it. Also put your name on it, unless you are making it for someone else. Then begin collecting tiny symbols of

American tribes embrace stories of the Little People, usually portrayed as informative supernatural beings rarely seen by humans except at times of great need. They especially appeared to children to help them.

Bella Coola creation stories describe the fierce Bear of Heaven guarding the place of Sunrise. In most native stories, Father Sun gave life to all creation on Mother Earth. Yet among the Yuchi, Cherokee, and Eskimos, the sun is considered female and the moon her little brother. Many legends tell of women and men becoming morning and evening stars. Groups of village children and certain animals dance, climb, or are chased into the night sky to become key constellations. The Navajo envision the spirits of their dead traveling across the Milky Way (the Great Sky Belt) to the Dance Hall of the Dead.

Stories relating a reverence for life on all levels are offset by trickster tales and flights of humor and imagination. Grandmother Spider is a beloved and highly valued creative

source of knowledge, as is Raven. But Raven also can be a trickster. Iktomi (or Iktome), the legendary spider of Plains Indian mythology, is often a trickster with many negative and humorous qualities. Trickster Coyote plays wickedly in countless native stories and certainly is the ultimate survivor.

The Great White Rabbit runs through Algonquian mythology, and as the human Manabozho, he helped found the Grand Medicine Lodge of the Midé. This is a common theme of many native stories, where animals often change into human form.

Some western tribal stories tell of people's evolution from the four winds. The winds are pinpointed as the cardinal points blessed in sacred prayers. There seems to be a story for every aspect of life and the world, and each has many things to teach us. The rich fabric and jewels of Native American stories are living traditions that continue to bless us, even as new stories are created and grow into being.

your favorite stories. Take your time and select things with care. Some storytellers spend a lifetime filling their story bags.

As you read the stories in this book, draw the characters that are most special to you on a piece of oak tag. Cut them out and put them in your story bag. Remember, a story bag is filled with story aids — items that jog the storyteller's memory.

When you are ready to tell some stories, gather your friends and family around you. Before you begin, open your story bag and let the youngest guest reach inside and pick out the first "story."

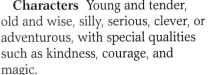

Recipe for a Story

by David Novak

For a basic story, you need some or all of the following ingredients.

Knowledge About the places, people, and times of your story. You can get this from experience, from your library, or from asking questions.

Characters Young and tender, old and wise, silly, serious, clever, or adventurous, with special qualities such as kindness, courage, and magic.

Setting(s) One or more places you can describe to make a world for your story. You'll need sights, sounds, moods, and feelings.

Trouble A conflict to fire up your story. Natural disasters, such as storms, earthquakes, cold, and heat. Human troublemakers, such as villains and fools. Supernatural beings, such as giants and wizards. Anything that can get in the way of your characters.

Changes A change of shape, such as growing up or growing wings. A change of mind, a change of way, a change of heart. A new day, a new home, a lesson learned.

Imagination To feel what your character feels, to see what there is to see, to make the impossible possible and the unlikely likely.

Spices Emotions, actions, moods, surprises, observations, and explanations to add flavor and keep your story interesting.

Begin: Mix and Blend

1. Drawing on your knowledge, describe the setting and characters you will use in your story. Give us a chance to know them and the world in which they live.

2. Use some of your spices to add flavor to the beginning. Develop a mood and explain the situation.

Midway: Preheat and Cook

3. Introduce the trouble, selecting one or more conflicts to force action into the lives of your characters. (You may add as many conflicts as you like, but too many will confuse the story.) The trouble may be large or small. The greater the trouble, the greater the story.

4. Use more of your spices: surprises and emotions. Let your characters get into action, using their special qualities or talents to solve their problems.

5. You may wish to change settings at this point, to keep your story fresh.

Last: Cool and Add Finishing Touches

6. Take the story out of the trouble. Describe the changes that have happened as a result of the trouble.

7. Let the entire story cool in your imagination. Add details and spices throughout.

8. Wrap up your story neatly. Watch out for loose ends (anything you started but did not finish). To do this, you may have to cut out parts that don't fit anymore. This is called *editing*.

I prefer to tell my stories before I write them down. After all, we learn how to talk before we learn how to write, so we're usually better at talking. Besides, telling your story to someone is a good way to cook it up. As you tell it, notice what makes people laugh, cry, or yawn. This will help you when you sit down alone to write it on paper.

DREAMS

by E. Barrie Kavasch

American Indian people believed that their souls could journey to other worlds and different realms of understanding in their dreams. Some even believed that their dream landscapes were more real than the waking world. Great value was given to subconscious states. Patterns, colors, and designs for ceremonial clothing and ritual objects came through dreams. Important elements of the ghost dance religion and sun dance ceremonies were received in dreams. Dream guessing was an important part of the Iroquois Midwinter ceremony. Indian healers often would receive curing rituals, songs, and specific plant uses in their dreams.

Dream incubation was practiced when a person seeking special knowledge concentrated on this goal and went to sleep in a chosen place of noted energy. Sometimes many nights passed before the requested details came through a dream. Occasionally, a series of dreams in one night or over the course of several nights would reveal the information. Medicine people and tribal leaders were consulted about special dreams. Children's dreams were given special significance, as children often received songs in their dreams to be sung at special times.

The vision quest was a ritual to induce spiritual dreams with symbolic animal totems as guardians to help shape one's life path. This was a central part of an American Indian's passage from childhood to adulthood. The child was prepared for this ritual over time so that success would come through fasting, prayers, and days spent alone in a remote, carefully chosen place. Today American Indian children are still guided on the vision path, much as their parents and grandparents were.

Indian men and women who received spiritual gifts of healing and insight during a vision quest might return to the same holy place throughout their lives, each time traveling ever deeper into their rich spiritual world. The Black Hills and Bear Butte in South Dakota were considered such holy places. Many other places throughout the United States, from the Grand Canyon to the Northwest Coast to Manhattan Island, were considered to have spiritual power.

Native people believed that during dreamtime, one could journey into the supernatural world, talk to the ancestors, and seek greater wisdom. They might even learn lost details of the past, and some could see into the future. Dreams also were ordinary excursions into good humor and fun. Most of all, dreams were respected and cultivated.

We all dream every night. Some of us can easily recall our dreams. Others need to train themselves to do so. Most artists, writers, and scientists know that dreams are fertile fields of inspiration. Sometimes, through dream incubation, we can work out problems that we cannot readily solve in our waking lives.

Everyday dreams hold important keys to understanding ourselves and our place within our family, group, and society. The following fragments from an Ammassalik Eskimo dream song give some evidence of how dreams can weave together the desires and necessities of life:

Last night I dreamed of you.
I dreamed you were walking
  on the shore pebbles
and I was walking with you.
Last night I dreamed of you.
And as though I were awake,
I dreamed that I followed you,
that I wanted you like a young
  seal,
that you were wanted by me
the way the hunter
wants a young seal
that dives when it feels it is
  being followed.
That's how you were wanted
  by me,
*who dreamed of you.**

*Translated from the Eskimo by Paul-Emile Victor, from *Memoirs of the American Museum of Natural History*, vol. 3. Courtesy of The American Museum of Natural History.

Dream Catcher

by E. Barrie Kavasch

One of the first gifts given to a newborn American Indian baby was a tiny dream catcher to hang above or from the cradleboard. Babies and children sleep much more than adults and so might have more dreams. It was very important to bless those dreams with love and a beautiful dream catcher to capture all bad dreams.

Cree and Ojibway (Chippewa/Anishinabé) artists made dream catchers out of bent ash splint hoops or hickory splint hoops. The webs were woven out of thin strips of wet rawhide, sinew, hemp, horsehair, or yarn. They looked like fine spider webs and would sometimes contain a bead or bundle, just like a real spider web might contain a fly or some other object.

Cheyenne, Navajo, Sioux, and Cherokee dream catchers often had a piece of turquoise, a glass bead, a shell, or perhaps a feather in the web, as well as some sweet grass for good luck and special blessings. Some dream catchers were woven on a circle of grapevine or a red dogwood, willow, crab apple, or plum branch. Some artists wrapped the hoop with soft buckskin or fur or attached long buckskin ties tipped with beads and feathers to catch the breeze and guide good dreams through to the dreamer.

Legends say that bad dreams have rough edges and get stuck in the web of the dream catcher; good dreams are smooth and can easily slip through the web. First light of morning destroys the bad dreams, leaving the dream catcher clean. You can make a dream catcher for yourself or to give to someone else.

You Need

30-inch-long grapevine or dogwood or willow branch

3 to 4 yards of artificial sinew, yarn, or cotton thread

beeswax

small beads, shells, or pieces of bone with holes

1- to 2-foot-long buckskin tie (optional)

small feathers (optional)

1. Curve and intertwine your grapevine or branch into a hoop (circle) 8 inches or less in diameter. Wrap and tie the sinew near the center where the ends of the branch meet and knot it securely. Wax the sinew by pulling it through the beeswax.

2. Going clockwise around the hoop and keeping the sinew taut, pass the sinew over the hoop rim. Pull the sinew out to the left, over and across, as you advance to the right, overlapping every inch over the hoop. Continue all around the circle (about twelve loops).

3. Continue in this manner and direction making netlike loops. The holes will get smaller as you weave toward the center of the circle. Stop to rewax your sinew and add a bead or shell in the second and third round. Keep your web taut, tightening toward the center.

4. Fasten the sinew with two small overhand knots at the center. Add a final bead or string several beads close to the center. Knot the sinew and cut off any excess.

5. If you want, tie a thin buckskin cord or strip on the bottom to hang free. Tie a bead and feather to the end of it if you like. Use your remaining sinew to tie a loop at the top so that you can hang the dream catcher.

The dream hoop represents the circle of life, the cycles of all living things in the natural world. The web represents the orb web spider's beautiful web in sweet-grass meadows of late summer. Some say that it symbolizes the web of Iktomi (or Iktome), the legendary spider of Plains Indian belief who sees everything and watches over us. Others suggest that it represents the web of life. Different tribes and individuals have their own personal beliefs. After you weave your dream catcher, write down your story of its symbolism, if you wish, and tie it to the dream catcher.

Listening to Our Dreams

by E. Barrie Kavasch

In an average eight-hour night's sleep, a person might have four to six dreams. The first dream might last only about five minutes. Each dream is a little longer than the one before, and the last dream of the night (usually in early morning) can last thirty to forty minutes. This is the one you will probably remember. You can easily train yourself to wake up briefly after each dream and record a line or two about it in a journal. (Be careful not to write over a previous entry.) Then you will go right back to sleep.

Our dreams have much to tell us. American Indians knew the importance of their dreams and remembered them carefully, sometimes sharing them in dream groups. Dreams entertain and tease us. Occasionally, a scary dream needs to be examined and understood so that it does not recur. Some of my adult friends had recurring nightmares as children. One woman had the same dream for almost nine years! American Indian children often were invited to talk about their dreams each morning to prevent this from happening.

Dream sharing is a great learning experience. We each have our own dream metaphors and landscapes of the night. The more we understand and respect this, the better it works to our advantage. Before you fall asleep each night, think, "My dreams are important. They are good, and I enjoy each dream. I shall remember my dreams and write them down." When you keep a dream journal over a period of time, you will see certain patterns and repeated ideas in your dream process.

Dream Journal

by E. Barrie Kavasch

To record your dreams, you can create a simple journal to keep beside your bed or under your pillow. (I keep mine under my pillow, wrapped in a small square of soft red flannel.) The handier and easier it is to use your journal, the more you are likely to reach for it, even in the dark when you are half asleep, and write down your dreams. You might want to practice writing in the dark (on scrap paper) or with your eyes closed to get the feeling of how easy it is to record dreams at night in the dark. Record

(in pencil) at least a sentence or two about your dreams, then go back to sleep.

You Need

stapler

10 sheets of 8 1/2- by 11-inch paper, cut in half

8 1/2- by 11-inch piece of oak tag, folded in half crosswise

colored markers or crayons (optional)

piece of flannel

pencil, short and not too sharp

1. Staple the 20 cut sheets of paper securely to the top of the right half of your oak tag cover (inside), allowing enough room for it to close (like a book).
2. Design and color the front and back covers (if you wish). Use an American Indian motif.
3. Take a square of flannel and fold your dream journal and pencil carefully inside. Place it near or under your pillow or beside your bed. It should be easy to open and write in.

SPIRITUAL OBJECTS

by E. Barrie Kavasch

American Indians considered dream-guided spiritual objects holy. Although some were very beautiful, they were not decorated solely as works of art in a classic sense. Some, such as medicine bundles and bags, medicine masks, and ghost dance attire, had an almost cryptic look and conveyed a feeling of great power. It was usually necessary to "feed" such items sacred tobacco and herbs and to keep them wrapped up and put away when not in ceremonial use. Songs and prayers were sometimes "given" to them.

Today most tribes feel that these powerful creations should not be seen outside their ceremonial use and should never be put on public display. Great care is taken never to reproduce exactly a sacred Navajo sand painting, an Iroquois False Face Mask or Husk Face Mask, various medicine shields and bundles, and numerous other tribal holy pieces. Otherwise, the replica will steal the original object's sacred power and bring everyone extremely bad fortune.

The Spirit Plate

by Wendell Deer With Horns

As a child in La Plant, South Dakota, I would walk with my mother up to the cemetery with food for our dear relatives who had "passed over." We would take some of our meat and bread, perhaps a cup of soup or a jelly jar of hot coffee, to place near the graves. It was especially hard to carry the coffee, and my mom would wrap a thick cloth around the hot jar so that I could hold on to it. She taught me how to pray to the good spirits to get this food before the bad spirits could eat it, because she said the latter were "hungry like wolves."

We would go to the cemetery every Sunday, and especially on Veterans Day and Memorial Day, as many of our relatives had been veterans. We would go to my grandmother's grave and those of the other relatives, and we would clean the gravestones and the area all around them. Then my mom would remember how my grandmother, Yellow Bird Necklace, used to sing the old honoring songs and memorial songs of our Lakota people whenever the soldiers would come through our reservation. Everyone was so proud of her!

I remember all the many ways in which my people celebrated life and death on the Great Plains, and especially on the Cheyenne River Sioux (Lakota) Reservation in South Dakota. We continue this remembrance when we set the spirit plate before each main meal. In this way, we think of and feed our dead relatives. In a way, it is a sacred ritual thanksgiving to the "ghost grapevine."

Setting the spirit plate is similar to our previous actions when we killed a buffalo. Something was always returned (in the spirit of the "gift") so that more would come back in its place. In killing and butchering a buffalo, we buried a small piece of a vital organ (usually the kidney or heart) in the earth to feed its spirit and honor the Creator.

To make a spirit plate, a small plate is selected, blessed, and carefully filled with a tiny portion of every food at the table. Then it is set near the center of the table and prayed over before anyone eats. Each food has its own spirit form and nourishment. Although you might not see anything disappear from this spirit plate, the good spirits eat the energy of the food. It nourishes them, along with the prayers, and they know that they are remembered and celebrated.

When I was a boy, the spirit plate was put outside near a tree, along with some tobacco and prayers, as in the old days. Sometimes it was set by the fire. Each family has its own way of setting the spirit plate. We consider the south to be the direction of the spirit world and the "Happy Hunting Ground," so prayers are often offered to the south.

You Need

small dessert plate

red, yellow, black, and white non-poisonous ink or markers

small paintbrush

1. Hold the plate carefully in front of you and paint a white circle (hoop) going clockwise around the inner rim of the plate. This symbolizes the Sacred Hoop of Life, around which the Ghost Nations roam.

2. Considering the four directions of the compass, paint a white feather marking the south. Paint a black feather at the west, a red feather at the north, and a yellow feather at the east. These four feathers represent the four directions and the sacred colors.

3. If you wish, you can paint other small Native American designs within the hoop. Then let the paint dry.

4. At your next major family meal, ask if you can set the spirit plate and explain its importance. Remember, do not put too much food on the plate. You might put a tiny glass of juice, milk, or cocoa beside it, because spirits like to have something to drink, too. Say simple prayers to your ancestors' spirits and give thanks to God. After the meal, wash the spirit plate with the rest of the dishes, then put it away until the next special occasion.

Make a Medicine Bag

by E. Barrie Kavasch

American Indian children make many kinds of bags for special uses. They learn by copying adults' examples of various tribal bags. By copying these fine bags, Indian children learn to create their own personal items, develop their attention to detail, and learn more about who they are and about their people and family.

Beautiful American Indian pipe bags and tobacco pouches, parfleches (folded rawhide pouches), possible bags (Plains Indian saddlebags), medicine bags, game bags, and sewing pouches were special items. Sacred and ceremonial bags often symbolized membership in secret medicine societies. Bags of fine-tanned leather, animal skins, soft wool, or velvet were painted or decorated with fringe and metal cones, beads and quills, dyed moose-hair embroidery, or wampum. These bags' colors and designs tell us a lot about the owner and his or her importance and tribe. Some personal medicine bags, worn around the neck or tied to a belt, were unadorned.

The term "medicine" can be extended to mean learning and understanding the mysteries of life. The medicine bag* is a symbol of private strength. It can be a symbol of who you are, as well as of your family relationships and love of life and the earth. When you make your medicine bag, put your special energy into it. Things created in this manner have more power, or "medicine," in them.

You Need

newspaper (optional)

soft leather or calico

scissors

ruler

leather needle (three-sided needle with a triangular point) or regular sewing needle

matching thread

24-inch strip of leather or ribbon about 1/8 to 1/4 inch wide

1. Cut a pattern from newspaper and transfer it to a piece of soft leather or calico, or use a precut 6-inch square of material.
2. Fold the leather or calico in half lengthwise, right sides together. Stitch along the bottom and open side, about 1/8 inch from the edges. Backstitch at the beginning and end so that your stitches will not pull out.
3. Turn the bag right side out so that the seams are inside. Carefully cut narrow slits near the top (1/4 inch down) for your leather strip or ribbon. Run the leather strip or ribbon through the slits at the neck of the pouch.
4. Select something tiny that symbolizes your birthday: a kernel of corn, a cherry seed, or a pine needle. Write your name and birth date on a small piece of paper or birch bark or on a small leaf. Wrap the item in the paper and place it in your bag.
5. Choose a few small items that represent your family, the earth, or where you were born: a pinch of earth, a small feather, or a tiny stone.

6. Put only a few things inside your bag at first. Keep it loose and light. As you wear it and experience more things in life, you will find other small objects to add. Remember, these items should represent your own special power, or "medicine." Wear the bag in good health!

*Medicine bags are sometimes called story bags because they contain mementos of special experiences and people and thus relate memorable stories.

Sacred Clowns

by E. Barrie Kavasch

Many Plains and Pueblo Indian peoples included clowns in some of their traditional healing and dance societies. Sacred clowns were important members of sacred sects. They wore grotesque (scary) or very funny masks and distinctive costumes. Some wore ragged clothes. Others painted their faces and bodies with mud.

The Fool Society of the Assiniboin tribe in Montana was one of many contrary (mischievous) fraternities. Clowns among the Arapaho and Crow were known as the Crazy Dogs. Some contraries were Thunder Dreamers, who followed

their dreams or visions of thunder and lightning. Membership in societies sometimes came through dreams that revealed and solved fears. The members played the contrary fool in rituals but were often celebrated warriors and occasionally women. A Cheyenne or Sioux might serve for many years in a contrary role, but not necessarily a lifetime. Some holy men, called *heyokas,* were contraries throughout their lives, as well as respected visionaries who saw their role as providing spiritual guidance for the tribe. Black Elk, a Lakota Sioux holy man, explained: "The *heyoka* presents the truth of his vision through comic actions, the idea being that the people should be put in a happy, jolly frame of mind before the great truth is presented."

Sacred clowns mocked tribal rituals, sacred objects, and dance rites in outrageous behavior that was embarrassing. They actually reinforced good behavior and respect for traditions by doing what was forbidden.

The Tumbling Koshare

by Ron Rundstrom and Pat Rosa

The tumbling paper toy is an old folk toy form that uses gravity as a means of movement. It was probably introduced into Europe from China and became a popular toy in the nineteenth century.

Many cultures have ritual clowns. The black and white banded Koshare are the clowns of the Pueblo Indians of the American Southwest. Their comic antics can be seen at many feast days and ceremonial dances in the villages of the Rio Grande in New Mexico. These spirit representa-

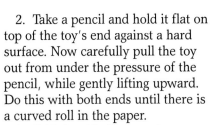

tives belong to sacred curing associations. They are "contrary" persons that can reverse roles and behave in ways that people should not. This mediator function takes the form of clowning that exaggerates incidents of village life or imitates the behavior and appearance of dance spectators. Their ritual ridicule serves to relieve tension, punish the misbehaver and maintain village harmony. They are ceremonial attendants that coordinate community tasks and promote fertility, rain and health with the best of satirical humor.

How to Make Your Toy

1. Transfer the toy pattern to a piece of lightweight poster board. Color it if you like, then cut it out. Remember the toy pattern may be used as a template to trace and cut out other tumbling toys with your own design on them.

2. Take a pencil and hold it flat on top of the toy's end against a hard surface. Now carefully pull the toy out from under the pressure of the pencil, while gently lifting upward. Do this with both ends until there is a curved roll in the paper.

3. Fold the side flaps as shown. Use the straight edge of a ruler for a sharper crease.

4. Cut slot "B." Insert tab "A" into slot "B." Glue or tape if you desire. The box shape should form a rubber band–like loop.

5. Place one or two marbles, smooth round stones, or a ball bearing into the box.

6. Close up the sides and insert side flaps under the box face. Put a little glue on the top of the flaps if you want more strength.

How to Make Your Toy Tumble

1. Place your clowns upright on an inclined surface and let them go.

2. If they slip, it means the slope is either too smooth or too steep. If the surface is too smooth, place a towel or piece of cloth over it.

A "cultural" toy from Reindeer Productions. Reprinted with permission.

PART II

People, Places,

ANCIENT CULTURES

A People Living in God: Early North American Cultures

We go deep into North America to visit many regional native peoples; listen to their legends, histories, and words of wisdom; and meet special individuals. Ancient ways of life give more meaning to early history on this continent. Many changes occurred throughout the historic period (the past five hundred years) for all native peoples and their places of origin, as well as their sense of place. Their legends are enduring threads that bind many of them together. They give us a better idea of who they are and how we all relate to each other.

by Randall H. McGuire

There were no "Indians" in North America when Christopher Columbus landed in the Bahamas five hundred years ago, but more than ten million people lived in what is now the United States. Among them were Diné, O'Odham, Lakota, Wampanoag, Ganiengehaka, and a host of other nations. They spoke hundreds of different languages. In most of these languages, the name they called themselves means "the people" in English. These people became Indians when Columbus called them *una gente en dios*, "a people living in God." In Spanish their name became Indios, or Indians.

The Indians' world was not a new world. According to archaeologists, the first Indians came to North America more than twenty thousand years before Columbus. During the last Ice Age, the great glacial ice sheets took up so much water that the oceans shrank. The Bering Strait, between Siberia and Alaska, dried up. A broad land bridge connected Asia and North America. Asian hunters followed game over the bridge into North America.

Many modern Indian peoples do not accept this theory of migration. They believe that the people were created with the land. The stories they tell explain who they are, where they came from, what the borders of their world are, and how they should live as humans. Each nation has its own creation story.

Archaeologists call the first peoples in North America Paleo-Indians. *Paleo* is a Greek word meaning "early." These early Indians found a colder climate than the one we know today. Great ice sheets covered much of Canada. The northern United States had an arctic climate. The deserts of the western United States were lush grasslands dappled with large lakes. Paleo-Indian hunters used finely made stone projectile points to hunt large animals such as mammoths (extinct elephants) and bison. By nine thousand years ago, the climate was becoming warmer. The ice sheets melted, and the lakes in the West dried up, leaving the modern deserts.

The lives of Indian peoples changed. Archaeologists call this new way of life the Archaic Phase. Archaic peoples adapted their way of life to the specific environment in which they lived. People hunted smaller game, such as deer and rabbits. They gathered wild grass seeds and ground them into flour. They collected shellfish along the rivers of the eastern United States and along the coasts. They threw the shells in large piles. In the far western United States and in most of Canada, the Archaic Phase lasted

22

and *Legends*

until the eighteenth century A.D.

In the eastern and southwestern United States, a new way of life, the Formative Phase, replaced the Archaic. These people lived year-round in one settlement, made pottery, and grew crops. They built great mounds and stone buildings that still dot the landscape.

"We Indians think of the earth and the whole universe as a never-ending circle, and in this circle, man is just another animal."

Jenny Leading Cloud, Rosebud Sioux

Archaeologists divide the Formative Phase of the East into the Adena, Hopewell, Late Woodland, and Mississippian periods. Adena people (500–100 B.C.) brought wild sunflowers, amaranth (pigweed), and squash into their gardens. They bred the wild plants to produce larger domestic varieties. They buried their dead in large mounds of earth. They built one mound in present-day Ohio to look like a snake eating an egg. During the Hopewell Period, people continued to build mounds, and they began a trade network that covered most of the eastern United States. This trade network fell apart in about A.D. 400, which marks the start of the Late Woodland Period.

By 800, people based their agriculture on corn, beans, and squash. These crops came from Mexico, where Indian peoples had grown them for thousands of years. The Late Woodland Period continued in much of the East until the Europeans arrived, but in the South, it changed into the Mississippian Period (700–1540). Mississippian societies divided people into nobles, priests, and commoners. The nobles and priests lived on high, flat mounds in great towns of up to twenty thousand people. The modern Cherokee, Creek, Choctaw, Seminole, and Chickasaw Indians are the descendants of Mississippian people.

Corn arrived in the Southwest before 1000 B.C., and by A.D. 100, three Formative cultures existed. The Anasazi culture began in the Four Corners region, where the states of Colorado, Utah, Arizona, and New Mexico meet. The Anasazi built large apartment buildings called pueblos and made white pottery with black designs. At the end of the thirteenth century, the Anasazi moved to the Rio Grande, where their descendants live today.

The Mogollon people lived in the mountains and made brown pottery with red designs. Around A.D. 1450, they moved north to become the Hopi and Zuni Indians. In the deserts of southern Arizona, the Hohokam built large canals to water their fields and made buff pottery with red designs. Their descendants, the Pima, still farm among the ruins of their ancestors.

In 1492, most of the Indian peoples of North America were farmers who lived in villages. European diseases and war destroyed the Mississippian culture and greatly reduced the farmers of the Southwest. Today almost two million Indian people live in the United States. Hundreds of Indian nations survive, and more than two hundred native languages are spoken.

The A:shiwi and Their Creation

by Edmund J. Ladd

In early May 1538, Estevanico, a Moorish slave and scout for Fray Marcus de Niza, a Spanish priest who was searching for the Seven Cities of Gold, was killed for spying at Hawikuh. [Hawikuh is one of six occupied villages where the present-day A:shiwi (Zuni) reservation is located in southwestern New Mexico.] When Fray Marcus reported back to Mexico that he had seen the fabled Seven Cities, Francisco Vásquez de Coronado launched a full-scale expedition in search of them. Coronado arrived at Hawikuh on July 7, 1540, which led to the first of many battles between invaders and Indians in the Pueblo world.

Since 1540, our people and our way of life have been altered by a number of outside influences: first the Spanish, then the Mexicans, and then the Americans. Now we are in the Modern Period. Through all these years, we have survived. We have our land, our language, and our religion — that is, our culture. This culture is a mixture of many borrowed elements, but it is uniquely our own.

We are the A:shiwi (I am a shiwi). We live at Ha/lona:itiwan/na, "The Center Place," in southwestern New Mexico, where our reservation was established in 1877. We speak a unique language classified by the anthropologists as Zunian. The Spanish gave us the name Zuni, which we are stuck with. From a population low of about twelve hundred in the late 1800s during the smallpox epidemic, we have now increased to nearly ten thousand tribal members.

Zunian is the first language in the home, with English and some Spanish also spoken. We have our own form of government led by an elected governor and tribal council composed of men and women who serve four-year terms. The nearest large town is Gallup, New Mexico, forty miles to the north on old Highway 66, now I-40.

What follows is a brief outline of an oral tradition of our creation. In the cultural context, the account is retold over four nights. It is not a story or a myth; it is the word of our origin as told for thousands of years.

In the Beginning

In the beginning,
there were no humans
on the surface of the earth.
Every day, Sun Father came up in the east,
traveled high over Mother Earth,
pausing overhead at high noon,
and then descended into the western ocean,
and it became night.
All night long, Sun Father traveled
under Mother Earth to arrive in the east in time
to bring a new day.
But the days were empty;
there was no dancing,
no laughter,
no singing.
There were no prayers,
no offerings.
Every day, as Sun Father traveled
high above Mother Earth,
he could hear the cries
of his children deep in the womb
of Mother Earth.

One day, as Sun Father was passing overhead,
he paused at high noon.
He created the Twin Gods
and said to them,
"Go, go into Mother Earth and
bring my children into my light."
The Twin Gods obeyed Sun Father.
After many trials and tribulations,
they brought Sun Father's children
up from the Four Worlds below
to his light.
That was the Beginning
(Chimegann/Kya).

The exact place of origin is not known,
but it was somewhere to the west
(to the west of modern-day Shiwinn/a).
People say, based on The Word
of the Beginning, that it was in the
Grand Canyon.
Names of places associated with the travel in
the search for The Center Place
are known:
Once the search began, from the place of origin,
the people traveled north and eastward,
moving, they said, "every four days."
A calendar had
not yet been developed; therefore, what the ancients
(the Eno:te:que) were really saying was,
"We moved every four years."

At first
all the people traveled together,
living in many different places.
Then the time for the people to divide and separate came.
The Gods presented the people with two eggs:
one, a very beautiful, shiny, turquoise blue egg;
the other, a brown, white, gray,
yellowed-speckled egg —
not very attractive.
The Gods gave the A:shiwi first choice.
   The other people (who were related to the A:shiwi)
   took the other.
   The Gods said to the A:shiwi,
   "If you had chosen the gray
   egg, you would have traveled to
   the south, to the lands of eternal summer
   where the Mu/la the Macaw
   lives. But because you
   chose the blue egg, you will
   travel north to the cold
      country where the K/walashi
      the Crow lives."
   When the A:shiwi continued
   their travels to the north and
   east, moving every four years
            in search of The Center Place,
            it came to pass that during these
            travels, various curing societies
            originated:
            The clans,
            the rain priesthood,
            the bow priesthood,
            the kiva societies,
            and the summer and winter
            ceremonial calendar, based on the
         winter and summer sun, the
         movement of Sun Father
         and Moon Mother,
         were created.
   When The Center Place was found
   (Ha/lona:itiwan/na),
all the people became settled —
some to the north,
some to the east,
some to the south,
and some to the west.

Today, from the place of origin,
we can see many places where the ancients (the Eno:te:que)
stopped over on their journey in their search for
The Center Place.
These places are still held sacred
in the collective memory of the
A:shiwi.

Rock of the Ages: Pre-Columbian American Music

by Franc Menusan

American Indian music has roots deep in the relationship between the sounds of nature and people's desire to communicate the emotions of the heart. Unlike European-influenced music, native music does not use familiar harmonies, key changes, or written music, nor do we know who composed most of our various songs or when they were created. We do know the songs came directly from the hearts of the people because the music retains its original power. We can feel it in our hearts even today, although the songs and dances are sometimes thousands of years old.

Our music developed from the power of rushing rivers and thundering herds of buffalo, the cries of the coyote, and the songs of birds. It is for indigenous people a sacred bond to the natural world, like a bridge connecting the beginning of time to the present and connecting native people today to our ancestors and other supernatural forces of this earth.

Each group of Indian people came into direct, prolonged contact with distinctly different forces of nature: the Aleut and Inuit with the cold, icy northern regions, the central plains people with vast open grasslands, the woodland people with the lakes of the East Coast, the desert nations with the Southwest, and the northwest whalers with the evergreen forests and cool water. Each region produced different music.

Our music also is linked to our oral traditions and histories. Songs and dances help the people to remember and associate important events with the whole body, not just the mind. Much of the music, as well as many of the instruments, have survived persecution and death.

In their search for gold, treasure, and archaeological information, the Europeans violated the graves of our ancestors. Strange as it seemed to the Native Americans, this activity has in some cases helped native people regain information about ancient instruments and cultures that might otherwise have been lost. Museums and private collections today contain flutes, drums, and horns made of bone, clay, gold, silver, wood, stone, and gourds.

These instruments are carved in an almost endless variety of shapes portraying plants, animals, fish, birds, and even people. Ancient murals and painted clay vessels show orchestras of trumpet players, percussionists, singers, drummers, and dancers. Even in remote villages of Mexico and Central America, archaeologists have found perfectly preserved wooden drums more than five hundred years old still in use in local festivals.

Our music, in both its longevity and its diversity, is a testimony to our survival as a people. Our drums beat strong, our flutes still sing like birds, and our rattles sound like rain. We still sing in the ancient tongues and perform the dances in the prescribed manner. As an ancient Aztec poet once wrote,

*I spread my wings
beside the flowery drums.
My song rises; it
spreads over the earth!*

The Boys and the Moon

by Margaret Bemister

Once there were two boys who were great friends. One lived in the middle of the village because his father was the head chief. The other lived at the end of the village because his father was a lesser chief. The boys spent a great deal of time together, making arrows to see who could make the most. Back of the village there was a hill. On the top of this hill there was a large grassy place which they called their playground.

One fine moonlit night they started up the hill towards their playground with their arrows. After they had gone a short distance, the lesser chief's son looked up at the moon and said: "Is not the moon just the shape of my mother's lip ornament, and it is just the size of it, too."

"You must not speak like that," replied his friend. "It is not right to speak that way of the moon. It is insulting."

At that moment it became dark; then a circular rainbow appeared coming down the hillside. It seemed to encircle them for a moment and then it disappeared, but when the head chief's son looked around, he saw that his companion had disappeared also. He called him in a frightened voice, but got no answer. Then he said: "My playmate must have been alarmed at the sight of the rainbow and must have run away from it"; so he began to climb the hill, calling his friend as he went. Still there was no sign of him. Looking up, he saw that the moon was again in the sky and he thought, "That circular rainbow must have been the moon. He was angry at my friend and came down and took him away."

Looking again at the sky, he saw that there was now a bright star by the side of the moon. "Ah!" he said, "that is my friend; the moon has taken him up to the sky — what can I do to rescue him?"

He had reached the top of the hill now and he sat down on the grassy place and began to cry. Then he thought he would try to shoot the star and perhaps his friend would fall out. He tried his bows one after the other and each one broke as he tested it. Then he tried his friend's bows and they all broke except one. Fitting an arrow in this, he shot at the star. It seemed to waver, but there was no sign of his friend falling from the sky, so he sat for many hours weeping at the loss of his playmate. At last he fell asleep. When he wakened, he noticed a long ladder that stretched from the star down to his side. Looking at it, he determined to ascend. But before he started, he gathered various kinds of brushes and put them in the knot of hair which he wore on the top of his head. He began to climb, and kept on climbing as fast as he could all day. When night came he camped upon the ladder, for he was still far from the star. When he awoke the second time, his head felt heavy. Reaching up he pulled out the branch of salmon berry bushes from one side. It was heavy with salmon berries. He ate these and felt greatly refreshed. Then putting the branch back into his hair he began to climb. By noon he felt hungry again, so reaching up he pulled out the branch on the other side of his hair. It was loaded with blue huckleberries, which he ate. He was now far up in the sky, and it was summer there. That was why the berries were growing on the branches in his hair.

The third day he climbed on until noon before he began to feel hungry. By this time his head was very heavy. Taking out the branch from the top of his head, he found it loaded with red huckleberries, which he ate.

At last he reached the top. Before him was a large lake, and on its shores grew moss and low bushes. Gathering an armful of brush and moss he made himself a bed and lay down to sleep, for he was very tired. Some time afterwards he was wakened by a little girl. She was neatly dressed in clothes made of the skins of animals and her leggings were trimmed with porcupine quills. When she saw that the boy's eyes were open, she said: "My grandmother sent me to get you. Follow me."

Rising to his feet he followed her to a small house wherein sat an old woman. She questioned him about his journey and asked him why he had come this long distance. He told her about his lost playmate and said he had come to find him.

"Your playmate is in the moon's house," she answered, and she pointed to a house not far away.

"I must go to seek him," he said quickly, turning to go.

"First of all you must eat," she replied. Then she brought him salmon berries, and meat. When he was ready to leave, she gave him a spruce cone, a rose bush, a piece of shrub called devil's club and a grindstone.

When he reached the moon's house he heard his playmate screaming with pain. He knew that the voice came from the top of the house near the smoke hole. Climbing to it, he reached down through the hole and pulled his playmate out. He put the spruce cone in his friend's place and told it to imitate his cries. Then they both began to run away as fast as they could. They had gone only a short distance when the cone dropped from the smoke hole and at once the people knew that the boy had escaped. Uttering a cry of rage the moon started in pursuit. He began to gain on the boys when the head chief's son threw back a piece of devil's club. This shrub at once

began to grow with great rapidity and its dense thorny stalks and its broad leaves with their thorny backs stopped the moon for some time. With much difficulty he at last succeeded in getting through and began to gain on them again. The chief's son next threw back the rose bush. This grew at once into a dense thicket and delayed the moon for several moments. Then the chief's son threw back the grindstone. This changed immediately to a high cliff from which the moon kept rolling back. Again and again it attempted to follow the boys, only to slip back every time.

By this time they had reached the old woman's house. She received them with joy and they sat for a long time talking to each other and to her. At last they felt tired and she told them to go and lie down at the place where the chief's son had first slept and think of their playground on the hillside. They went out and lay down on the bed of moss and brush and thought of their playground, but after a while the chief's son thought of the little house and the old woman. At once they were back to it. "Go back again," she said, "and lie down once more. Do not think of me. Think only of your playground."

So they went back and lay down again and kept on thinking of their grassy playground. At last they fell asleep. When they awoke they

found themselves on the hillside at the foot of the ladder. Running down the hill they came to the village, and when near the chief's house, they heard the beating of a drum. They knew at once what it was — a death feast was being held for them. It was now quite dark, for these feasts were always held at night, so they hid among the trees and waited until the feast was over. After a while they saw people come out, all with their faces blackened as a sign of sorrow.

When the people had gone back to their homes, the chief's son wished his younger brother would come forth. At once his younger brother came out of the house and stood near them, but when he saw the boys he was very frightened and ran back to tell his mother. Then his parents came forth, and when they found their son and his playmate, they carried them into the house, rejoicing very much. They sent for the lesser chief and his wife, and all the rest of the people in the village. They all came and held a feast over the safe return of the boys.

Marking the Months

by Diane E. Haspel

Indians marked the passage of months as the time from one full moon to the next. Many tribes added an extra moon when necessary to coordinate the moon's waxing and waning with the spring and fall equinoxes. That way, their calendar stayed in sync with the seasons.

Each full moon has many names. Most of those included here were used by the Indians when the first English settlers came to the New World.

January: Wolf Moon

The wolves were starving by January. Their usual prey was either hibernating or had already been devoured. Desperate, the wild animals scoured villages and towns, attacking anyone they could find. The howling January winds echoed the sounds of those hungry wolves, roaming the countryside by the light of the Wolf Moon.

February: Snow Moon

The cold light of February's full moon often shone on a frozen, snowy landscape. To the Passamaquoddy Indians of Maine, this moon was also known as the Hunger Moon, as food grew more and more scarce. Yet in the South, along the warmer Gulf of Mexico where spring came early, the Indians called it the Opening Buds Moon.

March: Maple Sugar Moon

The Anishinabé Indians of Minnesota knew, with the rising of this full moon, that it was time to get out the buckets, tap the giant maple trees, and start "sugaring" — boiling the sap down to make maple sugar. Other tribes called this moon the Worm Moon, probably because as the ground softened, the worms emerged.

April: Frog Moon

The Cree Indians lived in the region around Ottawa, Canada. Cree legend said that the number of months of winter was determined by the number of toes on a frog. With the rising of the Frog Moon, winter was over. The April moon was also called the Pink Moon and the Planter's Moon, referring to the start of spring.

May: Flower Moon

Flowers have always been part of May Day (May 1) celebrations. The Romans honored their flower goddess with freshly picked bouquets, and the English danced around Maypoles wound with flowers. In the area around Lake Michigan, the Huron Indians called the May moon the Budding Moon, since spring came a little later there.

June: Strawberry Moon

The Seneca Indians lived in the northwestern part of New York State. According to Seneca legend, during this moon strawberries were first given to them by the Jo-ge-oh, the Little People who took care of plants. The newly arrived English colonists thought the name most appropriate when they discovered the tasty fruit, abundant and ripe for picking under the Strawberry Moon.

July: Blood Moon

The Okanagon Indians of Washington attributed this moon's reddish color and name to the fierce hordes of hungry mosquitoes whose bites drew blood at this time of year. Another name, the Buck Moon, might have referred to deer blood, as deer were slaughtered and their meat dried in preparation for winter.

August: Moon of the Green Corn

In New England, August was the time to feast on the bounty from the fields. Roasting corn, which the Indians called green corn, was a favorite food. Some called this moon the Sturgeon Moon because the fish, too, were plump and good to eat.

September: Harvest Moon

For days, the moon rose early in the evening, riding high above the horizon. It provided the longest periods of moonlight of the year, and farmers made good use of it. They brought their fall crops in late into the cool September evenings, under the light of the bright Harvest Moon.

October: Hunter's Moon

The crops were harvested, the weather was crisp — it was time to go hunting. Man and dog headed out under the Hunter's Moon, its bright light lasting almost as long as that of the Harvest Moon. The Cree called it the Moon of Falling Leaves, another sure sign of fall.

November: Beaver Moon

Smart woodsmen and Indians, settlers and farmers, knew by the beavers' thick pelts that winter was coming soon. Busy as the beavers, they were finishing preparations for the cold months ahead by the time this moon appeared.

December: Cold Moon

The air, the ground, the sky — even the moon looked as cold as the ice reflecting it. The Hopi Indians of northeastern Arizona feared the cold December moon, calling it Kyamuya — "sacred but dangerous moon." The days were short, the nights very long, and the people worried that the sun would not return.

Hopi
Tuiqawi'taniq pam a'ne himu'u.
Aasapok tuiqawi itamui ngöyakiwta.
It huukyangwui nit kosngalawui
  pu 'o'omawtui
  pu' tuuwaq qachit aasapop'a.

English
Power is very mysterious.
Power is all around us
  in the wind
  and the clouds
  and the earth.

From *Little Hopi — Hopihoya,*
published by the U.S. Indian Service.

PUEBLO

The Pueblo Indians

The Pueblo Indians of America's Southwest have a rich and long history. Living in America for many centuries, the Pueblo are considered to be some of America's earliest farmers. Most of Pueblo life revolves around the land and the environment. To remind themselves of their dedication to the land and the environment, the Pueblo attach meaning to many things. Symbols play a vital role in their lives — in their ceremonies, designs, songs, and myths. Pueblo foods such as *piki* bread are eaten for special reasons and on special occasions.

The Pueblo have lived in North America for many years. Archaeologists are still uncovering many new facts about their past. Most Pueblo Indians in modern times have had to adapt to the ways of the non-Indian world. Although the Pueblo today live in a world of many different cultures, they still preserve the traditions of their ancestors.

How Rattlesnake Got His Fangs

retold by Jane Eppinga

Pima Indians tell stories at night after their work is done. Drums call the desert people and animals to hear the Wise One tell the legends of their ancestors.

Rattlesnake loved to listen to the stories. Sun God made Rattlesnake very beautiful with lovely patterns on his back. But he forgot to give the gentle snake any way of defending himself. Everyone tormented Rattlesnake, and he was miserable. Coyote was always playing cruel tricks on him. Everyone knows Coyote means no harm, but he is very foolish. His tricks cause pain and embarrassment. One night Coyote tied Rattlesnake in a knot. Then he threw him high in the air. When Rattlesnake came down, he got caught on a tree branch. Turkey Vulture grabbed him and threw him to the ground. Coyote and Turkey Vulture thought this was great fun, and they kept up their mischief all night. In the morning, Rattlesnake crawled home in great pain.

"I will never go back and listen to the stories," he promised himself.

But there came the drum call, and Rattlesnake could not stay away.

He tried to hide in a corner, but Coyote and Turkey Vulture found him. All night they threw the little snake up into the air and down to the ground. Rattlesnake again crawled home in great pain. But the next morning, things were different. Sun God was waiting for him.

Sun God spoke. "I will give you a way to defend yourself. I will put seashells on your tail and two of my powerful sunbeams in your mouth."

Sun God did this, and Rattlesnake felt much better. Now Coyote and Turkey Vulture would leave him alone. "Thank you, Sun God."

Sun God said, "From now on, you will be the most powerful desert snake. However, you must always first warn your enemy by shaking the shells on your tail. If he does not heed the warning, you may strike with your fangs."

"I will do as you command," said the happy little snake.

That night while Rattlesnake was listening to one of his favorite stories, Coyote pushed him. Rattlesnake shook the shells on his tail.

"Who do you think you are?" laughed Coyote as he kicked the little snake. Quick as a flash, Rattlesnake bit him. Coyote screamed in agony.

Everyone stared in amazement. Then Wise One spoke. "For too long, Rattlesnake has been abused by all of us. He has always been good and kind. I am glad Coyote got what he deserves."

Many others have since been cruel to Rattlesnake. No one should go near him, because he will rattle and bite in a flash. But whenever stories are told among the Pima, a happy little rattlesnake sits quietly and listens. No one bothers him.

Tewa Song of the Sky Loom

O our mother the Earth,
O our Father the Sky,
Your children are we, and
with tired backs
We bring you gifts you love.
Then weave for us a
garment of brightness;
May the warp be the white
light of morning,
May the weft be the red light
of evening,
May the fringes be the falling rain,
May the border be the
standing rainbow.
Thus weave for us a
garment of brightness,
That we may walk fittingly
where birds sing,
That we may walk fittingly
where grass is green,
O our Mother the Earth,
O our Father the Sky.

The Tewa are a North American Indian tribe of New Mexico and northeastern Arizona.

The Legend of Crooked Mountain

by William D. Hayes

The Desert People say that long ago the Gila River valley was not an arid land, but a green paradise. Where cliffs and desert are now, a forest of aspen, birch, pine and fir once thrived. Through this forest, sparkling streams tumbled down to the river, and from the streams men brought an abundance of fish. The needs of the people were few, and forest and valley furnished them with more than sufficient food and clothing.

Corn, maize, and cotton crowded one another in the fertile valley, while in the forest, hollyhocks, anemones and wild roses thrust their blossoms upward to the sun.

Birds, small and large, with feathers as brilliant as the sunset streaked through the trees. Deer and elk strutted about, while at their feet scampered the brownish gray ground squirrel. Bright green and orange lizards darted across the forest floor.

Life was pleasant, and the people lived happily in the valley, hunting and fishing and tending their crops. They worshipped what they saw — the majestic mountains, the forest, the river and the desert beyond the valley, the sunlight that glistened on their copper-colored skin. The sun was their life, and to the sun they dedicated many of their festivals and dances.

Always present to remind them that their lives were not to be abandoned to pleasures only were the medicine men, fierce in countenance and stern in guidance. Where many in the tribe found beauty and joy, the medicine men saw only gods and spirits — jealous deities as numerous as the trees of the forest, ever changing in form and favor, as shifting as the desert sands.

The people lived happily for many generations, but there came a time when they grew restless. Their valley was changing. For many days the sky was neither clear nor cloudy, but the color of the ground. The sun, red as distant fire, was ringed about with great circles of amber light. Anxiously the people watched while dark clouds gathered over Crooked Mountain. At night, flashes of lightning coursed through the clouds and silhouetted them against the sky.

At length above the distant thunder rose the rhythmic chants of the medicine men, and the murmuring voices of the frightened people.

"Someone among you has displeased the gods of earth and sky," said Cia-a-hei, the chief medicine man. "Some great disaster will come upon us."

And the people began to suspect one another and to quarrel among themselves.

There came a day when the sky was darker than before, and the mountains seemed suspended in mist above the desert. The people stood in small groups, talking in whispers. What was going to happen to them?

"Cia-a-hei was right," they said. "The gods of earth and sky are surely displeased. Who among us has displeased them? The sky is fearful to look upon, and Crooked Mountain hangs in the clouds. What are the gods going to do? What will happen to us?"

Cia-a-hei strode solemnly into their midst. He was in full ceremonial dress. When they saw the fiercely painted face and the many-colored feathers, the people stood for a moment as motionless as stones. Then they slowly backed away in every direction, until Cia-a-hei was left alone in the center of a huge circle.

He held his head high and chanted:
When the bowl of the crescent
* moon turns over,*
Then the rains shall rain down
* many days,*
And earth shall be no more.

As the wailing voice echoed through the valley, Cia-a-hei turned and pointed toward the mountains. They were dark blue against the clouds. He sang:
Away to Crooked Mountain,
To Crooked Mountain with my
* people,*
With my people I will fly.

For a moment all stood silently. Then they scattered and ran. The men ran to get their weapons, the women to pack the *seeu-haws,* or burden baskets, with fish, game, corn and pumpkin. The young children ran to their mothers, and the older children ran to help with the packing.

When all were ready to begin the long journey out of the valley and across the desert, they stood again in silence. They watched while Cia-a-hei, with solemn gestures, held his magic crystal over his head and stepped into a large earthen vessel.

The vessel rose above the valley and carried Cia-a-hei away toward the mountains. He was followed by the burden baskets, which in like manner rose and flew away.

The clouds, that had hung for many days above the mountains, now rolled over the valley, covering the sun and making the day dark. There was a rustle through the forest, for even the animals and birds knew of the danger. Through the half-light the long column of people and animals marched out of the valley and into the desert.

The dark sky swirled over their heads, but no harm came to them on their journey. At last they walked wearily up the western slopes of Crooked Mountain. They looked up, and saw Cia-a-hei standing far above them on a red rock. He was pointing upward. Raising their heads higher, they saw the dark clouds part, and there, hanging upside down, was the crescent moon, pale yellow in a blue-green sky.

As they watched, the opening in the clouds closed with a roar of thunder that shook the earth beneath their feet. Released by the thunder, drops of rain spattered onto the ground. Soon the rain came

down so hard that the people were forced to climb above the rising water. Huge waves, as dark as malpais stone and covered with white foam, hammered against the mountains, and again the people felt the rocks shake beneath them.

Through the driving storm the people struggled slowly upward to the highest peaks. There they huddled, lashed by wind and rain. Some cried out in terror as the waters rose...higher and ever higher. After many days, the mingled voices of the people were as one voice, wailing to their medicine men. "Save us!" the people cried. "Save us from the storm!"

Then into the midst of the frightened people, Cia-a-hei led the medicine men. They tore their hair. They shook their brightly painted rattles and waved their ceremonial feathers through the rain, splashing as they danced.

The wind and rain stopped. All was calm. Where a moment before peals of thunder echoed through the mountains, now voices rose in song, offering thanks for deliverance. The people moved about in a wild and joyous dance, beating out the cadence on tomtoms. But even as

they danced, great thunderbolts split the sky, and once more rain began to fall.

Again Cia-a-hei led the medicine men in a dance of appeal to the earth and sky. The rain stopped. But now a clap of thunder louder than before shook the mountain, and the rain poured down again.

Twice more, with frenzied dances, the medicine men stopped the fury of the storm, but twice more it resumed.

Now, in the driving rain, Cia-a-hei held his magic crystal high above his head. In a high wailing voice he called:

I stand on Crooked Mountain,
To escape the rising waters,
To escape the rising waters.

Then he turned to the rest of the people and said, "Only one thing more I can do. My power is almost exhausted. Even this can give us only a little time, for the end cannot be avoided." Standing on the edge of the precipice, he looked down at the dark water and chanted:

Rise, rise, O Crooked Mountain,
From the evil waters, rise.

Then the immense boulders rose and lifted the people high above the water. But still the rain came down, and soon the waves lashed at the people as before. Three more times the mountain lifted the people above the flood. Yet the rain continued to fall and the waters to rise.

For the last time, Cia-a-hei stepped before his people. Raising his crystal above his head, he chanted:

Rise, O mighty waters, rise,
We turn to stone,
We turn to stone.

And he dashed the crystal against the side of the mountain. A tongue of flame licked and hissed at the rain, and a roar shook the mountain as the crystal broke in many pieces.

But the light from the flame fell not on men, women and children, animals and birds, but on their images in stone. They had become part of the mountain itself.

When you travel through the Gila River valley on a summer afternoon, look over the Superstition mountains to the clouds banked high above. This is Crooked Mountain. In the light of late afternoon, from the western and northern slopes of the mountain, you can see deep canyons and the grotesque beauty of massive rocks. The rocks rise, one upon another, until the highest are fused in the purple distance.

Across the western face of the mountains, when the late afternoon sun touches them, streaks of gold cleave the massive heights. Some of the Desert People say these streaks were etched there by a great flood that once destroyed the world.

The setting sun is a capricious deceiver. Searching shafts of golden light play upon the sculptured peaks. With beckoning fingers they trace imaginary shapes in the towering rocks. "Over there," they seem to say, "are those not men of stone? And those rocks rising like temples above the others, do you not see images of men and animals and birds carved in them? Are these dead stones not mocking us with a life of their own?"

With one last consuming burst of light, the sun embraces the entire mountain range, and the weird images seem to glow from within. Another glance and they are gone; for the sun is gone, and the sun is their life. Already the mountains are gray against the luminous sky.

From *Indian Tales of the Desert People* written and illustrated by William D. Hayes (David McKay Company, Inc., New York). Copyright © William D. Hayes. Used by permission of Kathryn Hitte Hayes.

The Transformation of Cliff-Dweller

The mean, bad-hearted Cliff-Dweller was known for stealing young, pretty girls. He also shut them up in caves. But one day the girls shot arrows through Cliff-Dweller's heart, and he died. Cliff-Dweller's bones grew white in the desert. His friend Storm-Cloud missed him and grieved for him. Storm-Cloud was so upset that he forgot to send out his rain clouds. Storm-Cloud forgot to laugh and to play. The Indian people no longer heard his voice thundering in the mountains.

So the Indian people danced to please him. They begged Storm-Cloud's mother, Reason-Spirit, to make her son send them rain to water their corn fields. Reason-Spirit agreed to speak with Storm-Cloud.

"Why do you not drop rain upon the corn for the Indians, my son?" she asked.

"Because I am so unhappy that I forgot them," he answered. "I miss Cliff-Dweller so much. He never comes to play and hunt with me anymore."

"I will find out what happened for you," Reason-Spirit said. She took a ball of dust, moistened it, and covered it with a cloth. She chanted, "Come forth, my little messenger, come forth!" A fly came out from under the cloth. It flew into the desert to find Cliff-Dweller.

Soon the fly returned with a speck of dried bone. Reason-Spirit knew Cliff-Dweller had died. She told her sister, Memory, to bring his bones to her. Memory soon came back with the bones. Reason-Spirit then made a good heart from the desert clay. She placed the heart upon the pile of bones. Then she covered them with her magic cloth and sang, "Bones come together, together, together!" The cloth moved. Reason-Spirit chanted, "Rise up bones, and good heart beat! Let us give Cliff-Dweller a seat."

Just then, Cliff-Dweller stood up and threw aside the magic cloth. He was the same Cliff-Dweller on the outside, but inside he had a new heart made of clay from the earth. Reason-Spirit told him that his mean heart had caused him to die. She warned him to use his good heart to do good things.

Cliff-Dweller went out hunting with Storm-Cloud. Storm-Cloud was so happy that he thundered all day. He sent heavy rain showers down upon the fields of the Indian people. Their corn grew tall and green and full of ears. Cliff-Dweller returned to his mother, who was very happy over his new clay heart. He never again stole a young girl or shut one up in a cave.

Excerpts adapted from "Cliff-Dweller and the Corn Maiden" and "The Transformation of Cliff-Dweller" from *Taytay's Memories: Collected & Retold* by Elizabeth W. De Huff. Copyright © 1924 by Harcourt Brace & Company and renewed 1952 by Elizabeth Willis De Huff. Reprinted by permission of the publisher.

To Feed My People: The Coming of the Corn

told to Alice Marriot by informants who prefer their names withheld

Zuni, in southwestern New Mexico, is the largest of all the Pueblos, and probably the most conservative, with the exception of the Hopi villages....

Zuni religion and philosophy are extremely complicated, and have furnished lifetimes of study for some of the greatest of American anthropologists. What is told here is only a fragment of the immensely detailed origin myth.

The origin myth is recited annually, by two priests speaking in unison, in midwinter. Then the Shalako, great birdlike supernatural beings, also known as the Divine Ones, come to bless the houses of Zuni in a night-long ceremony of song and dance. The recital of the entire myth occupies two to four hours early in the performance, and if a single syllable is missed or slurred the dance will not result in health and well-being for all the people.

The first people who came into this world were the Áshiwi, and they were very queer-looking. They had short tails, with no hair on them, and very long ears. When the Áshiwi lay down at night to go to sleep, they lay on one ear and covered themselves with the other. Their hands and feet were webbed, and their heads and bodies were covered with moss, with a big tuft of it sticking out in front of their foreheads like a horn.

All the same, the Áshiwi were human people, who moved about the earth, looking for the place that was to be their home. At last they found a place they liked, beside a spring, and agreed that they would settle there. Then the Divine Ones visited the Áshiwi and cut off their tails and shortened their ears. They told the people to bathe in the spring and become clean, and when the Áshiwi came out of the water all the moss had been washed away from their bodies and heads, and they looked like any other human beings.

After the Áshiwi came out into this world, other people followed them. First came the Hopis, who had been neighbors and friends of the Áshiwi in the underworld. Then came the Mexicans, and then the Coconino and the Pima, and finally the Navahos and the other Apaches. Now the world was populated indeed. The Áshiwi found the middle place of the whole world, and there they established Zuni, where it is today.

Now on the way up from the underworld, some of the Áshiwi had become tired and had fallen behind the others. Once there was a settled place for them to come to, these people began coming out, sometimes a few at a time, sometimes many at once. Each time some Áshiwi joined the others, the earth would rumble and tremble, as a sign that the people were coming out. Then the people above would say, "Here comes my younger brother," or, "Look, my little sister is coming out." And they all rejoiced, and were happy to be together again.

This went on for a long time. It would be too hard to say how long it took in years, but four magic cycles were completed before the last of the people emerged from the underworld.

The last to come out were two witches, a man and a woman. In their hands the witches held all power, for good or for evil. The Divine Ones heard the rumbling before the witches emerged and came to meet them. The supernatural beings were surprised to see two people with their heads covered with hoods of coarse fibers, which blew loosely about their shoulders in the breeze.

"Where are you going?" the Divine Ones asked. "We don't know whose relatives you are."

"We would like to join your people at the Middle Place of the World," answered the witches.

"We don't want you with us," the Divine Ones said.

"Oh, but you will," the witches answered. "See how we hold our hands, clutched under our armpits? In our hands we grasp all the seeds of the world. If you do not let us go to the People of the Middle Place we can destroy the world, for we hold all the seeds, and without them men will starve."

"Perhaps the People of the Middle Place will not want you," the Divine Ones insisted.

"We have all sorts of precious things here," the witch went on as if he had not been interrupted. "I will give these seeds to the leader of the village, but in return he must give us two of his children, a boy and a girl. When he gives us the children, the corn and other seeds will belong to him."

"Why must he give you his children?"

"So that they may die. If they do not die, the rains will never come and the seeds will never grow."

"Wait here," directed the Divine Ones, and they hurried away to the Middle Place. They came to the head man of the village, and told him what the witches had said.

"Will they really hold back the rain if I don't give them my children?" the head man cried.

"So they said," replied the Divine Ones.

"Then it is well," he assented, and he bowed his head.

When the witches reached the Middle Place they went to the head man. "We have come for your children," the witches told him.

"I have no small children," the head man informed them. "I have only a youth and a maiden, but you may have them if you wish. What do you want to do with them?" For he still hoped that his children might be spared.

"We wish to destroy those young people," said the witches.

"Must you? Must you really destroy children? Why do you say that?"

"If we don't destroy them the rain will never come," answered the witches. "It is only by destroying those children that rain can come for all the people. We have wonder-ful things to give you, but there must be much rain if those things are to be of value to you."

"It is well," the head man repeated, and he led the witches to his house, where his son and daughter were sleeping in an inside room.

The witches touched each child over the heart, and shot their magic power into the young bodies, so the children died.

"Now bury them in the earth," the witches instructed the head man, and he did as he was told.

Four days and four nights the male rains fell, heavy and strong, soaking the earth and making it ready to bring life to the seeds. Then on the fifth morning the earth began to rumble. The Divine Ones, watching, saw the young man rise from his grave, alive and well.

Again the rains, the female rains, fell, soaking the earth, gently stroking it so it would bring life into the seeds. On the fifth morning the earth rumbled again, and the girl stepped out of her grave, unharmed.

That night the witches planted their seeds, and by morning the corn stood in rows above the earth. "Come and see," the witches called to the Áshiwi, and everyone came and stood beside the field, watching the corn grow through the day. By evening the corn was ripe and ready for harvest, and the witches called to the Áshiwi again. "Come and eat," they said.

The Áshiwi tasted the food, but it was hot, like chili pepper, and they did not like it. "It isn't fit to eat," they said to the witches.

So one at a time the witches called the crow, the owl, and the coyote, and those three tasted the crops. As the birds and the coyote ate, the food became milder and mellower, so that at last it was just right. The Áshiwi ate the crops, and liked the food.

But from that time forth the people had to watch their fields, for the crow and the owl and the coyote like the food so much that they will steal it all from the farmers if they can.

"To Feed My People: The Coming of the Corn" from *American Indian Mythology* by Alice Marriot and Carol K. Rachlin. Copyright © 1968 by Alice Marriot and Carol K. Rachlin. Reprinted by permission of HarperCollins Publishers, Inc.

NAVAJO
Diné: The People of the Navajo Nation

The Navajo cannot say when the first people came to live in the land amid the four sacred mountains. They tell how the mountains were created by First Man and First Woman, who, with other Holy People, made fire, designed the first hogan, and provided day, night, seasons, and harvests. One dawn First Man and First Woman heard a cry and found a baby girl. They named her Changing Woman, and she taught many things to the animal beings. Before she went west to live with the sun, she created four Navajo clans from the skin of her own body. They lived amid the mountains and followed the teachings of the Holy People.

Archaeologists believe that the Navajo came to live in the American Southwest as a result of migrations over a long time. Their language is one of a group of related languages called Athabascan, centered in northwest Canada. Beginning a thousand years ago, small groups of Athabascan-speaking peoples migrated south. Moving over several hundred years and many generations, the descendants of those people reached the Southwest by the mid-1500s.

The Pueblo already lived in the area where they settled. The people from the North adopted some of the Pueblo's settled ways, learning to live by agriculture as well as their own hunting and food gathering. They built roundish homes called hogans. In the 1500s, when the Spanish came, they called these people Apache de Nabaju, "Apaches of the cultivated fields," and the name Navajo stuck.

They called themselves Diné, "the people." They called their land Dinétah, "land of the people." It is also called the Navajo Nation.

The Navajo Nation was hard won. The Diné were not one tribe but scattered related groups. They were united in their shared history and beliefs and their feelings that Dinétah is a sacred land. White people nearly drove them from that land in the 1800s, but today the Navajo are united under an eighty-eight-member tribal council and elected tribal chairman. Their twenty-five-thousand-square-mile nation has been governed by the council since the 1920s from an immense hogan-shaped building in Window Rock, Arizona.

In this century, income from oil, coal, minerals, and timber sales has led many Navajo to change from their traditional occupations as farmers, sheepherders, and craftsmen. The Navajo Nation now includes industries, schools, hospitals, and museums, but it is not a wealthy land. Although the Navajo are the largest and most prosperous Native American group, many people live in poverty, have a hard time finding work, and experience the same social problems related to alcohol and drugs as other Americans. Many Navajo now live in modern homes and go to college in faraway places; others still live in hogans and follow traditional ways.

Navajoland

by Jean Milne

The Navajo Nation, which extends over a large section of Arizona and smaller parts of New Mexico and Utah, covers about thirteen million acres, or an area about the size of Massachusetts, Connecticut, Delaware, and Maryland all put together. Bounded by the Colorado River and Grand Canyon National Park on the west, the reservation is adjacent to two other national parks and several national monuments.

Although the area has about a dozen major highways, towns of any size are few and far between. But wherever you look are some of the world's most awesome natural wonders. This is a land that has been carved by wind and water. Its colors are so vivid that people who have seen only paintings or photographs can hardly believe they are true.

Visitors to Navajoland often feel that they are in the presence of the supernatural; the Navajo know they are. Almost every mountain and sandstone formation has a religious significance. The Navajo believe, for example, that the 278-foot-wide natural arch called Rainbow Bridge was once a rainbow that one of the Holy People turned to stone to help another supernatural being escape from a flood.

Four sacred mountains form the four corners of the holy land where the Navajo believe their legendary ancestors emerged from beneath the earth many years ago. Each mountain represents one of their sacred colors or steps in their creation: La Plata Mountain (Colorado) represents the Black Underworld, Mount Taylor (New Mexico) the Blue World or Second Level, San Francisco Peak (Arizona) the Yellow World or Third Level, and Blanca Peak (Colorado) the White (Visible) World.

You have probably seen Monument Valley (the northernmost section) several times because it has served as a backdrop for more than a hundred western movies. From the mile-high floor of the plateau rise tall, odd-shaped, red sandstone mesas, buttes, and towers. Totem Pole, the most famous of the slender spires, soars five hundred feet, almost as high as the Washington Monument. The lofty buttes, with their chiseled sides, resemble ancient Greek temples.

Very little vegetation grows on this high desert land — only scattered bunches of sagebrush, greasewood, piñon, and juniper. In some areas, not even the smallest plant mars the surface of the golden, wind-rippled sand dunes.

In the southwestern part of the reservation is the Painted Desert, where low sandstone hills are banded in various shades of pink, yellow, and blue, becoming lighter or darker as the light changes.

The narrow gorges that were cut into the eastern part of this high plateau are as spectacular as the land above. Canyon de Chelly (pronounced "Shay") and Canyon del Muerto slice through perpendicular red and tan sandstone walls that rise to more than a thousand feet in places. Although some of the walls have been sculptured by erosion, most are as smooth as those in your home.

The fertile soil in the bottom of the canyons provides good grazing and agricultural land. But even here you find gigantic towers such as Spider Rock, which is more than eight hundred feet high.

Almost on the eastern border of the reservation is an area of high mountains with thick forest of poplar, yellow pine, and cedar trees.

Below the ground are vast deposits of coal, natural gas, and uranium, which contribute greatly to the tribe's economic resources. In spite of the wealth these bring, many Navajo wish that the land could be left as it originally was.

The Navajo's land is a place of fascinating beauty. Sometimes harsh, it is where Navajo people have lived, prospered, struggled, and returned. For Navajo people, this land amid the sacred mountains provides a foundation for all that is Navajo. People who come from other places may find it too hot in summer, too cold in winter, or too windy all the time, but Navajo people find the beauty in a land that is home.

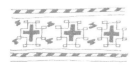

The Hideout at Fortress Rock

by Sally M. Crum

In the early 1970s, grandchildren and great-grandchildren of Navajo who lived during the time of the Long Walk were interviewed. Stories their ancestors had told them were recorded by other Navajo and translated into English. The following account related by Teddy Draper, Sr., concerns the experience of his great-grandmother. It is told as she related it to Teddy's grandmother before he was born.

I was fifteen years old when I heard that American soldiers were forcing all Navajo to leave their homes and go to Fort Sumner, New Mexico. We were living near the rim of Black Rock Canyon (part of today's Canyon de Chelly National Monument). One day our leader, Dahghaa'i (Mustache), told us we should move to a safer place, a nine-hundred-foot-high island of rock near the junction of two canyons. We called this rock Tsélaa´ (Fortress Rock).

"Our warriors were sent to Fort Defiance to steal mules and oxen so the soldiers would have to travel on foot. This gave us time to prepare our hideout. Poles were carried from twenty miles away and placed between ledges on the cliff face. Notched, they could be used as ladders and pulled up when the enemy came.

"We killed many of our sheep because they couldn't be taken up the rock. The meat was dried and, along with lots of dried fruit and berries, was hauled up to the top of Tsélaa´. Water was taken up in pitch-lined baskets. We were also counting on natural basins in the rock to provide water as the snow melted.

"In Ghąąji (October), our leader told us to climb up Tsélaa´ because it would snow soon and then the poles would be too icy to climb. I helped a little girl named Asdzáá Ashįįhí (Salt Lady) who had no immediate family. Although it was very difficult to climb, all of us, numbering over two hundred, made it to the top.

"It wasn't until Yasniłtééz (January) when the lookout watchers saw about sixty soldiers coming down the canyon toward Tsélaa´. We all were very quiet. We thought they didn't see us, but apparently they did because four days later they were shooting at us from the canyon rim. Fortunately, they were too far away for the bullets to do any harm.

"The soldiers returned to the base of our fortress and shot at our warriors stationed on a ledge closer to the canyon floor. The white men fired at our men all day long. We could hear them shouting at each other and heard the moans of our wounded.

"On top of the rock, some of our people were dying from the cold. Food was scarce, and our water supply was running out because it had not snowed in a while. The soldiers remained for six days, keeping us from getting food and water. They fried bacon so the smell would encourage us starving Navajo to surrender.

"One night our men lowered water jars by ropes to pools right next to the sleeping soldiers. The moonlight was bright, so this was done on the north side of Tsélaa´. The soldiers did not notice.

"The next day we were surprised to see the soldiers leave. They had also run out of rations. The poles were replaced, and the men went down first to bury our dead. When we were certain the Americans were gone for good, we all climbed down and said, 'One of our best Earth Mothers is Tsélaa´.'"

Editor's Note: If you visit Canyon de Chelly, take binoculars to Fortress Rock. Just below the rim, you will see one of the log ladders placed by the Navajo more than 125 years ago.

The Navajo and the Stars

by Toni A. Watson

Since people first became the "Two-Legged Ones" and stood erect to gaze at the heavens, they have been fascinated by the stars. In this regard, the Navajo are no different.

The Navajo think of the stars as friendly beings. They believe the laws by which they should live are written in the patterns of the stars. These people use their star-watching skills to know when to hunt, when to plant, and when to harvest.

The stars even assist the Navajo in their healing rituals. In sand paintings, the singer uses symbols for stars, star constellations, and the sun and moon. The stars of these dry paintings receive their healing powers from a bright star that shines through the smoke hole in the roof of the hogan where the ceremony takes place.

Because the night sky (called the "dark upper") and sky phenomena are essential parts of the Navajo universe, references to the "dark upper" are common in the art, ceremonies, and storytelling of the Navajo people.

To the Navajo, it all began before there were any men, before Monster Slayer had killed the monsters. At that time, Black God came into the hogan where Earth and Sky lived. He had a small group of stars known as Dilyehe tied to his ankle. Black God stamped his foot vigorously, and Dilyehe jumped to his knee. Another stamp brought the stars to his hip. The other assembled gods nodded approvingly. He stamped once more and brought Dilyehe to his shoulder. A fourth and final stamp of his foot caused the circle of stars to lodge along his left temple, where he commanded them to stay. They remain there today. The constellation Dilyehe, which we know as Pleiades, is displayed on the left temple of the mask of Black God.

Thus Black God demonstrated to Sky and Earth his power to beautify the dark upper by placing stars in ordered patterns. They encouraged him to continue. Black God owned a deerskin pouch that contained crystals for making the stars. Standing under the dark upper, he reached into his pouch, drew out the crystals one by one, and carefully and deliberately placed them in the sky. In the east, he first placed the constellation Man With Feet Ajar (a large, irregular square in Vorvus). Then, slowly in succession, up went the constellations Horned Rattler, Bear, Thunder, and, in the south, First Big One (Scorpio). In the north, he stationed the Pole Star plus Revolving Male (Ursa Major, or the Big Dipper), Revolving Female (Ursa Minor, or the Little Dipper), Slender First One (part of Orion), Pinching or Doubtful Stars (Aldebaran, lower branch of Hyades), Rabbit Tracks (near Canis Major), and, finally, Dilyehe. Then he took some fine crystal dust from the pouch and created the Milky Way.

Having completed this part of his task, Black God was about to rest for a bit when Coyote, the trickster and troublemaker, approached him. Coyote complained that he had not been consulted about placing the stars. Black God knew that Coyote meant mischief, but before he could prevent him, Coyote grabbed the pouch of crystals, emptied it, and blew the contents across the sky. (That explains why only the stars put there by Black God have names and those scattered at random by Coyote are nameless.) Coyote had saved the brightest crystal from the pouch, however, and he placed it very carefully in the south (perhaps Antares). Today the Navajo still refer to this star as Coyote Star, and before they close their eyes in sleep, they glance to the south and see its mischievous wink.

CALIFORNIA INDIANS

The First Californians

by Jane Harrigan

Long before the first Spanish explorer arrived in the place we now call California, the land was home to thousands of Indians. In fact, there may have been as many as 275,000 Indians in California — more than anywhere else in North America — when the Spanish arrived there in 1542.

California was a wonderful place for the Indians to live. The climate was warm, the ocean and streams were full of fish, and everywhere there were animals and plants for the Indians to use for food, clothing, and shelter.

California Indians were organized into approximately one hundred tribes who lived in small villages. They spoke six or seven different languages, and there were more than one hundred varieties, or dialects, among those languages. Pomo, Yurok, Miwok, Chumash, and Yuman were the names of some of the California Indian groups. Sometimes the members of different villages could not understand each other because of their different dialects. Indians from different villages rarely saw each other because the villages were often separated by mountains, rivers, deserts, and other land formations, and this prevented the Indians from learning their neighbors' languages.

The California Indians knew how to make the most of nature. They did not have horses or cows, and only a few of them planted crops. Instead, they made their food and tools from the things they could find.

Indian men used bows and arrows to hunt deer, rabbits, squirrels, and mice. The men also did the fishing, using nets most of the time instead of poles and hooks. For fishing in the ocean, the Indians used dugout canoes made from redwood trees or boats made of planks tied together and covered with tar. For smaller bodies of water, they made rafts from bundles of reeds.

The Indians ate all kinds of fish, including shellfish and freshwater fish. And if a whale came close enough to spear, there was food for everyone.

The men did most of the hunting and fishing, but Indian women also provided food for their people. They gathered seeds, nuts, and plants in big baskets they carried on their backs. The baskets had long handles that the women wore around their foreheads. When they went on food-gathering trips, the women wore special woven caps so that the baskets would not hurt their heads.

The California Indians were very good at making baskets for all kinds of uses. Some baskets were woven so tightly that they could be used to carry water or cook food. Others had very beautiful colored designs that told stories. The Indians also were skillful at making tools, pipes, and musical instruments, especially flutes.

The Indians did not wear many clothes, but they liked jewelry made of rocks and shells. They also decorated themselves with tattoos by pricking designs into their skin with cactus needles, then rubbing in charcoal or dye from plants. Many Indian women were given tattoos that symbolized beauty or that they were married or about to be married. The meanings of these tattoos varied from village to village.

In different parts of California, the Indians lived in different kinds of houses. The designs of the houses were determined by the climate and

the building materials found in the area. In the colder, northern areas where there were forests of oak and pine, houses were made of wooden planks. Sometimes these houses were built in a pit, which helped them to stay warm in winter. In other areas, houses were made of tree bark or poles covered with mats made of brush or reeds. These mats could be covered with mud to keep cold air out. Most Indian houses had an opening in the roof to let out smoke from the fire that was built in the middle of the floor for heating and cooking.

Some of the Indians' customs may seem strange to us. For example, they used strings of shells for money, but often they just traded for what they wanted. Indian children were not given a name until they were six years old. And when an Indian died, no one was ever allowed to say that person's name again.

The first Spanish explorers were surprised to see the California Indians, and the Indians were very surprised to see the white men. But the Indians continued living as they always had until the Spanish began settling in California and building missions in the 1760s.

The Spanish thought they were helping the Indians by bringing them to live at the missions and teaching them about farming and Christianity. But many of the Indians did not want to leave their homes and ways of life. Many died from diseases they caught from the white people. Others ran away from the missions, and if they were caught, they were punished.

Things became much worse for the Indians when the Mexicans and people from the eastern part of the United States began claiming land and settling in California. The discovery of gold sent thousands of people into the hills where the Indians lived. They cut down the trees and panned for gold in the streams where the Indians had

fished. By this time, the Indians were angry. They began to steal from the prospectors and to fight back. But their bows and arrows were no match for the white men's guns, and many Indians died in the fighting.

Finally, in the 1850s, the U.S. government set aside pieces of land called reservations for the twenty thousand Indians who remained in California. But many were too proud to take help from the government, so they stayed in the hills and lived very poorly.

Today many Indians have married white people, and their children know little about the customs of their ancestors. But some Indians take pride in the traditions and stories of their great-grandparents and in the role they played in the history of California

How Animals Brought Fire to Man

by Anne B. Fisher

On cold nights when all the Karoks along the Klamath River were warm around the fire, the story-teller waved his story-telling staff and told how Karoks got their fire.

In the beginning, Fire was given to two old hags, because they were the very oldest people on earth. These hags were to share *Oh*, the Fire, with the Indians. Instead, the old hags kept Fire for themselves.

The Karoks shivered with the cold. They needed Fire to warm their hands and backs on cold nights. They wanted their children to see the pretty yellow flames dance. So they tried in every way

they could think of to get Fire away from the two greedy old hags.

The old women were fearsome creatures. One had four teeth. She gnashed her teeth together and they rattled like stones.

The other had five teeth in her flabby old mouth. The sound she made was far worse than stones rattling.

The hags had stringy hair, tied in a knot on top of their heads with a string of nettles. They were so thin their bones clattered when they walked.

The old hags rattled and growled every time an Indian came near the hut where they lived. They chased Indians with clubs in their bony hands. They threatened to claw Indian eyes out with their fingers that had nails on them like claws of Eagle.

One winter night when it was colder than it had ever been before, the Karoks were desperate. Shivering, they went to Coyote and told him their troubles.

"Unless we get Fire we will be so cold we will shake our bones apart, then the bones will rattle out of our skins and we will be dead," they told Coyote. "You are crafty and clever and cunning. Please steal Fire away from those hags for us."

Coyote felt sorry for the Indians, because he was warm in his yellow coat of fur and they had no snug fur

coats to keep them warm. He thought of taking off his coat and giving it to them, but it didn't have any openings through which he could get out.

He rubbed his whiskers and thought and thought. But no idea for a way of stealing Fire came to him.

Then he shook his tail hard, so hard that the earth around him shook too. Only, shaking his tail didn't shake a thought into his head about how to steal Fire from the old hags.

His fleas bothered him. If he could just get rid of those miserable fleas, he mused, maybe he could think better. He rolled on the ground, stirring up clouds of dust. The dust blinded the fleas and choked them. They stopped biting Coyote while they sneezed and coughed and tried to wipe the dust from their eyes.

While the fleas were wiping themselves off, an idea came to Coyote.

He called the Indians and animals together and told them he had a plan for stealing Fire.

Then, from the land of Karoks to the house of the old hags, he stationed a great company of animals, each animal at a distance from the other. The strongest animal was placed nearest to the den of the hags. The weakest animal was the farthest away. Last of all, Coyote hid a Karok Indian to wait near the hags' hut.

Coyote told the Karok exactly what to do, then trotted up the mountain to the door of the old hags.

Coyote knocked softly, politely, on the door.

The hags didn't hear him. They were fighting, and rattling their teeth at each other.

Coyote knocked again, more loudly.

The door opened and the hag with four teeth stuck her head out.

"What do you want?" she asked through her teeth.

"Would you please let me in out of the cold?" Coyote asked politely. He shivered a little to show her how cold he was, though he really was very warm with excitement.

The old hag suspected nothing. After all, he was polite. She had no grudge against Coyote, except that he "Ye-owed" too loud and too long on moonlight nights and kept her awake.

"All right, come in," she grumbled. "But for my poor ear's sake don't start 'ye-owe-owing' tonight."

Coyote had learned a long time ago when to sing and when to be quiet. This certainly was the time to be quiet. Everything depended on his manners.

He tip-pawed as softly as he knew how on every one of his four paws, to the hearth. He lay down before the crackling fire and made himself comfortable. Now all he needed was to wait for the Karok hiding in the woods to do his part.

Coyote's ears perked up. He heard the Karok coming along the trail.

Suddenly the Indian made a furious attack on the hut. Crash! Bang! His club thudded against the place, rattling the walls.

The old hags rushed out, gnashing their teeth.

That was Coyote's chance! He seized a half-burned brand in his mouth and fled from the hut like a comet, and down the mountain.

The two hags had sharp ears and eyes. They saw Coyote and took after him.

Coyote ran as fast as he could. But he had eaten more than the hags and was fatter.

They were so thin they had only bones to carry and they could run very, very, *very* fast.

Coyote's breath was giving out! The hags were so close he could feel their breath blowing on his tail. He could hear their teeth rattling.

Gasping, Coyote looked around

for help. He couldn't run any more. Just as one old hag grabbed at his tail, something leaped from the bushes. Mountain Lion! Mountain Lion seized the flaming brand between his white teeth and raced on.

Coyote sank down, clearing his sooty eyes and throat and catching his breath. Through the roaring in his own ears, he heard the old hags scream in anger and gnash their teeth more wildly than ever as they rushed by him and after Mountain Lion.

Mountain Lion went so fast that he left a trail of sparks in the cold damp night.

Even Mountain Lion could not out-race the fleet hags. They were about to catch him by the tail when Bear jumped out of a cave! Bear grabbed the torch in his great claws and took off with it.

But Bear couldn't go as fast as Mountain Lion, because he had robbed too many bees of their honey that year and was big and fat.

"Kerthunk — wobble," he waddled. Bear got winded very soon. The old hags soon caught up with him. They had only knots of hair and bones to weigh them down and they didn't have as heavy teeth as Bear had.

Bear was so near to being caught

that he had to throw the torch toward the place where Rabbit was supposed to be hiding.

"What if Rabbit isn't there?" Bear thought. "What if Rabbit doesn't catch the brand and the hags get Fire back?" Bear was sorry he had eaten so much honey and was so fat. If Indians lost Fire they would blame him and the honey inside his fat belly.

But Rabbit was there in his place by the bush. He caught up the torch and didn't mind a bit that his whiskers were singed.

"Hoppity-hoppity-hop" he went, right from under the bony, reaching fingers of the old hags, and down the mountain path as hard as he could hop.

On went the torch from one animal to the next with the old hags after it.

Poor Squirrel, the next to the last animal on the trail to the Indian village, burned his tail so badly that it curled up over his back — where it remains to this day.

Last came Frog, who didn't get the brand until it had burned down to a very little piece. He hopped along so heavily that the old hags gained on him.

They kept coming nearer and nearer and NEARER and faster and faster and FASTER!

Frog pulled his back legs up very tight and made a great spring.

Still the hags gained on him.

They were about up to him. He could feel their breath on the back of his neck! He stretched himself at each leap until his poor muscles went "crackety crack."

Then he was caught! His smoke-dried eyes bulged out of his head. His little heart thumped like a club against the cold bony fingers that closed over his body.

He made a wild "Croak!" the first croak he had ever made in all his life. "I'll make one more hop for the Karoks! One more hop for Coyote who trusted me in this great thing!" he vowed.

With a mighty gulp, brave little Frog swallowed Fire, tore himself away from the bony old hands that held him, and leaped into the river.

He dived deep and swam furiously until he reached the other side of the river where the hags could not follow. There he sank down, gasping with his last breath. But alas, he had left his beautiful tail in the hands of one old hag. Worse, there was only his ghost left to spit out a burning ember onto some sticks.

It is because Frog's ghost coughed out that ember that Indians can make Fire by rubbing two sticks of wood together. And it is because Frog lost his tail that, ever since, only the young Frogs called tadpoles have tails.

Although Coyote ran until his paws were raw — and Rabbit singed his whiskers — and Squirrel scorched his tail so that it curled up over his back — and Frog lost his tail forever — not one of the animals has ever spoken of the sacrifices made in bringing Fire to the Indians by the Klamath River.

From *Stories California Indians Told* by Anne B. Fisher, illustrated by Ruth Robbins. Copyright © 1957 by Anne B. Fisher (text) and Ruth Robbins (illustrations). Published by Parnassus Press, Berkeley, California. Reprinted with permission.

The Iroquois: Men Lead, Women Choose

by Trudie Lamb Richmond

The Six Nations of the Iroquois are eastern woodland Indians whose territory at one time stretched from the Great Lakes through New York State and over large portions of land on the Canadian side of the St. Lawrence River. For centuries, they lived in longhouses, each shared by several related families, and they still call themselves Haudenosaunee, "people of the longhouse."

The land of the Iroquois was rich and fertile, and the people depended mostly on farming for their food. As with many societies, men did the hunting and fishing and provided protection. In turn, women maintained the village, tended the crops, prepared and preserved the food, and raised the children.

Long ago, five nations, or tribes — the Oneida, Mohawk, Cayuga, Onondaga, and Seneca — formed the League of the Iroquois to protect their trade routes to the west and to keep peace among themselves. Later, a sixth nation, the Tuscarora, joined the league.

The idea of the league originated with Dekanawida many generations ago. He had been searching for a way to bring peace and unity to his people, whose warring and quarreling were dividing them at a frightening pace. Dekanawida's league and the Great Law of Peace still unite the Six Nations of the Iroquois and have enabled them to preserve their identity and culture. There are many unique factors of the Great Law. One of these is the political power of Iroquois women. Not only do the women decide who will be the leaders of each nation, but if a leader fails in his duties, only the women have the power to remove him.

In Iroquois society, the woman is the center of the family and the heartbeat of the nation. The creation story explains how Sky Woman fell from the Sky World, landing on the back of Turtle. As she began to dance and sing her ceremonial songs, Turtle's back grew larger, creating our great continent — Turtle Island (North America). When she died, she became part of the earth. Almost from that moment, the role of women, the Givers of Life, was clear. That is why Indian people say, "The earth is our mother; treat her with great respect."

Indian people describe all natural forces in kinship terms, as they believe that they are related to all

Word Lore: From the Longhouse

by David Richmond

Saigo ("Greetings!")

People of the longhouse called themselves by slightly different names than the ones we use today. We live with unique Iroquois names, and the English or French versions of them, which help connect us to our Indian heritage. Like precious strings of wampum, these names weave us into Native American understandings, linking the past with the present.

Iroquois From the Algonquian Iriakhoiw with the French suffix -ois. This was a term of fear meaning "real adders" or "poisonous snakes" used by the Algonquians to refer to the Iroquois people. We call ourselves the Haudenosaunee ("people of the longhouse") and by the names of our nation.

Mohawk An Algonquian term of fear meaning "cannibals," "wolves," or "man-eaters." The Mohawk call themselves Ganiengehaka ("people of the flint country"), the keepers of the eastern door for the Six Nations.

Oneida "People of the standing stone" or "stone people."

Onondaga "People of the hills"; keepers of the wampum, fire keepers, name bearers.

Cayuga "People of the marsh"; keepers of the great pipe.

Seneca "People of the great hill"; keepers of the western door.

Tuscarora "People of the hemp."

Other Iroquois Words

Akwesasne "Land where the partridge drums" (Strong wing beats by some game birds are called "drumming.")

Adirondack "Bark-eaters" (Indians living in the Adirondack region were known to eat the inner bark of trees, which is good survival food.)

Canada "Group of houses or dwellings"

Genesee "Beautiful valley"

Hiawatha "Maker of rivers"; also, a famous Iroquois chief

Kentucky "Meadowlands"

Niagara "Thunder of waters" or "neck-shaped region"

Ohio "Beautiful river" or "big river"

Susquehanna "Turbulent river"

Ticonderoga "Where two rivers meet"

Onen ("It is finished.")

living things. For example, they call the moon Grandmother and the sun Elder Brother. All within the animal kingdom are relatives. This belief creates a sense of unity not only in a spiritual sense but also in the sense of managing society. And it is with this outlook that the Iroquois link themselves in a series of circles. At the center is the family. The next circle is made up of clans, the next of tribes, and the largest of the nation. These circles explain how groups are related and define their responsibilities to one another. For example, the people within a clan are all descended from a common ancestor, and each clan is named for animal relatives such as the turtle, bear, wolf, deer, or snipe (a bird).

Women are the heads of clans as well as households. They are called clan mothers. Children belong to their mother's clan rather than their father's (people within the same clan do not marry each other). When a young man marries, he goes to live with his wife's family.

The women within each clan appoint the male chiefs, who, in turn, speak for their clans in tribal councils. Consulting with the other women within their clan, the clan mothers decide on issues and questions to be debated and acted upon in the council. They recommend to their male spokesmen what view to express and push for. The clan mothers look for certain qualities and strengths in their leaders. Besides loyalty and trustworthiness, a leader must be a skilled speaker.

The women have great political power. Not only do they have authority over their homes, the land, and the children, but they also determine a person's name, which does not belong to the person but to his or her mother's clan. Each clan keeps a record of names, maintained by the women. When a child is born, he or she receives a name not in use; when the person dies, that name goes back in the record and

Algonquian Indian Place Names

by E. Barrie Kavasch

Connecticut, Algonquian for "long tidal river," and Massachusetts, Natick for "at the great hills," are only two of many U.S. states that bear American Indian names. Although most of the native Algonquian (spoken) dialects in New England are gone, the Anglicized versions of many Algonquian place names remain.

These Indian names, from Nova Scotia to Virginia, speak about features, fears, foods, medicines, colors, water uses, and survival. Indian tribal names usually mean "the people" or "people of a particular place." Other names refer to distinctive associations, activities, or manners. A few northeastern tribal names translate to key foods. For example, Passamaquoddy (Abenaki) means "those who pursue the pollack" (a particular native fish); Nipmuc (Algonquian) means "freshwater fishing place"; Menominee (Algonquian) means "wild rice people"; and Mashantucket (Mohegan/Pequot) means "a well-wooded country."

The Algonquian Indians of the Northeast called the White Mountains of New Hampshire Agiockochook ("crystal hills") because they were considered the home of Manitou, the Great Spirit, whose anger was the lightning and whose voice the thunder. This region is still alive with

native legends and spirits.

Native place names seem to reflect an ancient resilience and integrity with nature and the land: Androscoggin (Abenaki) means "fish-curing place"; Apponagansett (Narragansett) means "oyster bay"; Apponaug (Narragansett) means "place to roast oysters"; Damariscotta (Abenaki) means "plenty of alewives" (a particular fish that was very important in native diets); Cataumet (Algonquian) means "great fishing place"; Cohasset (Algonquian) means "at the small pine trees"; Cotuit and Coonamessett (Algonquian) mean "pine woodland"; Skunknet (Algonquian) means "a fishing place for eels"; and Cuttyhunk (Mohegan) means "land opened or broken up," as for farming.

The Algonquian words *moccasin, squaw,* and *papoose* often are used to denote special medicinal plants, such as squawmint, squawbalm, papooseroot, and moccasin flower. Many Algonquian words are commonly used today in relation to food: succotash, squash, quahog, wampum, sumac, tamarack, skunk, muskrat, caribou, wapiti, squirrel, and opossum. Succotash is from the Narragansett word *msickquatash,* meaning "boiled whole grains (corn)," and squash is from the Narragansett/Massachusett word *askootasquash,* meaning "fruits from the vine." In some ways, we are still speaking Indian languages today.

becomes available again.

When a man is selected as chief, he is given a chief's name. Each clan has a long list of chief's names, which, like the chief's position, must be treated with respect. Among these are Shononses, meaning "his house is long"; Skanaawadi,

meaning "across the swamp"; and Dayohronyonkah, meaning "it reaches or pierces the sky."*

As with U.S. Supreme Court justices, a council position is for life. But if a leader fails to carry out his

*The names were obtained from Elizabeth Tooker, *Handbook of North American Indians,* volume 15, 1975.

  46

About the Little People

by Jesse J. Cornplanter

"We will rejoice with our own ceremony, which will also be yours from now on. This ceremony is called 'Dark Dance' and really belongs to us, you must observe everything that takes place and remember everything so you can carry it back to your people, which will bring them good luck. They in turn will remember us and our relation by getting up the ceremony for our enjoyment. So I command you to watch now."

The old man of the Little People to the Seneca boy

---

responsibilities or considers himself more important than his people, the women can use their power to remove him from his position. He is given three warnings. If there is no change, the leader is stripped of his right to rule in a "dehorning" ceremony.

And so it has been for many generations that the voices of Iroquois women are not only heard but also listened to with great respect. What is even more remarkable is the fact that the democratic principles of the Iroquois were of great importance in the founding of the U.S. government. The U.S. Constitution was modeled after the Iroquois' oral constitution, the Great Law of Peace. The founders of the United States ignored one very important aspect of the Iroquois League, however. American women did not win the right to vote until 1920, more than 125 years after the Constitution was adopted.

In the olden times when my people lived more or less with nature's own way, when they were able to converse with animals, when strange things happened, when great beasts and birds were common, these little people lived their various modes of habitation; they were very close friends of the "Ong-weh-ohn-weh" [or] "Real Humans" as we are called. They made contact with our people in many different ways. To us, they are known as "Djo-geh-onh," and were considered more powerful even though they were very small. They had a way of making friends to little boys of our people, often taking [the boys] with them to their homes, which may be some place among the Rocky places or Caves.

One of the legends tells of an Indian boy about the age of seven [who] was out hunting little birds. He had his little bow and arrow to shoot what he [might] see, as it was the custom in those days to teach their growing boys all the sports of the hunt and chase as a major part of their early training, — it was their schooltime. This little boy was wandering on, when he finally came to a river to see if he could see some water-fowl to shoot. He had no sooner reached the edge of the water, when he heard a swishing noise to the direction of up-stream. Looking up, he was surprised to see a tiny canoe shoot around the bend of the stream at a rapid speed. In the canoe were two of the tiniest

  47

little men that the boy ever had seen. They came right up to where the boy stood and stopped. Both had a tiny bow and a quiver of arrows.

They both greeted the boy, then one of them asked him thus, "How would you like to trade your bow and arrows with one of us?"

Then the boy thought how foolish it would be to do so, as their bows and arrows were much smaller than his; so he said, "How foolish it would be to do so — why, yours are so much smaller than mine."

Then one of them took a bow and strung it and taking an arrow he shot it straight up, the arrow disappeared into the sky and did not come down at all. Saying at the same time, "That may be true, but all great things on earth are not always the biggest; you may live to learn that." Then they took their canoe-paddles and with one stroke disappeared around the bend of the river.

The boy was surprised; so he went back to his home, where he was staying with his grand-mother. He told her all about what happened. Then his grand-mother scolded her grand-son, saying: "You made a big mistake by your refusal to accept the trade. Had you taken one of their bows and arrows, you could take any game that you desired, as they are magic. Hereafter never be too hasty in judging people as you see them, for you never know who or what they may be."

Excerpt from *Legends of the Longhouse* by Jesse J. Cornplanter. Copyright 1938 by Jesse J. Cornplanter and Namee Price Henricks. Copyright renewed © 1966 by Mrs. Jesse Cornplanter. Reprinted by permission of HarperCollins Publishers, Inc.

CHEROKEE AND OTHER SOUTHEASTERN TRIBES
Indian Cultures of the Southeast

by E. Barrie Kavasch

Southern Indian cultures flourished in the warm temperate regions of our country for thousands of years. In these diverse areas, various chiefdoms ruled complex native societies. Many had capital towns, often located on surrounding massive mounds and other notable earthworks, which supported temples and council lodges.

The first recorded European encounter occurred in 1513, when Juan Ponce de León encountered a hostile reception from the native people of southern Florida. Hernando de Soto's disastrous, meandering intrusion among southeastern peoples in the years 1539 to 1543 ended his life but was even more devastating to the native tribes, many members of which were killed, kidnapped, enslaved, and raped. Countless later died of European diseases, to which native populations possessed almost no resistance. The English established the colony of Jamestown in 1607, the first permanent English settlement in North America. They encountered the powerful Indian chief Wahunsonacock. Because they could not pronounce his name, they called him Chief Powhatan, the name of his tribe and confederacy of about thirty different bands inhabiting possibly as many as two hundred villages in the tidewater region that came to be called Virginia.

The Cherokee people originally lived in the regions that are now parts of Georgia, Alabama, Tennessee, Kentucky, North and South Carolina, Virginia, and West Virginia. Noted farmers and

hunters, they worked the fertile bottomlands along the rivers, where they cultivated corn, squash, beans, sunflowers, gourds, sunchokes, tobacco, and cotton. Southeastern forests were full of deer, bears, mountain lions, bobcats, beavers, raccoons, opossum, wild turkeys, quail, grouse, ducks, pigeons, and countless other animals and birds, as well as valuable medicinal plants.

The Cherokee, Creek, Choctaw, Chickasaw, and Seminole of the Southeast have shared very similar ways of life, political restrictions, and conflicts. Other southeastern

tribes include the Catawba of South Carolina; the Alabama, Chitimacha, and Koasati of Mississippi; the Mikasuki (Miccosukee) of Georgia and Florida; the Tunica-Biloxi of Louisiana; and the Yuchi of the Appalachian highlands.

Most of these native peoples were pushed beyond their ancestral homelands by American settlers. Many chose to live among other tribes and confederacies in Texas, Mexico, and Canada. Many others walked the Trail of Tears during the U.S. government's shameful forced removal of the southeastern tribes to Arkansas and Oklahoma in 1838–39. Still others remained in the Southeast; hid out; intermarried with other tribes, African slaves, and white Americans; and tried to "live white" where they could. Many native people of the Southeast are now biracial or triracial and proud of their mixed heritage, although early laws forbidding inter-racial marriage prevented many of our ancestors from talking about their cultural histories.

Today the Five Civilized Tribes are centered in Oklahoma. They have gathered considerable strength and pride as they have watched their populations grow and flourish. The Cherokee Nation is located in Tahlequah, Oklahoma, and more than ten thousand eastern Cherokee live on their reservation in North Carolina. The Choctaw Tribal Center is in Durant, the Muskogee Creek Capitol in Okmulgee, the Chickasaw Council Center in Ada, and the Seminole Nation Museum in Wewoka (all in Oklahoma). Various tribal centers also are located in Texas and Florida.

How the Rabbit Stole the Otter's Coat

retold by Elizabeth M. Tenney

A very long time ago when the earth was new, all things were not as they are now. The animals were very different from one another. Some wore short coats, others long. Some had dark-colored fur, others red or gray. Some had rings on their tails; others had no tail at all.

The animals were forever arguing about who looked the best. Finally, to settle the dispute, they agreed to hold a council. Everyone was to be invited to decide, once and for all, who had the finest coat.

Otter, who lived far away on a distant creek, was not present. Although the animals had not seen him for a long time — he seldom came for a visit — it was known that Otter had a very fine coat. Surely, when he heard about the contest, he would come to the council to show it off.

Rabbit quietly listened while the others talked. He did not like what they were saying. It seemed to him that the animals already had more or less agreed that Otter's coat was the finest. That would never do! Rabbit was determined to have the honor himself.

Hmmmmm, he thought, I shall have to come up with a good trick to cheat Otter so that he will not be chosen. But what shall it be?

Rabbit thought about it all night and finally came up with a plan. Slyly, he asked questions about where Otter lived. No one knew for sure, but Rabbit was able to learn the general direction of Otter's creek.

Without saying anything to

anyone, Rabbit slipped away. For four days, he traveled until he arrived at Otter's dwelling. Rabbit recognized Otter at once by his beautiful soft coat of dark brown fur.

"Good day to you, Rabbit," said Otter. "Where are you going?"

"I've come to see you," said Rabbit. "The animals have sent me to bring you to a council. Because you live so far away, they were afraid you might get lost."

"How kind of you to come," said Otter, very pleased to have a special messenger sent for him. He invited Rabbit into his home, fed him a good supper, and prepared a bed for him. The next morning, the two of them set out for the council grounds. Rabbit led the way.

They traveled all day, and when night came, Rabbit selected the campground because Otter was a stranger to that part of the country.

Rabbit cut down bushes to make their beds and fixed everything neatly for their camp.

The next morning, they started out again. As they went along, Rabbit began to pick up pieces of wood and load them on his back.

"Why are you picking up bits

of wood?" asked Otter.

"It may be chilly tonight," replied Rabbit. "The wood will keep us warm and comfortable."

"That's a good idea," agreed Otter.

When it was near sunset, they stopped to make camp. Again Rabbit made all the arrangements. When supper was over, Rabbit picked up a piece of wood and sat down by the fire. He began to whittle a paddle.

Again Otter asked what he was doing.

"I have good dreams when I sleep with a paddle under my head," said Rabbit.

Otter thought this was very strange, but he said nothing. When the paddle was finished, Rabbit began to cut away the bushes to make a clear trail down to the river.

"Why are you making a trail to the river?" asked Otter.

"This place is called Di' tatlaski' yi (the place where it rains fire). Sometimes it rains fire here."

Rabbit scanned the sky and looked worried.

"The sky looks that way tonight. You go to sleep, and I'll sit and watch. If the fire does come, as soon as you hear me shout, run down this trail I have made and jump into the river."

Otter thanked Rabbit for taking such good care of him and prepared to go to sleep.

"Oh, one more thing," said Rabbit. "You'd better hang your coat on a limb over there, so it won't get burnt."

Otter took off his coat and did as

Rabbit told him. Then he lay down and went to sleep. Rabbit kept awake. After a while, the fire burned down to a red glow.

"Otter!" called Rabbit. But Otter did not answer. He was fast asleep.

In a little while, Rabbit again called, "Otter!" But Otter did not stir.

Then Rabbit pulled out his paddle and put it into the fire. He filled the paddle with glowing hot coals. With a big swing, Rabbit threw the coals high into the air and shouted, "It's raining fire! It's raining fire!"

The hot coals fell all around Otter, and he jumped up afraid.

"Run!" cried Rabbit. "Take the path to the water!"

Otter ran and jumped into the river. He has lived there ever since.

Rabbit took down Otter's coat from the tree limb and put it on. Then Rabbit proceeded to the council grounds.

In the meantime, all of the animals were waiting and watching for the arrival of Otter. At last, they thought they saw him coming in the distance.

"Otter's coming! Otter's coming!" they called. They sent out one of the small animals to show Otter the way to the best seat. They were all glad to see him, and each, in turn, went up to welcome him.

But Otter kept his head down and held one paw over his face. The animals thought Otter was very bashful.

Then Bear came up. Bear was very wise and a little suspicious. Why would someone with such a beautiful coat hide his face? Bear pulled Otter's paw away and saw that it was really Rabbit with his split nose!

Rabbit jumped up and started to run. Bear reached for him and caught hold of his tail. Rabbit pulled away so hard that his tail came off in Bear's hand! Rabbit got away but even today has only a small tuft of a tail.

GREAT LAKES AND MISSISSIPPI VALLEY TRIBES

Peoples of the Great Lakes and Mississippi River

by E. Barrie Kavasch

The heartland waterways of North America nourished the homelands of diverse prehistoric native peoples, ancestors of today's Great Lakes and Mississippi River tribes. Four of the Great Lakes bear American Indian names: Erie, Michigan, Ontario, and Huron, although the French take credit for Huron, which is the name they gave to the Wyandot. Lake Superior, which French explorers called *le lac superieur,* is the largest and westernmost of the Great Lakes.

The five sparkling lakes form a giant geographical stairway stepping down some six hundred feet from the middle of our continent to the Atlantic Ocean (via the St. Lawrence River), as the water flows from one lake into another. Lake Huron is the second-largest lake in this dynamic system and the fifth-largest freshwater lake in the world. French explorers gave this name to the Wyandot Indians, whose name for themselves means "islanders" or "peninsula dwellers." But the French thought that the Wyandot looked "rough" and "wild," hence the name Huron. These northern Iroquoian-speaking Indians were great hunters and traders. Their Canadian homeland was called Huronia.

Lake Michigan is the third largest of the Great Lakes and almost a twin to Huron, which it joins at the Straits of Mackinac. Michigan is Ojibway for "big water" or "great lake." Erie, the fourth-largest lake, is Iroquois for "wild cats." This Iroquoian-speaking tribe, "the nation of the cat," was decimated by the Iroquois in the mid-1600s, as they sought to control the rich fur trade. Lake Erie narrows at its eastern end, spilling into the Niagara River, which thunders down the 326-foot vertical drop of Niagara Falls into Lake Ontario. Ontario is another Iroquois word, meaning "sparkling or beautiful water." It is the smallest, but third deepest, of the scenic lakes. Ontario empties into the St. Lawrence River more than a thousand miles from Duluth, Minnesota (at the western end of Lake Superior). The river travels another twelve hundred miles to the Atlantic Ocean.

The Kickapoo, Sac (Sauk), Fox, Chippewa (Ojibway), Ottawa, Potawatomi, and Menominee were among the Great Lakes peoples. The Sioux recall their distant origins in the Great Lakes region, before they migrated to the broad plains. The more socially organized Great Lakes tribes had two chiefs — a peace chief and a war chief. Some tribes also had a ceremonial leader, who was usually a medicine person and led religious rituals. The Grand Medicine Lodge, or Midéwiwin, of the Chippewa is an ancient, and continuing, medicine society, whose sophisticated rites, healing formulas, songs, prescriptions, and other healing paraphernalia are respected throughout the Americas.

The Chippewa (called Ojibway in Canada) called themselves the Anishinabé, which means "first people." The Chippewa, Ottawa, and Potawatomi were known as the Council of Three Tribes.

Algonquian Indians named the great river that divides our country Mississippi, which means "big water," "father of waters," or "great river." Flowing from its source in northern Minnesota approximately twenty-three hundred miles south to its mouth in the Gulf of Mexico, this powerful river is more than a mile wide in some places. As the mighty Mississippi meanders and

turns back on itself in some places, it drains forty percent of the American heartland. Devastating floods continue to devour additional land.

The river has influenced the shape, history, economics, and politics of our country since long before it was called America. Prehistoric Indians built their villages in its fertile valleys and on its prominent bluffs. Early hunters, gatherers, farmers, fishermen, and craftspeople left haunting remains in various settlement areas, some of which were inhabited for more than eight thousand years. Sophisticated Mound Builder cultures built immense cities, effigy mounds (in the shapes of snakes and turtles), and various earth mounds. These earliest Mississippian and Hopewellian cultures traveled and traded along the great river system and beyond. Centuries ago, the ceremonial center of Cahokia (in Illinois) was home to perhaps twenty thousand people, ancestors of many of today's Native Americans. The lower Mississippi was central to the settlements of the distinctive Natchez people.

Hernando de Soto reached the Mississippi in 1541. One hundred years later, French, then English, explorers, traders, and missionaries began to encounter many different Mississippi River tribes. Large villages of Natchez, Alabama, Choctaw, and Chickasaw came under attack. Soon the Illinois Confederacy and the Iroquois Confederacy were at war. The Shawnee, Sac, Fox, and Kickapoo worked to organize a confederation in the early 1800s, but the swelling tide of American expansion saw the removal of most southern tribes to areas west of the Mississippi by 1839. Thus, the mighty river became the political/geographical dividing line for a young nation unable to come to terms with its diverse ethnic origins.

The Curse of a Manitou: A Chippewa Legend

retold by Joanne Swords

In the Chippewa* wigwams around the shores of three of the five Great Lakes — Superior, Michigan, and Huron — the storytellers of long ago passed the hours with spellbinding tales. The Chippewa told these stories not just to amuse listeners but also to explain what was happening in their world. The tribal shaman, or medicine man, would tell the stories, which eventually grew into legends.

*The Chippewa are also known as the Ojibway.

Each tale would place the blame or credit for some occurrence on one or more of the Chippewa's gods or manitous (spirits).

The depth of the Great Lakes has fluctuated greatly over the years. Recorded all-time lows occurred in the 1920s and 1930s and again in the 1950s. Modern residents whose lake property has been left high and dry by these lows have had a hard time understanding what was going on, so just imagine what the Indians of long ago must have thought. During one great low, a shaman spun this tale of Manabozho, the spirit of the winds and waters of the Great Lakes.

One warm summer day, a stately Indian walked slowly along the shores of the Great Lakes

---

Word Lore: How the Lakes Were Named
by Betty H. Little

Many U.S. place names — cities, states, and bodies of water — are English spellings of Indian words. For example, the names of more than half the fifty states come from various Indian languages. Of the five Great Lakes, three names come from Indian languages:

Michigan The Ojibway, an Algonquian Indian tribe, lived on the shores of Lake Michigan, the largest body of fresh water situated entirely within the United States. To the Ojibway, the lake was "big water." The word "Michigan" comes from the Ojibway word *michigami*, a combination of *michhaw* (great) and *sasigan* (lake).

Erie The Iroquois Indians along this lake's shores used the long-tailed wildcat as their totem, or symbol. The tribe was known as "the nation of the cat," or *erieehronous*. French explorers named the lake *lac du chat* (lake of the cat), but English takes its name from the Indian word.

Ontario This name comes from the Iroquois word *onitar-io*, meaning "sparkling or beautiful water."

The names of the other two Great Lakes come from the French:

Huron The bristly hair on the heads of the Wyandot Indians living along this lake reminded early French explorers of the wild hair of a boar. In the French language, *hure* means "head (of a wild boar)." Although the hairdo probably caused the French to use this term, perhaps it also referred to the Wyandot's "bristly" nature.

Superior French explorers called this *le lac superieur*, meaning that it was located higher than, or upstream from, the other Great Lakes. This is the only lake name that lacks any Indian association.

looking for food. He was Manabozho, one of the Chippewa Nation's great magicians and manitous. Being in no hurry, he looked out over the water, drinking in its beauty, then turned to survey the pine trees and grasses of the region.

After a time, when the sun was high in the sky, Manabozho came upon a patch of lake weeds that he especially liked to eat. He ate and ate until his stomach was rock hard and could hold no more. Having eaten so much and walked so far, Manabozho grew sleepy, so he lay down on the warm sand and slept a very deep sleep.

A strong wind arose over the Great Lakes and saw Manabozho sleeping on the sand. Deciding to play a trick on him, the wind blew the water into violent waves with caps of white froth. They crept nearer and nearer to the sleeping Manabozho.

When one very high wave crashed down, drenching Manabozho, he awoke in a terrible temper. He rose to his full height and shook the water from his body. His dark eyes snapping like lightning, he held his hands out, facing the water. The strong wind stopped blowing and became a breeze. The water quieted, washing over his feet.

In a voice reaching to the farthest regions of the Great Lakes, he shouted, "Hereafter, so that you may treat no one else in this rude manner, you will become smaller and smaller. One day you will be like the little water held in the palm of my hand. And the strong wind will play no more."

The waters of the Great Lakes have retreated from Manabozho's anger many times since that day. The next time the water of one of the lakes is especially low, remember the manitou's curse.

PLAINS INDIANS

Peoples of the Plains: Early Days

by Stanley A. Freed

Blackfeet, Cheyenne, Comanche, Crow, Dakota (Sioux). The very names of the Plains Indian tribes call to mind vast herds of buffalo and mounted warriors of legendary courage. They symbolize the American frontier, which, though long past, still retains a prominent place in national history and mythology.

Long before European settlers introduced horses and guns to the Great Plains, Indians inhabited the heartland of North America. They lived in places from southern Texas to southern Canada and from the Mississippi River to the foothills of the Rocky Mountains, a region of about one million square miles.

Before A.D. 1300, drought drove most of the original inhabitants, mainly hunters who traveled on foot, into other regions, and the plains became largely depopulated. Then the tribes we know today began to drift into the region from all directions. Migration to the plains continued for five hundred years. Population growth and the lure of the buffalo may have encouraged this migration. Pressure from Europeans, who were firmly established along the East Coast by the mid-seventeenth century, also pushed the Indians onto the plains.

The Plains Indians entered a great grassland with two major zones differing chiefly in rainfall. The eastern prairie zone had enough rainfall to make farming possible. West of the prairie, the drier high plains were generally unsuitable for agriculture, but the region's short grass (buffalo grass) was excellent for great herds of buffalo. Therefore, the tribes living in the high plains were strictly nomadic buffalo hunters, while the prairie tribes also farmed.

For part of the year, the farming tribes of the plains remained in permanent villages, living in large, solid, earth-covered lodges. Built mainly by women, earth lodges were domed structures forty to fifty feet in diameter. Because these lodges were considered sacred, ceremonies accompanied their construction. Several related families lived in one lodge. Beds were fitted with canopies for privacy.

The farmers raised the common Indian crops: maize (corn), beans, squash, melons, gourds, and sunflowers. Although men occasionally assisted in clearing the land or husking corn, women did most of the farming. Planting began in April and continued into June. Then the Indians left the village for the summer buffalo hunt, leaving behind only the aged and the disabled, with a few able-bodied adults to care for them, tend the crops, and protect the village. Laden with meat and hides, the Indians returned to their villages in September for the harvest. Often a fall/winter buffalo hunt followed the harvest. Some tribes returned to pass the winter in temporary villages built along rivers on low-lying land protected from the wind. Although the farming tribes sometimes lived away from their main village for many months every year, they considered it their home.

During the summer, all the plains tribes followed the buffalo, hunting them to build up a supply of meat for the winter. They lived in tipis, conical skin tents made of a dozen or so buffalo hides sewn together. Easy to erect, take down, and transport and designed to withstand strong winds, the tipi was ideally adapted to a nomadic life on the windswept plains. Especially for the tribes of the high plains, who passed the harsh

winters in separate small bands, summer was the time for a tribe to assemble for ceremonies such as the sun dance, the major annual ceremony for most of the tribes.

The summer buffalo hunt was a communal activity. Before the Indians had horses, they hunted buffalo by driving a herd over a cliff or into an enclosure where they could be shot with bows and arrows. The idea was to kill as many buffalo as possible before the herd moved on.

The Indians found ways to use every part of the buffalo: The meat was their staple food; bone and horn provided tools and utensils; the hair was used to make bags, ropes, and padding and the hide to make clothing, bedding, tipis, and storage containers; dried dung, or buffalo chips, served as fuel. The Indians also made ceremonial objects from parts of the buffalo. However, not all the buffalo that were killed could be used. Because the main hunting methods involved mass killing, hunters sometimes killed more animals than the people needed.

Buffalo hunting changed after the Indians acquired horses. The basic technique became the exciting and dangerous pursuit on horseback of individual animals. The horses and firearms that Europeans brought to the New World changed not only

hunting techniques but also transportation and warfare. The travois, a platform for baggage mounted on two poles, was originally dragged by a dog. Horses quickly replaced dogs, as they could drag much heavier loads. Tipis became larger. People accumulated property. The old and the sick, who formerly had to be abandoned when a family moved, could now be carried along. Mounted warriors replaced raiders on foot. They were skilled enough to give the U.S. Cavalry fits.

The full-blown, legendary hunter-warrior culture of the Plains Indians lasted only about two hundred years. Plains Indian culture in its best-known form, based on the buffalo, horse, and gun, began to develop in the second half of the seventeenth century, long before white settlers appeared on the plains. Whites were living all around the plains, however, and horses, guns, and other useful items found their way even to Indians in the heart of the region, many of whom might never have seen a white person.

Horses came from the Spaniards moving north from Mexico to found settlements in the Southwest in the seventeenth century. Although horses spread slowly among the Plains Indians, most tribes had them by the end of the eighteenth cen-

tury. Guns came from whites living in the East. Traders supplied them to Indians, who were increasingly drawn into the fur trade. England and France also armed their Indian allies in the Colonial wars.

The Indian wars on the plains began with the Grattan Massacre in Wyoming Territory in 1854 and ended at Wounded Knee, South Dakota, in 1890. Although the Indians fought bravely and well, they were worn down by vastly superior numbers and resources. After the buffalo were nearly exterminated, mainly by professional white hunters, the Indians lost their staple food and were subject to starvation. Further resistance was futile, and the Indians were settled on reservations. After a period of disorientation, they began to recover. Today they take part quite successfully in modern American society while at the same time preserving important parts of their own cultures.

Lone Boy and the Old Dun Horse

retold by Josepha Sherman

Once, in the long-ago days when the Pawnee wandered freely on the Great Plains, there lived a boy named Lone Boy. He was the poorest in the tribe. He ate only what others didn't want and wore only what others threw away. His little lodge was made of scraps of leather and bits of bark. He owned no horses and had to walk wearily after the tribe whenever they moved.

One day, Lone Boy heard a feeble whinny. He hurried down into a small ravine, where he found the saddest, oldest dun (brownish gray) horse he had ever seen. Every rib showed on its skinny body, and its mane and tail looked like bits of tangled yarn.

"Poor old horse!" Lone Boy said. "I'll take care of you."

Everyone laughed at him for bothering with such a sad-looking animal. But Lone Boy took good care of that horse. He fed it the best grass he could find and groomed it well.

One day, the tribe's scouts came hurrying back to camp. They had found a large herd of buffalo, and one of the buffalo was a spotted calf! The hide of a spotted calf was powerful medicine indeed.

"Whoever brings me the spotted hide," cried the Head Chief, "will wed my daughter."

Off raced all the hunters on their swift horses. Lone Boy went, too, mounted on his old dun horse. The other hunters laughed at him and left him far behind.

When the other hunters were out of sight, the old horse stopped. "Don't worry," he said.

Lone Boy gasped. "You — you spoke!"

"Don't be afraid of me, either. Come cover me with this nice, cool mud. That's right; plaster it all over me. Give me the strength of the earth. Now wait till we hear the hunters' call."

The call came. The old dun horse shot forward like the wind, far ahead of the other hunters. Again and again, he dove into the buffalo herd. Again and again, Lone Boy used his bow. The spotted calf fell to his arrows and so did a fat buffalo cow.

"You have enough meat here," the old dun horse said.

Lone Boy agreed. He took the hides and meat before any of the other hunters could see him. The old dun horse carried it all with ease. Lone Boy gave the other poor people of the tribe all the meat they could eat. Then he took the magical spotted hide to the Head Chief.

The Head Chief's daughter smiled at Lone Boy, but the Head Chief would not let her wed a boy who owned nothing but one old horse. "I will let her marry only a true hero," he said.

"Never mind," the old horse whispered to Lone Boy. "You will prove yourself a true hero."

The next day, the tribe was attacked by an enemy war party. Lone Boy rode out with the others

to defend his people.

"Charge the enemy only four times," the dun horse warned.

Lone Boy charged the enemy. Each time, the arrows flew till they darkened the sky, but Lone Boy was unhurt. Each time he rode, he counted coup, striking down the warriors. He did this once, twice, three times, four times.

But the battle wasn't over. "I rode four times without harm," Lone Boy told himself. "I'll make one more charge."

He rode into the battle a fifth time, but an arrow struck the old dun horse. The battle ended. The tribe celebrated their victory. But Lone Boy couldn't celebrate.

"If only I had obeyed you!" he mourned over the old horse's body. "You would still be alive!"

Rain poured down, hiding the horse. When the storm finally ended, the old horse stirred, then scrambled to his feet.

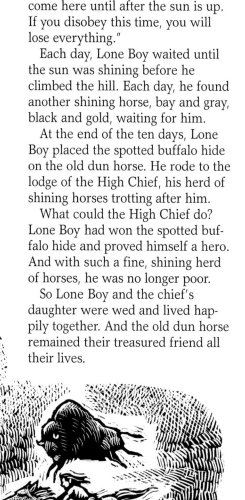

"That was a close thing!" the horse said. "If you had not been so kind to me when you first found me, and if you had not shared your meat with the poor people of the tribe, you never would have seen me again. But your good deeds were stronger than your disobedience, so here I am."

The old horse switched his tail. "It's time to get you settled as a hero. Each night for ten nights, you must leave me on this hill. Do not come here until after the sun is up. If you disobey this time, you will lose everything."

Each day, Lone Boy waited until the sun was shining before he climbed the hill. Each day, he found another shining horse, bay and gray, black and gold, waiting for him.

At the end of the ten days, Lone Boy placed the spotted buffalo hide on the old dun horse. He rode to the lodge of the High Chief, his herd of shining horses trotting after him.

What could the High Chief do? Lone Boy had won the spotted buffalo hide and proved himself a hero. And with such a fine, shining herd of horses, he was no longer poor.

So Lone Boy and the chief's daughter were wed and lived happily together. And the old dun horse remained their treasured friend all their lives.

Small Deer and the Buffalo Jump

by Peter Roop

Small Deer threw back the buffalo robe covering the lodge entrance. He kicked viciously at a dirty dog sunning itself nearby. The surprised animal yelped and scampered to a safer place.

Small Deer picked up his bow and arrows from where he had thrown them. He knew a brave must always treat his weapons with respect, but now he didn't care. An angry fire flared inside him.

He notched an arrow and aimed it at a raven winging its way over the Indian camp. Before he let it fly, Small Deer remembered that Mastoa the Raven was good medicine for his people. He would only bring bad luck upon himself and his family if he harmed the bird. Still, Small Deer wanted to strike out against something, anything to make him feel better.

When he saw his friend Morning Eagle coming his way, Small Deer ducked behind a lodge. However, Morning Eagle had seen him disappear and easily discovered him.

"Why do you hide from me, Small Deer?" asked Morning Eagle.

"I do not wish to see anyone," growled Small Deer.

"Why is this? Am I not your friend?"

"Yes, Morning Eagle, you are my friend. But even a friend can do nothing for me."

"Tell me what Spirit causes you anger. Maybe my medicine can chase it away," offered Morning Eagle.

"It is no Spirit that makes me angry. It is my father!"

"Your father?" asked Morning

Eagle. "What has he done that his son storms around camp like someone possessed by evil?"

"He has chosen Straight Arrow to be the *ahwa waki*, the buffalo runner. He will stampede the buffalo over the jump tomorrow," Small Deer said angrily.

"Why does this anger you? Straight Arrow is your brother. He will bring glory to your family."

"Because I can run faster than he can," Small Deer cried.

"Your father does not know this?"

"He does. He still says that Straight Arrow will lead the buffalo over the jump because he is the eldest son of the chief. As second son, I must stay behind the stacked stones and only help frighten the buffalo."

"Small Deer, your father has spoken. You must obey him just as all his people do," Morning Eagle said.

"But my father is wrong. Straight Arrow may be as fast as the young antelope, but I am as fast as the wind. So it is I who should lead the buffalo over the jump."

Small Deer paused and then quickly added, "And besides, I am tired of my name. I wish to change it, like you did. I hate the papoose name Small Deer."

Morning Eagle looked closely at his friend. He saw the disappointment on his face. He saw the anger in his heart. He felt he must try to help Small Deer.

"There is nothing to be done, my friend," said Morning Eagle. "You can't change your name until you do something brave. You must forget your anger. Come, let us hunt along the river for deer. Mastoa the Raven gives us his good luck."

"No!" Small Deer said. "I wish to be by myself. You go."

Morning Eagle looked once more at his friend before heading away from the circle of lodges. He knew now that Small Deer must be left alone to chase his anger away.

Small Deer watched Morning Eagle until he was out of sight. Then he turned and walked in the other direction.

At first, Small Deer walked fast. Soon he began running, and he threw away all thoughts of his brother and the jump and just let his feet carry him where they would. As he ran, Small Deer felt his anger fading away just as a crackling fire dies out at night.

Before he knew it, Small Deer found himself at the top of the buffalo jump cliff. He stopped at the cliff's edge and looked down. Far below he could see the smoke-white buffalo bones from his tribe's earlier jumps. He kicked a rock over the edge, watching as it bounced down the steep slope.

Many times before, Small Deer had seen his people drive a buffalo herd over the cliff. It was an important event, for it meant food for his people and new buffalo skins for robes and lodges. It was also a chance for him to earn a new name. If only his father would let him lead the jump.

Small Deer turned away from the cliff. He walked between the stacks of stones that marked the entrance

57

to the jump. From where he stood, the twin rows of stone stacks opened wider and wider, like the jaws of a hungry wolf. He knew that tomorrow he would be standing behind one of the stone piles waiting to jump up and frighten the charging buffalo.

Suddenly, Small Deer turned around and began running with all of his might to the edge of the cliff. A startled jack rabbit hopped nimbly out of his path. Small Deer ran faster and faster. All he could see in front of him was the empty air beyond the cliff's edge. Far in the distance, he could see where the earth and the sky met once again.

Without stopping, Small Deer ran over the edge of the cliff. The hot afternoon air whizzed by. Then, as he knew he would, Small Deer landed in a small cup of rock jutting out from the cliff face. Many braves had landed on this thin ledge as hundreds of buffalo had flashed by to their deaths far below.

Small Deer lay in the cup catching his breath and dreaming that he was leading the herd tomorrow. If only he could be the *ahwa waki*, the buffalo runner. He already knew what his new name would be.

However, it was only a dream, for his father had spoken.

The sun was sinking behind the Backbone-of-the-World Mountains when Small Deer returned to camp. He ate his dinner hastily and lay down on his buffalo robe bed. That night he had no desire to listen to the old braves talk about their heroic deeds of the past.

In the morning, Small Deer went with all of the other braves for their daily swim. Then, after a quick breakfast, he joined the camp as it followed the trail to the buffalo jump.

Straight Arrow had gone in search of the buffalo long before the sun had rolled into the sky. No one knew exactly when he would find a herd to drive back. But they must

all be prepared when Straight Arrow returned with the thundering herd.

His father, the chief, gave each brave a position behind one of the standing stacks of stones. Small Deer was to hide with Morning Eagle behind the seventh stack. At just the right moment, they were to jump up waving their robes to frighten the running buffalo.

All morning the sun burned down brightly on the two boys. Flies buzzed and bit Small Deer and Morning Eagle, who had long ago given up battling them. The rising heat made the brown land dance and swirl in the distance. Both boys strained their eyes for the telltale sign of dust that meant the herd was coming.

It was Morning Eagle who saw the cloud of dust first.

"There, far beyond the last pile of rocks," he said excitedly to Small Deer.

Small Deer leaned forward, squinting his eyes until he saw it, too. Then he jumped up and ran to his father.

"They come! Morning Eagle and I can see their dust," Small Deer told his father as he pointed far out over the plains.

"Hyi! You are right, my son. Your

brother leads a good herd. Now quickly get back to your place."

Small Deer sprinted back. Before long, he could see Straight Arrow running swiftly in front of the small brown herd of buffalo.

"Ah, we will eat well tonight, Small Deer," whispered Morning Eagle.

"Yes, it is a good herd," Small Deer said with only a hint of sadness in his voice. "I only wish it was me out in front."

"Maybe next year your father will choose you," suggested Morning Eagle.

Small Deer grunted and kept looking at the approaching herd. He could see Straight Arrow very well now.

Suddenly, he grabbed Morning Eagle.

"Something is wrong with Straight Arrow," he said with fear in his voice.

"What?" asked Morning Eagle.

"Straight Arrow is not very far in front of the herd. They are much too close to him."

"Hyi! You are right. If he cannot make it to the edge of the cliff, the buffalo will surely run him down!"

The stampeding herd was a long arrow's shot behind Straight Arrow when he reached the first stack of stones. All at once, the braves behind those piles leaped into the air waving spears and robes and shouting. The frightened buffalo bellowed and entered the funnel of rocks.

By now it was clear that Straight Arrow was in great danger. The hard hoofs of the buffalo beat the earth with the sound of the thunder in the sky. Straight Arrow was beginning to slow down just when he needed to be running his very fastest.

Straight Arrow passed the third, then the fourth, then the fifth stone stacks. At each one, new braves rose shouting and waving. The buffalo gained on Straight Arrow until they were less than a spear's throw behind his tiring feet.

As Straight Arrow neared Small Deer's stack, he turned and looked back. He never saw the sharp stone sticking up in front of him. Straight Arrow hit the rock running full speed and tumbled into a heap on the ground.

Like an arrow shot from a well-pulled bow, Small Deer dashed to his brother. He grabbed Straight Arrow under his arms and yanked him to his feet. The ground rocked with the crash of the buffalo. Small Deer could almost feel the hot, foamy breath of the first buffalo.

Using all of his strength, Small Deer began running with Straight Arrow to the edge of the cliff. The buffalo got closer and closer. Then, like stones dropped into a pond, the two boys disappeared over the cliff. The stampeding buffalo followed. One by one, the herd plunged over the edge.

Once in the narrow cup, Small Deer hugged his older brother close. Inches from their heads, sharp hoofs clawed wildly for the suddenly missing ground. The earth shook with anger as the buffalo's great bodies crashed into it far below the huddled boys.

Slowly, a strange silence filled the air. Small Deer looked up. No more buffalo hurtled past them. He lifted Straight Arrow to his feet. Side by side, the two braves watched their tribe gather beneath them to begin butchering the dead buffalo.

Then they heard a voice call from above them.

"Come, my sons. Let us celebrate this good jump. The Sun Spirit certainly has shone on our tribe. And let us celebrate the brave deeds of my children."

That night after a huge meal of boiled buffalo ribs, Small Deer was called before his father.

"Small Deer, today without thinking of your own safety, you ran in front of the buffalo and saved your brother. As you know, when any brave does a deed of courage, he may choose to change his name to honor that act. Do you wish to change your name?"

Small Deer could scarcely believe his father's words. His dream was coming true. He felt a warm glow spreading through his body like sunshine after a storm.

"Yes, Father, I wish now to be called Charging Bull."

"Hyi! Charging Bull, that is a good name. And it is a name that will be spoken with pride around our camp-fires for many moons to come."

"Small Deer and the Buffalo Jump" copyright © 1981 by Peter Roop. Used by permission of Northland Publishing (Flagstaff, Arizona), publisher of Peter Roop's forthcoming *The Buffalo Jump*, a picture book available in the spring of 1996.

NEZ PERCE
Joseph, a Chief of the Nez Perce

From time immemorial, a small group of people who called themselves Nee-me-poo (the real people) roamed the plateau lands of what is now eastern Oregon and Washington and western Idaho. They fished in the waters of the Snake, Salmon, and Clearwater rivers. They hunted in the hills and valleys of the Blue Mountains. And they gathered berries and dug the roots of camas lilies on the prairies at Wieppe and Camas. These people loved their homeland.

Then one day in 1805, American explorers led by Meriwether Lewis and William Clark came upon this group of fewer than six thousand people. They were met with friendship. In time, more white men followed, among them French Canadian trappers who, upon seeing some tribal members whose noses were pierced for decoration, called the native group Nez Percé (pronounced "nay pairsay"), which is French for "pierced nose." Soon all the white men were calling the Indians that, and over time it came to be pronounced "nez purse."

The Nez Perce welcomed the white men and the goods they had to trade, but as more and more white people came to the area to hunt, mine gold, and settle, the Nez Perce found themselves pushed from parts of their homeland. Farmers planted in the fields; miners camped by the rivers and in the mountains. For seventy years, the tribe lived peacefully with the newcomers, but as more settlers came, less land was left for the Nez Perce. When the U.S. government tried to move all the Nez Perce to a small reservation, a conflict now called the Nez Perce War began.

One man, called Joseph, became known as the leader of the Nez Perce bands that resisted the government order to move. He was not their war chief, nor was he even a warrior. Joseph was the civil leader of one band of the tribe, responsible for that group's daily welfare and spokesman for the band in meetings with others. In council with the war chiefs and leaders of other bands, Joseph helped make the decisions that took the Nez Perce on a long flight for freedom during the war. In council with U.S. officials before and after the war, he spoke for his people with eloquence and dignity. He earned the respect of many Americans, who considered him to be the main leader of the entire tribe.

When the war ended, Joseph led his people in their efforts to return to their homeland from the exile that defeat had brought. Today he is considered a hero for his long struggle to maintain peace, his wisdom in helping lead his people on their difficult journey, and his determination after the conflict to bring them back to their homeland.

Cunning Coyote and the Monster of the Clearwater

retold by Ada S. Howell

On cold winter evenings, Young Joseph and his friends would gather around the fires in the longhouse and beg for stories from the old men. "Tell us again how our tribe got started," Joseph called. And this is the age-old story the elders told.

In the beginning, when the earth was new, there were no people here, only animals — Grizzly Bear, Rattlesnake, Cougar, and many others. But Coyote, Iceye'eye, was the smartest and craftiest of them all.

A huge monster from the sea, the great Ilt-swi-tsichs, roamed the Kamiah Valley (in what is now northern Idaho). So enormous was his appetite that he sucked everything into himself. Soon he had devoured so many animals that there were more inside him than out. Filled with fear, those who were left sent Silver Salmon down the rivers to ask Coyote for help. Iceye'eye came up the Columbia and Snake rivers to the Clearwater River. There he saw the monster, so big and bloated that he filled the whole Kamiah Valley.

Quickly, Coyote made a rope out of wild grapevines, tied himself to the highest peak, and howled a challenge. The monster answered and tried to suck him in as he had all the others. Coyote did not move.

"O horrible monster, it is I, Iceye'eye, the great Coyote. I have come to destroy you with my powerful medicine. Suck me in if you can."

"Coyote, I have been waiting for you for years. I will swallow you," the monster replied.

That is what Coyote wanted to hear. He cut the rope and let the monster's breath pull him down the mountain. At last, he was near the mouth, the huge jaws opened wide, and down Coyote went, swallowed like a worm. There he found many of his friends, some starving.

Coyote took from his bag five flint knives. The first four broke. With only one knife left, he cut and cut and finally severed the cords that fastened the heart to the body. The heart fell down, and the monster

was dead. All the animals trooped out the gaping jaws.

"How shall we get rid of him?" asked Brown Bear.

"You help me," Coyote said. "Get some flint knives. We'll soon be rid of this fellow."

Coyote cut off a leg and threw it over the mountain. "This will be the Blackfeet and the Sioux. They shall be long-legged people."

From the scalp, he made the Crow Indians. "They shall be proud of their long hair," he said.

Fox asked, "Who is going to live in this, the most beautiful country of all?"

"Why didn't you ask me sooner? Bring me some water," answered Coyote. "This will be my greatest creation."

So he took blood from the monster's heart, mixed it with water, and sprinkled it up and down the valley. People sprang up — stronger, taller, nobler, and wiser than any others.

"They will be the Nee-me-poo (the real people)," he said.

The Great Spirit above was pleased with Coyote, so he turned the heart into a large basalt mound, which can still be seen on the east slope of the Kamiah Valley.

SIOUX
The Sioux

The Sioux once occupied the vast plains region of the United States, from Minnesota west to Montana and from Canada south to Oklahoma. For food, they hunted buffalo, elk, deer, and small animals and birds. They also gathered nuts, root vegetables, fruits, and berries. Sometimes they had to fight to protect their hunting grounds from rival Indians, but they fostered friendships and formed strong alliances with other neighboring tribes. Their beliefs focused on the natural world, and their god, Wakan Tanka, the Great Mystery, tied all living things together. Humans, they believed, were related to the earth, plants and animals, and other natural phenomena.

The nineteenth century brought traumatic changes to the Sioux and other Native Americans. White settlers moved west with an appetite for land and little regard for the Indians' way of life. Sioux chiefs tried to establish boundaries for their people, to protect their hunting grounds and sacred places. Treaties were made, in white men's terms, but as the demand for land increased among whites, many of these treaties were broken. In the course of a few decades, the Sioux were confined to a few reservations, a fraction of the land they had previously called home.

Perhaps the most unfortunate thing about America's westward expansion was the lack of interest on the part of so many white soldiers, settlers, and government officials in finding out who the Sioux were and how they had lived in balance with nature for hundreds of years. A century later, the Sioux still must fight to protect their way of life. However, more and more people are learning the wisdom of

Sioux beliefs and recognizing the need to carry on their traditions. In learning from the Sioux and helping them to preserve their culture, we can make our own lives richer.

Tatanka

by Karen E. Hong

Long, long ago, in the days of the oldest grandfathers, *tatanka* (buffalo) lived under the earth. In those times, a young man was out hunting when he came upon a steep hill. As the man looked at the hill more closely, he found a large opening.

The man entered the doorway and found many bracelets, pipes, and ornaments scattered on the floor. Perhaps, he thought, these are offerings to some great spirit. Careful to leave everything as he had found it, the man passed into a second room. This chamber was so dark that he could not even see his hands before his eyes. Scared, he rushed from the cave and hurried home to tell all he had seen.

When the chief heard the young man's story, he chose four brave warriors to return with the man and investigate the hill. They found the

hill as the young man had described it. In the dark second room, the warriors felt their way along the walls. Finally, they found a narrow opening. One by one, they squeezed into another chamber. Once again, they felt their way, finding a small opening so close to the ground that they had to crawl through it.

In this chamber, the warriors smelled a sweet odor. They explored the room on their hands and knees, locating a hole in the floor that seemed to be the source of the sweet smell. They decided to venture no farther, but to return to the camp and report their findings.

Sometime later, the young man returned to the hill. He found buffalo droppings in the cave. Buffalo tracks covered the floor. Soon he came upon fur that the buffalo had rubbed off against the walls.

The next day, a huge herd of buffalo moved near the Indian village. The tribe, eager and grateful for this bounty, killed many buffalo in the hunt. Now they would have food and all the other necessities the buffalo provided, including clothes, tools, and skins for tipis.

Some said that the cave foretold the tribe's successful hunts. Others held that the cave was the source of the buffalo herds that roamed the earth. The cave, they said, was the way the Great Spirit provided a steady supply of food for his people. Each spring, great herds emerged to satisfy the Indians' needs.

Tales Around the Campfire:
Native Americans Remember Their Past

by Brandon Miller

"I was born in the Moon of the Popping Trees (December) in the Winter When the Four Crows Were Killed.... A long time ago my father told me what his father told him."

Black Elk, 1863–1950

When Black Elk of the Sioux tribe recounted the history of his life, he used a traditional and ancient manner of keeping the past alive — not through the written word but through storytelling. Native Americans passed on their tribal legends, songs, stories, and visions during long nights around the campfire. The "Old Ones" would relate tales of creation and tribal life. Their stories of brave and wise deeds gave the young people a challenge to live up to in their own lives.

A woman of the Blackfeet tribe thought this was a fine way to learn. "The old folks usually sat around and had time and patience for the little ones," she said. "Imagine how different was the education kids got, coming as it did from people who have to be somewhat wise about life just to have survived into old age."

History was as much a part of Indian life as waking each day or hunting for food. Listening to stories of the old ways began at birth and continued throughout life. Because there were no books to record the tales, people had to remember them so they could pass them on. There was so much to be remembered — the rituals, dances, poems, names, and deeds — all of the tribe's explanations for why the world was the way it was. How had the buffalo come to the plains? How did the four-leggeds and the two-leggeds live together on Mother Earth? How had a brave warrior been given the "medicine" that kept him safe in battle? The powers of the Great Spirit were felt everywhere and never forgotten.

Native Americans mixed legend and lore with history. Things were justified or explained long after the event had taken place. Time was not marked by the same stepping-stones of dates as white men use in recording their history. Descriptive phrases and words set the time and the event. These things would be remembered for many winters (years) around the campfire.

Native Americans preserved their history in other ways, too. One painted buffalo robe holds a record of the Dakota Sioux from 1800 to 1871. The pictures highlight battles, trade, and the epidemic illnesses brought by the white people. In the Northwest, Indians told their stories in the carvings on their totem poles. Woodland tribes drew pictures on strips of birch bark, carved posts, and painted the inner walls of their bark houses.

White historians of the past often depicted American Indians in a harsh light. Books and papers written by white traders, scientists, and soldiers are colored by their own theories and prejudices. Interpreters often misinterpreted Indian words that carried meanings too deep to be translated into English.

Fortunately, that is changing. Today many books retell the Native Americans' stories in their own words. This trend began in the 1930s, when many of the Old Ones could still remember the days when the plains tribes followed the buffalo. Others recalled the ways of the peoples along the rivers and in the forests before they had to move and live on reservations. They remembered, as Black Elk did, the stories their fathers told them and repeated their peoples' histories to researchers and historians who wanted to preserve the Indians' ways on paper.

When Black Elk recalled the death of his cousin, the great Sioux chief Crazy Horse, his simple words carried an emotion not found in history books: "Crazy Horse was dead. He was brave and good and wise. He never wanted anything but to save his people, and he fought the Wasichus (whites) only when they came to kill us in our own country. They could not kill him in battle. They had to lie to him and kill him that way."

For many years, Indian children were taught only the "white man's" version of history in schools. But at home, the stories of the Old Ones were repeated with pride. A strong sense of their own history has helped many tribes hold together their tattered heritage.

In 1960, the Northern Cheyenne people were in danger of losing more of their reservation land. In response to this threat, they expressed the ties they have with the past: "Our people are proud to be Americans and Northern Cheyennes. That is all we have to be proud of today, except our honorable past.... We think of our past as we write this plan for our future." In that past "are the names of great and generous hunters who fed the people, fighters who died for freedom,...holy men who filled us with the power of God.... We will do good things as a tribe...that we cannot do as individual men cut off from our forefathers."

The Sacred Pipe

by Toni A. Watson

There are many versions of this legend, and this is a brief compilation of several. The only people who can truly tell this and other sacred legends are medicine people. Their tellings, too, are considered sacred and are not written down or recorded in any way.

In the beginning of all beginnings, the Great Spirit called all his people together. Standing on a cliff of red stone, he broke a piece from the wall and, kneading it in his hands, made a huge pipe. He smoked this great pipe over them and to the four directions. He told them that this stone was red, as was their flesh, and from it they might make their pipes of peace. But it belonged equally to all. The war club and the scalping knife must not be raised on this ground.

He smoked his pipe and talked to them till the last whiff, and then he disappeared in a cloud. Immediately, two great ovens opened up, and two women (guardian spirits) entered them in a blaze of fire. They are heard there even today and answer the call of shamans, or medicine men, who consult them on their visits to this sacred place.

The place is the Sacred Pipestone Quarry, the main place where North American Indians obtain material for their pipes. All Indians who camp near the quarry maintain peace, even if they are bitter enemies at home. Many have carved their sacred symbols on nearby rocks in memory of their stays at the quarry. Located in Pipestone County, Minnesota, near the town of Pipestone, the quarry is now a National Monument reserved for Indians.

Legend of the Dream Catcher

Long ago when the world was young, an old Lakota spiritual leader was on a high mountain and had a vision.

In his vision, Iktomi [or Iktome], the great trickster and teacher of wisdom, appeared in the form of a spider.

Iktomi spoke to him in a sacred language that only the spiritual leaders of the Lakota could understand.

As he spoke, Iktomi, the spider, took the elder's willow hoop, which had feathers, horsehair, beads, and offerings on it, and began to spin a web.

He spoke to the elder about the cycles of life...and how we begin our lives as infants and move on to childhood and then to adulthood. Finally, we go to old age, where we must be taken care of as infants, completing the cycle.

"But," Iktomi said as he continued to spin his web, "in each time of life, there are many forces — some good and some bad. If you listen to the good forces, they will steer you in the right direction. But if you listen to the bad forces, they will hurt you and steer you in the wrong direction."

He continued, "There are many forces and different directions that can help or interfere with the harmony of nature, and also with the Great Spirit and all of his wonderful teachings."

All the while the spider spoke, he continued to weave his web, starting from the outside and working toward the center.

When Iktomi finished speaking, he gave the Lakota elder the web and said, "See, the web is a perfect circle, but there is a hole in the center of the circle."

He said, "Use the web to help yourself and your people to reach your goals and make good use of your people's ideas, dreams, and visions.

"If you believe in the Great Spirit, the web will catch your good ideas — and the bad ones will go through the hole."

The Lakota elder passed on his vision to his people, and now the Sioux Indians use the dream catcher as the web of their life.

It is hung above their beds or in their home to sift their dreams and visions.

The good in their dreams is captured in the web of life and carried with them, but the evil in their dreams escapes through the hole in the center of the web and is no longer a part of them.

They believe that the dream catcher holds the destiny of their future.

From the Wounded Knee School District, where Sioux artists create their dream catchers and legends as fundraising enterprises to help improve their schools in South Dakota.

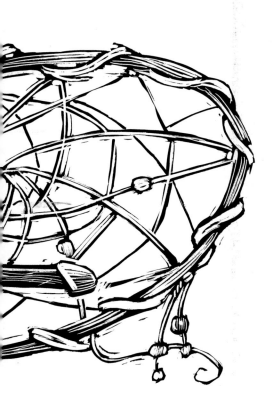

The Vision Quest

retold by E. Barrie Kavasch

The vision quest is an important tradition among many Indian peoples. If a young man or woman needs to solve a personal problem or find out what to do or be in life, he or she might go on a vision quest. The choice to go might be made during the coming of age rites. Sometimes it involves staying alone on a hilltop or inside a vision pit, without food or water, for up to four days and nights. The vision quest is a test of strength and endurance, but if the spirit voices or dreams reveal a vision that shapes the person's life, the quest is worth the effort. Some people can go on several vision quests during their lifetime.

Once a young Sioux wanted to seek a vision or dream that would give him the personal power to be a medicine man. He was very proud of himself and was sure he had great talents. All he needed was a vision.

His family were good people, wise in the ancient ways. All winter they worked to prepare the young man, feeding him plenty of corn, herbs, and meat to make him strong. They also set aside a small offering for the spirits at each meal so that they might help him gain a great vision.

In early spring, when the weather turned beautiful, two medicine men took him to the sacred Black Hills. They built a small sweat lodge in which to purify and prepare him. They bathed him with the incense of sweet grass, rubbed his body with wild sage, and fanned him with an eagle's wing.

Finally, the medicine men took him to a lonely plateau and prepared a vision pit with offering

bundles of herbs, cedar, and tobacco. They told the young man to be humble, to ask for holiness, to cry for power, and to pray for a sign from the Great Spirit. He was to crouch on a blanket and pray for a gift that would make him a medicine man. After they had prepared him, they left him there alone.

Fear kept him awake the first night, as he trembled in the pit and cried out loudly for the power he wanted. He was cocky and ready to wrestle with the spirits for a vision. But no dreams came to him.

Before sunrise, he heard a voice speaking to him out of the white mists of dawn. It said, "Young man, you disturbed us all night, all the animals and birds; you even kept the trees awake. Why should you cry here? There are other hills you could have picked. Why don't you go elsewhere to cry for a dream? You're a brash young man and not yet worthy to receive a vision."

But the young man was determined to stay there, and he clenched his teeth, resolving to force a vision to come. He stayed another day in the pit, hoping for enlightenment, which did not come. The second night he was paralyzed with fear, cold, and hunger. Shadows moved everywhere around him, and the wind screamed and wailed through the Black Hills.

Then in the predawn half light, he saw an enormous boulder towering over his vision pit. It moved toward him, and just as it seemed about to fall in on him and crush him, it stopped. Speechless, he watched as the boulder rolled back up the mountain, all the way to the top. He sat motionless, numb with fear, as this immense boulder came roaring down at him. At the last moment, he managed to leap out of his vision pit and run off, just as the boulder crushed and obliterated the pit.

But again the boulder rolled up the mountain and hurtled down on him. "I'm leaving, I'm leaving!" the

young man screamed, running away. This time the boulder leap-frogged over him and bounced down the slope, crushing everything it touched. He ran on in terror, barely noticing that the boulder was once more rolling up to the top of the mountain. The fourth time it came crashing back down, crushing things in a fearful descent. It flew through the air in a giant leap over him and struck the earth, planting itself right in front of him. This shook the earth fiercely, and the young man was flung over the boulder and thrown to the ground.

Bruised and badly shaken, he finally ran back to his village. Angrily, he told the medicine men that he had gained no knowledge and received no vision. The medicine men returned with him to the mountain and dug a new vision pit, into which he climbed. He cried for a dream until dawn, when he again heard the voice in the white mists saying, "Stop disturbing us; go away!" This same thing happened on his second and third mornings. By this time, he was weak with hunger and thirst; even the air seemed to be fighting him. No dreams had come, but he was determined to endure one last night. He cried out in the dark loneliness until he lost his voice, yet still no dream came to him. Just at daybreak, he again heard the voice, very angry now: "Why are you still here?"

The young man began to realize that he had suffered in vain and would have to return to his people and confess that he had failed in his vision quest. Angrily, he shouted, "Who are you to give the orders? I don't know you. I can't help this, and I'm going to stay right here until my uncles come to get me!"

Suddenly the mountain began to rumble and shake. The wind began to scream louder than ever. The trees were swaying in great anger. As the young man looked up, he saw an enormous boulder perched

on the summit of the mountain. Lightning came down on it, and it began slowly moving down the mountain. It quickly picked up speed, snapping off trees and splintering other boulders as it rushed right down toward him. Then he realized that he had truly angered the spirits and could gain nothing this way. He leaped out of the boulder's path and raced, falling over rolling rocks, back to his village.

The medicine men listened to his sad story, then explained that he had gained some knowledge: Suffering brings no vision, nor does will power and courage. A vision must come as a gift born of wisdom, patience, and humility. Only then can you reach greater understanding.

From *American Indian Myths and Legends* by Richard Erdoes and Alfonso Ortiz, editors. Copyright © 1984 by Richard Erdoes and Alfonso Ortiz. Adapted by permission of Pantheon Books, a division of Random House, Inc.

Coyote, Spider Man, and the Rock

adapted by Nancy Boatwright

Once Coyote was walking with his friend Iktome, the Spider Man. They came upon Iya, the rock.

"This is a nice-looking rock," Coyote said. "Look at the lines of spidery green moss that cover it. These lines could tell a story. I think this rock has power. But he must feel cold. I will give him my blanket."

So Coyote removed the thick blanket he was wearing and laid it on the rock. "Here, friend rock, take this as a present."

"Ah, that is a fine blanket," Iktome said. "So many colors, and so thick. You are certainly in a

giving mood today."

"I am always giving things away," Coyote answered. "Now, doesn't Iya look fine in my blanket?"

"It's his blanket now," Iktome said.

Coyote did not reply, and the two friends walked on. Soon a cold rain began to fall. Before long, the rain turned to hail. Coyote and Iktome found a cave where they could wait out the storm. However, the cave was cold and wet. This did not bother Iktome, for he had his thick buffalo robe. But Coyote had only his shirt. He began to shiver, and his teeth chattered.

"Oh, friend of mine," Coyote said to Iktome, "go back and get my blanket for me. I need it now, and that rock has no use for it. He has gotten along for years without it. Hurry, I am freezing."

Iktome ran back to the rock. "My friend needs his blanket back. May I have it, please?"

But the rock said, "No. I like having this beautiful, thick blanket. What is given is given!"

Iktome returned to the cave. "He won't give it back," he told Coyote.

Coyote became angry. "I'll go get it myself. After all, it was I, not he,

who paid for it. Ungrateful, no-good rock!"

"Friend, be careful," warned Iktome. "There is power in that rock. Maybe you should let him keep it."

But Coyote could not be talked out of it, and he set off to get his beautiful blanket.

"Hey, rock!" he called to Iya. "What need have you for this blanket? I am freezing. Let me have it right now!"

"No," said the rock. "What is given is given!"

Then Coyote jerked the blanket away from the rock and wrapped it around himself, saying, "I need it more than you, so that's the end of it."

"Not the end," said the rock.

By and by, the rain and hail stopped. The sun came out, and Coyote and Iktome sat in front of the cave, sunning themselves, while they ate pemmican and fry bread.

They were feeling warm and peaceful, when suddenly Iktome said, "What's that noise?"

"What noise? I don't hear anything."

"There's a rumbling and crashing from far off."

"Yes, I hear it now," Coyote said. "It's getting louder and nearer. What can it be?"

"I have a pretty good idea," Iktome replied. "Friend, I think we should get out of here."

And then they saw it. The great

rock, Iya, was rolling, thundering, crashing toward them.

"Run, friend! Iya means to kill us."

Coyote and Iktome ran as fast as they could, but the rock came on, steadily gaining on them.

"Let us swim across the river," Iktome shouted. "The rock is heavy. It will sink to the bottom, and we will be saved."

They swam to the other side, but the rock came rolling right behind. It rolled across the river as if it were a dry bed.

"Quick, into the trees!" Coyote cried. "These great timbers will surely stop Iya." So into the thick forest they ran, but the huge rock came rolling after them, splintering everything in its path.

Coyote and Iktome managed to stay just ahead of the powerful rock, but when they emerged from the forest and saw the flatlands stretching before them, they stopped. How could they hope to escape now?

"Friend Coyote," Iktome said, "I have no quarrel with the rock. And I have just remembered some pressing business I must attend to. So long!" Iktome rolled himself into a ball, became a spider, and disappeared down a mouse hole.

Coyote ran on, but he soon grew weary. The rock thundered right over him and flattened him. Then Iya, the rock, gathered up the blanket and returned to his own place.

Coyote lay, lifeless it seemed, on the flat ground. But he, too, had power. He could bring himself back to life. This time it took the whole night for him to return to his usual form. That was fortunate, for it gave him time to think. And while he was thinking, he decided that it was a good thing to be generous of heart.

"If you give something, give it forever," he concluded.

Adapted with the permission of the authors, Richard Erdoes and Alfonso Ortiz, from a tale related in *American Indian Myths and Legends*, Pantheon Books, a division of Random House, Inc., New York, 1984.

White Buffalo Calf Woman

Most American Indian tribes have creation legends for the features of their landscape: how this river came to be, when those mountains were formed, how that coastline was carved. These stories are told for adults and children alike, in solemn ceremonies or as spontaneous creations. The people learn how to live their daily lives by these legends: how to catch fish, how power is divided between men and women, how food is prepared, how honor in war is celebrated. The most important legend of the Sioux people is that of White Buffalo Calf Woman.

I t happened a very long time ago, even before the Sioux had horses. Perhaps it was in the Moon of Red Cherries (July) that the seven tribes of the Sioux Nation came together and camped...."* There was no game, and the people were starving. Every day they sent scouts to look for game, but the scouts found nothing.

Early one morning, as two scouts climbed a high hill, they saw something coming toward them. But the figure was floating instead of walking, and they knew it was *wakan* (holy).

As it came nearer, they realized it was the most beautiful young woman they had ever seen. She wore a white buckskin dress that shone in the sun. It was embroidered in sacred designs of porcupine quills and in radiant colors no ordinary woman could have made. This wakan stranger was Ptesan-wi, White Buffalo Calf Woman. She carried a large bundle and a fan of sage leaves.

She told them, "Go tell your people I carry a message from the buffalo nation. I am bringing them something holy." The people put up their big medicine tipi and waited for four days. White Buffalo Calf Woman approached the gathered tribes, singing and carrying her bundle before her. As she sang, a white cloud that smelled good came from her mouth.

Halting before the chief, she opened the bundle. The holy thing it contained was the *chanunpa,* or "sacred pipe." She held it up for all the people to see. She was holding the stem with her right hand and the bowl with her left, and thus the Sioux have held it ever since.

White Buffalo Calf Woman showed the people the right way to pray. Filling the pipe with red willow bark tobacco, she taught them how to sing the pipe-filling song, how to lift the pipe up to the sky toward Grandfather and down toward Grandmother Earth. She told them that the smoke rising from the bowl was the living breath of the great Grandfather Spirit.

"With this holy pipe," she said, "you will walk like a living prayer. With your feet resting upon the earth and the pipe stem reaching into the sky, your body forms a living bridge between the Sacred Beneath and the Sacred Above. Wakan Tanka smiles upon us because now we are as one: earth, sky, all living things, the two-legged, the four-legged, the winged ones, the trees, the grasses. Together we are all related, one family. The pipe holds us all together."

She spoke to the women, telling them that what they were doing was as great as what the warriors did. She also talked with the children, because they have a wisdom beyond their years. She told them, "You are the coming generation. Someday you will hold this pipe and smoke it. Someday you will pray with it."

The sacred woman then left the people, saying, "I shall see you again." She walked off in the same direction from which she had come, outlined against the setting sun. As she went, she stopped and rolled over four times. The first time, she turned into a black buffalo; the second time into a brown one; the third time into a red one; and finally, the fourth time she rolled over, she turned into a white female buffalo calf. A white buffalo is the most sacred living thing to the Sioux.

*From a telling by Lame Deer of the Rosebud Reservation in 1967.

NORTHWEST COAST INDIANS

The Peoples of the Northwest Coast

by Wallace H. Olson

The area known as the Northwest Coast extends from northern California through the southeastern part of Alaska. In most of this region, coastal mountains rise up from the ocean shore. This is a land of mists and rain. As the warm ocean breezes climb over the mountains, they drip their moisture on the rich, lush temperate rain forest below. Large stands of evergreens — spruce, hemlock, fir, and cedar — go on for miles. This forest also supports a variety of other trees and bushes, including many kinds of edible berries. The woodlands are home to deer, bears, wolves, and a wide assortment of smaller animals.

The clear, fast streams are the spawning grounds for five species of Pacific salmon. Trout and other fish also live in the streams. The nearby ocean abounds with a variety of saltwater fish and sea vegetables, which some people call seaweeds. Sea mammals such as seals, sea lions, sea otters, killer whales, and other animals make their home in these coastal waters. Along the shore are clams, cockles, oysters, and crabs.

In the past, the Northwest Coast provided an abundant food supply for the Indians who lived there. Today, even with a much larger population and big cities such as Seattle and Vancouver, Native Americans and others still find places to hunt, fish, and gather food.

Archaeologists are not sure when the first people arrived on this coast, but some ancient sites are about ten thousand years old. By three thousand years ago, a distinct way of life was developing. This came to be known as the Northwest Coast Culture. Year after year, the adult salmon moved into the freshwater streams to lay their eggs and start a new generation. Salmon were the basic food of the Indians. Some groups had special ceremonies to welcome back the first salmon of the year. In addition to the salmon, the people used many other natural resources. The beautiful cedar and other evergreen trees provided the logs and planks for their homes and canoes. Their diet included berries, fish, meat, and seafood. With so many resources, the people had time for singing, dancing, storytelling, and ceremonies. They also had time to travel up and down the coast for trade or warfare. Long, tubular shells known as dentalia were harvested near Vancouver Island and traded south to California and north to Alaska.

The people of the Northwest Coast are famous for their large gatherings, which the Chinook Indians of the Columbia River called potlatches. After the arrival of Europeans, who brought new and exotic trade goods, some societies began to "fight with property" by giving huge amounts of gifts and food to their guests. The guests were then obliged to repay their hosts for the gifts they had received. To the far north, among the Tlingit Indians, the potlatch remained primarily a memorial to honor the dead, and gifts were given to others in the name of those who had died.

With all the necessities of life at their doorstep, the people had time to develop highly stylized art forms. Each family had a special creature as its crest, such as the eagle, raven, bear, or killer whale. A crest is like a coat of arms, a symbol of the family. In this land of totem poles, large carved statues are reminders of great events, the legendary past, and historic figures. Many of these poles contain crest designs.

With the coming of the Spanish, British, French, Russian, and American explorers in the late 1700s, the Indians' world began to change. The sea otter was hunted almost to extinction. The newcomers brought new diseases, and

thousands of people died in the epidemics that followed. Soon the settlers arrived, and the Indians signed treaties that reserved some of the land and resources for them. The Indians struggled to survive and preserve their culture, but much was lost. In the wake of new technology, new religions, and new societies, the old languages and cultures began to disappear.

Today a cultural revival is under way. Northwest Coast Indians are bringing their culture into the modern world in new and exciting ways. Old stories and legends are being rewritten and produced as theatrical plays. Crests are worked into stylish designs on dresses, coats, and jackets. Carved masks and panels, made in a combination of traditional and modern designs, are sold and displayed in exclusive art stores and galleries.

Many of the Northwest Coast Indians know their history and traditions. They are proud to be descendants of the first Americans. As they tell their stories and share their lives with you, they hope that you may have a better understanding of the Northwest Coast Culture.

Survival and the Sea
by Karen H. Dusek

"Hi! Hi! Hi!
Go straight to my wife.
She's a magic treasure."

So sang the Makah whalers of the Olympic Peninsula to turn their harpooned prey toward shore.

Whaling was very dangerous and required skill, bravery, and strong magic. Killing a whale provided large amounts of food for the people and prestige for the hunters. For these reasons, and because it was costly to carve and outfit a canoe, only high-ranking chiefs could hunt whales.

The tribes followed many rituals to bring the hunters success. The chief bathed in cold water and perhaps asked his wife to join him. As he sang, she imitated a whale, spouting and diving. Seven men were carefully chosen as crew members to follow in canoes, but the privilege of being the first to harpoon the whale belonged to the chief.

The hunters left the shore armed with heavy wooden harpoons. During the hunt, they expertly paddled their canoes along the whale's left side. Standing in the prow of the boat, the chief waited until just the right moment, then thrust his weapon deep into the blubber behind the fin.

As the whale tried to escape, it pulled the long cedar bark–sinew rope attached to the harpoon. Tied to it were floats made of sealskin. Eventually, the drag from the floats and repeated harpoonings wore the mighty animal out. When it could move no longer, the hunters swiftly killed it.

Triumphantly, the hunters returned home to a great feast. The villagers welcomed the whale as a guest and divided it among themselves. They ate the skin and blubber, used the blubber oil as a dip for fried fish, used the sinew to make rope, fashioned the intestines into bags to store oil, and shaped the bones into tools.

When Fog Woman Made the First Salmon

retold by Margaret Johnston

Once, in a far northern land where rivers ran sparkling and cold, no salmon yet splashed in the streams, in the bays, or in the wind-tossed sea. The Tlingit Indians who lived on this land and fished in its waters found only a poor fare of cod, sculpin, and, now and again, a herring or halibut.

Raven, a mythical adventurer (sometimes represented as an Indian man, sometimes as a bird or in another form) lived with the Indians in the northern land. One day Raven and his two servants paddled his canoe out into the bay to fish. Soon heavy fog settled in, and Raven lost his way.

Suddenly, the ghostly mist began to clear from Raven's canoe, and he saw a shadowy woman, lovely as a dream. "I am Daughter of Fog," she said. "Give me your spruce-root hat."

She turned Raven's hat upside down, and waving her slender arms, she pulled all the fog into the hat, where it disappeared. Soon the sun shone hot again.

Like the sun, Raven's heart burned with love for Daughter of Fog. He took her to his camp alongside a stream that rippled down to the bay. Soon Raven and Fog Woman were married.

For three moons, the couple lived in harmony, but Raven grew tired of his quiet life. One morning he slipped away from camp and paddled upriver. Fog Woman, angry at Raven's sudden absence, called to a servant: "Bring me Raven's spruce-root hat and fill it with water from the freshwater stream."

When the servant brought the water, Fog Woman dipped a finger into it and said, "Pour it out toward the sea."

The servant obeyed, and immediately, on the ground where he had poured the water, there flopped a new kind of fish. "A salmon," Fog Woman said to the frightened servant. "Hurry and cook it. We must eat it before Raven returns, lest he discover my powers."

The servant followed Fog Woman's command, and soon they feasted on the salmon. Later, when Raven came home, he noticed a bit of red-colored meat between the servant's teeth. He stormed until the servant confessed that Fog Woman had created a salmon.

Raven grumbled to Fog Woman, "What is this delicacy you hide from me?"

But Fog Woman would say only, "I will go upstream and return on the fourth rising of the sun. While I am away, you must build a large smokehouse." Then she vanished.

Raven scowled, but a strange force drove him to obey his wife's orders. By the time the sun disappeared for the third time, he had finished the smokehouse.

On the fourth dawning, when the sun peeked over the edge of the earth and slanted its rays toward the heavens, Fog Woman returned. Upon seeing the smokehouse, a smile, fleeting as a moonbeam, parted her pale lips. She waved her hand toward the bay and the stream and bid Raven, "Search in the water for salmon."

Raven stared in awe as darting salmon leaped and splashed over each other in the foaming water. Jubilant, he began scooping up the fish. By the time the sun had journeyed three times across the heavens, Raven and Fog Woman had caught, cleaned, dried, smoked, and stored a winter's supply.

For a time, Raven and Fog Woman were happy. Before long, though, Raven boasted of his wealth and angrily denied to all that Fog Woman had created the salmon.

Raven began to mistreat Fog Woman. One day he struck her with the backbone of a salmon, and the sharp spines pierced her side. She cried out in pain — a cry sad as the sound of the wind moaning through the forest. She ran toward the sea.

Raven raced after her. Again and again, he reached out for her. Each time, she slipped through his arms like fog, and she floated out over the sea.

Raven watched sadly as his wife disappeared, then he heard a curious sound. He spun around and gasped in disbelief. The salmon he and Fog Woman had dried suddenly came to life, flopping down to the sea and into the water. Raven screamed in fury. He scrambled to catch the tumbling salmon. Over and over, they slithered from his grasp. The smoked salmon also came alive, streaming from the smokehouse and joining the strange procession of fish following Fog Woman out to sea.

Raven stood frozen in shock. Now he was poor again. He would have no salmon — only his former fare of cod, sculpin, and, now and again, a herring or halibut. Raven wailed in despair. Fog, thick as storm clouds, settled over his camp, and his cries were lost in the mist.

It is said that soon after the day when all the salmon followed Fog Woman out to sea, Fog Woman's many daughters, the Women of the Creek, went to live at the head of each freshwater stream. They still live there today. And because Fog Woman created salmon in a freshwater stream, salmon return from the sea every year and fight their way to the headwaters of these streams for one last look at the Women of the Creek before they spawn and die.

The Legend of Wishpoosh

retold by Elizabeth M. Tenney

Beavers held an honored position with many tribes of Native Americans. Some tribes believed that beavers had created humans. Others believed that persons who died came back to life as beavers. Beavers were eaten by some tribes, but only on special occasions. Indian hunters always traveled far from home to capture beavers for these feasts because the beavers living near an Indian community were considered friends of that community.

When the fur traders came, Indians' attitudes toward beavers began to change. The traders offered the Indians goods in exchange for beaver furs the Indians captured. The more pelts captured, the more goods the Indians received. Although the Indians had survived for many years without the kinds of goods the white traders brought, they soon grew dependent on the goods. The need to capture beavers to obtain the goods they wanted and needed led some Indians to violent confrontations with other Indians and with white people.

This legend, about a great beaver named Wishpoosh, was told by Indians of the mid–Columbia River region of the Pacific Northwest. It had two purposes: to explain a great flood the Indians believed had once taken place and to explain the origins of the tribes in the region. Many of the locations mentioned in the legend can be found on a good map of present-day Washington State.

Long ago when the world was very young, no people lived on earth. Only the Watetash — the animal people — roamed the land.

One of the Watetash was an enormous king-beaver who went by the name of Wishpoosh. Wishpoosh resided in Lake Keechelus* high in the snowcapped Cascade Mountains.

Now Wishpoosh was a very destructive beaver. He had a great appetite and ate absolutely everything that came his way. Soon he had eaten all the smaller creatures in the lively mountain lake, as well as those that lived on the shore. Then he began devouring all the trees and the plants that surrounded the lake.

Wishpoosh was destroying so many creatures and so much vegetation that Speelyei, the coyote god of the mid-Columbia region, decided that he must do something to stop Wishpoosh.

Speelyei jumped into Lake Keechelus and struggled with Wishpoosh. They rolled and twisted and fought each other, causing the water of the lake to boil. Wishpoosh became so violent that he tore out the banks of Lake Keechelus, and the water flooded down the canyon, sweeping everything before it. At the bottom of the canyon, the water stopped and held against the rocky ridges, forming another lake. This lake was larger than Lake Keechelus and covered the Kittitas Valley.**

But the struggle between Wishpoosh and Speelyei was not over yet. Wishpoosh continued to thrash about madly, eating every-

*Lake Keechelus (spelled "Kichelos" in the early literature) still exists as a mountain lake. It is situated near the summit of the Snoqualimie Pass, along the main east-west highway (U.S. 90) that crosses the state of Washington, leading to Seattle. Lake Keechelus can be clearly seen from the highway, which skirts its shores for several miles.

**Kittitas is a well-known valley in central Washington that surrounds present-day Ellensburg. Kittitas was once the territory of the Kittitas tribe.

Bountiful River

by E. Barrie Kavasch

Rivers and streams were valuable highways of life commonly traveled by Indian peoples throughout North America. This is still the case in many areas. Rivers have long been routes of commerce and trade, as well as pathways to adventure and new life. Many North American rivers bear their original Indian names, or Anglicized versions of them. Some of these names tell us more about early native concepts and uses of these vital waterways (see pages 45, 46, 51, and 52).

Let's take a canoe trip on an imaginary river and examine life along its banks. The water, the shoreline, and the land all hold many wonderful surprises. Many river plants have very special values, and American Indian peoples used these various plants in fascinating ways.

Think about what you might have eaten for your day's meals if you were an American Indian living here more than five hundred years ago. How would you have brushed your teeth? How would you have prevented poison ivy and insect stings from irritating your skin?

Following are some plants you are likely to see on your journey.

American lotus This plant was used like arrowhead. The ripe seeds also were cracked and eaten like hazelnuts or almonds.

Arrowhead Indians collected these starchy tubers underwater, then roasted and ate them. The leaves were used to wrap foods, bandage skin wounds, and soothe burns.

Blue flag iris Poisonous. The roots served as strong medicines and bandages on certain wounds. The dried iris leaves were used to weave baskets and mats and to make cords and braided ropes.

Boneset The leaves and blossoms were valuable in medicines, as bandages, and in tea to treat flus and bad colds. The stems were used as toothbrushes.

Cattails All the plant parts are edible in the right season: Green shoots were eaten like asparagus in spring, pollen in late spring, unripe flower heads in early summer, and the starchy tubers throughout the winter.

Giant reed The ripe seeds sometimes were used as a cereal or pounded into breads; the creeping roots were pounded into flour and used to sweeten other foods.

Groundnut The pealike pods and seeds were eaten as vegetables, and the delicious small tubers were eaten like potatoes.

Jewelweed The leaves, flowers, and stems were crushed and rubbed on the skin as treatment for poison ivy. This also helps relieve insect stings and makes a nice green dye.

Poison ivy Poisonous; do not touch. American Indians pounded the leaves and bark to make ink and a black dye for baskets and mats. All plant parts can cause itching and a red rash. If you get into poison ivy, look for jewelweed and rub it on your skin right away.

Raspberry The leaves were brewed as tea, and the ripe fruits were used in foods and drinks and for dyes and inks.

Red osier dogwood Twigs were important as toothbrushes and paintbrushes, and the long stems were used to weave baskets and containers. Do not eat the white fruits.

Sassafras Green twigs were chewed as toothbrushes and used as small paintbrushes. The distinct leaves also were pounded to use in medicines, salves for the skin, insect repellents, and foods. The bark was used in tea and root beer and as a brown dye.

Wild grape The leaves were used to wrap foods and medicines and to shape into toys. Shedding bark was twisted into cords and ropes, vines were woven into baskets and dream catchers, and the clear sap was a sweet source of water during drought. The ripe fruits were good in foods and drinks and were used to make dyes.

Wild rice The ripe seeds of this aquatic grass were roasted and enjoyed by many American Indian tribes as a delicious wild cereal grain.

thing that he could find, growing larger and larger as he ate.

For a while, the rocky ridges restrained the flood, but Wishpoosh had become so large and so strong that at last even the ridges gave way, and the loosened water swept down to fill the great basins of Cowiche, Naches, and Ahtanum.

Yet even these basins, surrounded by their hills, could not hold the monster beaver. Before long they, too, gave way, and the water flooded down in a torrent through the Yakima area. The water cut a passage through barren hills and filled the level plains of what are now Simcoe and Toppenish.

For a long time, this water was dammed by the Umatilla highlands, but Wishpoosh did not give up. As before, he continued to thrash about, eating everything he could find in the water and on the land. Finally, again he broke the rocky hills that kept the water in, and the water flooded to form the greatest lake of all between the Umatilla on the east and the Cascade Mountains on the west. The entire area was underwater.

Yet even this huge lake could not hold the frenzied beaver. After a time, the mighty Cascades gave way before his onslaughts. The water then flowed to the sea, draining all the valleys behind.

But even that was not the end of Wishpoosh. Once in the ocean, Wishpoosh laid about with such fury that he devoured all the fish, even the whales! He threatened all creation.

Speelyei saw that he must bring an end to Wishpoosh, or the world would be lost. Transforming himself into a floating branch, he drifted to Wishpoosh and was soon swallowed up.

Once inside the beaver, Speelyei turned back into himself, drew out his knife, and began to cut out all of the giant beaver's vital organs.

At last, this was too much even

for Wishpoosh. He life ceased. His huge carcass was cast up by the tide onto the beach at Clatsop near the mouth of the Great River.

Speelyei stood looking at the carcass. What should be done with it? The coyote god took his knife and cut off the beaver's head. From it, he fashioned a group of people — the Nez Perce — who were great in council and oratory. From the beaver's arms, he made another people — the Cayuse — who were powerful with the bow and war club. The beaver's legs became the Klickitat, a people who were swift runners. The belly of the beaver became the Chinook, whose lands offered much to eat. Finally, there remained the hide and the insides. Speelyei picked these up and, turning toward the east, hurled them as far as he could. These became the Snake River Indians.

Thus were formed the various tribes of people who lived in the northwest corner of the land.

How Raven Made the World

retold by Grant Lyons

The Indians who lived along the Pacific coast of North America have a story about how the world was made, and how it came to be the way it is. The old people told this story to their children, who grew up and told it to their children, and so it passed down through the generations and is still told today. This is what they say:

Before there were human beings on the earth, other more powerful beings lived here. They were the First People. They knew many things human beings will never

74

know, they had powers human beings will never have, and they never died. But Raven, the great trickster, changed everything.

Everyone knows the raven is a lazy, wicked — and clever — bird. The Raven Spirit that rules the world is just the same. And he made the world to suit himself.

In those days of the First People the world was completely dark. There was no sun, no moon, no stars, no green trees. Raven himself had no color. Then Raven heard that one family had all the light in the world, but they kept it for themselves. Raven was a thieving rascal then as now, and he decided to steal the light for himself.

The family with all the light had a young daughter who was just reaching the age of marriage. Her family watched over her very carefully to make certain she spoke to no strangers. Raven knew he had to find a way to become a part of this household. The best way, he decided, was to become the baby of the young girl. But how was he to get inside her body and make her think he was her baby?

He made himself into a leaf of a cedar tree and dropped into the family's basket of drinking water. But the girl's mother saw the leaf and threw it out. So Raven made himself even smaller, into the tiny needle of the hemlock tree. This time no one noticed him. The girl drank the water and swallowed the hemlock needle in it.

Once he was inside the girl's body Raven immediately made himself into a baby and began to grow. Neither the girl nor her parents understood what was happening. Very soon Raven was born, a perfect baby, and the family accepted him.

Raven began to cry all the time. He drove the family crazy with his strange wild screams. What is the matter? What does he want? they asked each other. Raven rolled his tricky little black eyes and pointed to a bundle hanging on the wall. They gave him the bundle to play with and he was very quiet for a while.

But when no one was looking Raven tore open the bundle. It was full of the light of the stars. As soon as it was open, the stars scattered, flying up through the smoke-hole of the lodge into the sky.

This was the first light in the world.

Raven began to cry again. He pointed to another bundle on the wall, and again, to quiet him, the family gave Raven the bundle. Inside he found the round, silvery moon. He played with this until the family stopped paying attention to him. Then he threw the moon up through the smoke-hole and into the sky with the stars.

This was the second light in the world.

Raven began crying again. This time he pointed to a handsomely carved cedar box in the corner of the lodge. The family, unable to bear his screaming, gave this to him too. Raven peeked inside and saw that this was the most powerful light by far. It was the sun.

As soon as no one was watching him, Raven turned himself back into a bird, and with a loud, laughing "Ca-aw!" snapped up the box and flew out through the smoke-hole with it.

He flew to the lodge of his cousin the seabird, Petrel. There he would be safe. But Raven could not control his desire to steal and play tricks. Petrel owned all the water in the world, and Raven decided to steal this too. So when Petrel was sleeping, Raven took the water into his beak, grabbed the sun-box in his claws, and started to fly away. But Raven's heavy burdens slowed him down.

Meanwhile, Petrel woke up and called on the spirits of his smoke-hole to help him catch Raven. The spirits seized Raven and held him in the smoke-hole while Petrel piled his fire high with pine and spruce pitch. As Raven fought with the spirits, the smoke changed him from snowy white to pitch black.

Finally Raven escaped and flew away. But he found it difficult to fly with the water in his beak, so he began to spit it out. First he spat out the lakes, then the rivers, and finally the sea. And when he saw what he had done, he laughed.

All the First People were now angry with Raven. They came out of their lodges and began shouting at him, saying terrible things about him. This made Raven very angry. He warned them to stop or he would make them sorry, but they paid no attention to him.

Raven opened the cedar sun-box just a little. Some of the sunlight slopped out. It knocked the First People flat on their backs. But still they would not stop shouting and cursing at him. So Raven opened the box all the way.

Sunlight flooded the world. The First People were blasted every which way — some up into the heavens, some into the sea, and some down below the earth.

Raven laughed a long time at what he had done. He thought it was a great joke.

One day Raven decided the world was too empty, so he made human beings. He considered carving human beings from stone so they would last a long time. But he saw that this would take a lot of work. He was too lazy. So he carved them out of twigs and sticks instead. And that is why human beings must die in their season like the leaves of trees, instead of living forever.

Once he had made human beings, Raven saw that they were weak and helpless. So he went to the First People up in the heavens, in the sea, and beneath the earth. He made a deal with them. If they would help the poor weak people he had made, then his people would honor and respect them always. So the First People agreed to return to the earth as the animals and plants human beings need to live — the salmon, the whale, the elk, the deer, the fir and spruce and salmonberry, and many others.

That is why the world is the way it is. Raven made it and it is his world, full of tricks and lies and many jokes on the poor human beings who live in it. Nothing is quite what it seems, and people must die. But friendly spirits are everywhere, ready to help those who honor and respect them.

ESKIMOS
The Arctic Peoples
by E. Barrie Kavasch

For thousands of years, the Eskimos' ancestors inhabited the vast frozen Arctic. Most of these Arctic peoples lived along the coast, from the North Atlantic, Hudson Bay, and Arctic Ocean to the Pacific Ocean, stretching more than five thousand miles across the snowy North. They called themselves Inupiat (or Inupiaq) in Alaska, Inuit in Canada, Yupik in Siberia, and Kaladlît in Greenland, all of which mean "the real people." We called these hardy people Eskimos, an Algonquian word for "eaters of raw meat." The Aleut inhabit the Aleutian Islands, a string of volcanic islands stretching from Alaska across the Bering Sea to Siberia. Diverse Indian peoples also live and thrive in Alaska and in some of the polar Arctic regions.

Centuries ago, these rugged northern natives lived as seasonal hunters, following the movements of seals, sea lions, walrus, whales, caribou, musk oxen, polar bears, and numerous birds and fish. They were skilled craftsmen, who invented ingenious tools such as knives, sewing implements, oil lamps, snow goggles, showshoes, bow drills, dogsleds, and several kinds of harpoons, spears and spear throwers, and bows and arrows. They were especially known for their light, maneuverable boats of

seal or walrus hides stretched over curved driftwood and ivory (or antler) frames. *Igloo* is Inuit for "house," and it has come to mean the circular domed snow dwelling that many Arctic peoples used as temporary winter shelters. They also lived in many other types of dwellings, from hide-covered hunting tents to large, subterranean turf-covered houses in their winter villages.

The native peoples of Greenland were the first in this hemisphere to meet Europeans, around A.D. 984, when Vikings established contacts that may have lasted for hundreds of years. English explorers recorded contacts with Eskimos in 1576. Since the 1700s, continual exploration and exploitation of these peoples and their environments have significantly altered native ways of life, yet hunting and fishing are still central to their economies.

Arctic peoples believed that everything in the natural world possesses its own spirit *(inua)*. Traditions honored in festivals, dances, prayers, foods, songs, and games helped unite, strengthen, and maintain their ties to the land and sea and to all creatures. Even their tools, snares, weapons, and household items transcended their utilitarian needs to become imaginative, compelling works of art honoring the inuas.

The Old Man of the Volcano

by Roy J. Snell

There was once a boy who lived with his mother in a place called Kopkina's Igloo. There was only one house on that side of the river, but on the other side there were many. Down the river was the sea where men went hunting and fishing. On each side of the river was the tundra where the grass grew long in summer and wild ducks came to lay their eggs and where red foxes came down to steal them. Men hunted down the river, on the ocean, and on the tundra, but they never went up the river. Far away up the river was a great smoking mountain. If ever a hunter was daring enough to go up the river he never returned. The people did not know what happened to these hunters, but they were sure it was something too terrible even to be talked about.

When this boy, whose name was Iyokok, was old enough to think about it he said to his mother:

"How is it that I have no father?"

"You had a father," replied his mother, "but one day he went hunting and never returned. He was a daring hunter, so men say that he went up the river and there met with a terrible fate. As for me, I do not know about that. He never returned."

For a long time after that Iyokok sat by the seal-oil lamp, thinking. At last he said to his mother:

"Mother, when I am grown and have become a skillful hunter, I shall go up the river."

"No! No! No, my son," cried his mother; "you must never, never do that!"

"Yes, Mother, I shall go," said the boy. "I will be very wise and skillful, and I shall come back; then perhaps it will never again be dangerous to go that way."

Nothing more was said about it for a long, long time. Then one day, when the boy had grown large and strong, he said to his mother:

"Mother, to-morrow I shall get in my skin-boat and shall go up the river."

For a long time his mother tried to persuade him not to go, but when at last she saw he would go, she said:

"Very well, then, if you must go, take these with you."

She gave him a feather, a pebble and a needle. Then she said to him:

"When in trouble, think of the feather. If you get no comfort from this, think of the pebble. If you are very hard pressed, use the needle."

That may seem a very simple thing for her to do, but this mother was a woman of great magic, so it may not have been so bad, after all. We shall see.

Leaping into his kiak [kayak], the boy paddled away. For several hours he pushed steadily forward until of a sudden he came to a great whirl of water which carried him toward a cliff. In the cliff was a cavern. Into this cavern the water was running with such force that, whether he wished it or not, he was carried, skin-boat and all, right down beneath the rocky wall and into a great dark grotto which was nearly filled with water. The air in the place was warm.

Seeing a sandy beach, he drove his kiak upon it and went ashore. Hardly had he done this than he saw a very large old man approaching him. Out of his mouth, as he breathed, there came fire.

"That is the old man of the mountain," Iyokok told himself, as he shuddered with fear. "Now I shall be killed!"

After thinking of his feather, his pebble and his needle, he was not quite so much afraid.

The large man, however, offered to do him no harm. He only said: "Follow me."

Iyokok followed.

They left the grotto and continued upstream a long way. When they had come to a narrow place where there was a high cliff on one side and a steep precipice on the other, the man said to Iyokok:

"If you are going to live with me you must leap off the precipice."

At this he gave him a great shove that sent him spinning headlong toward the rocks hundreds of feet below.

Iyokok was so frightened he could not scream. "Surely now I shall be killed," he thought. Just when matters were at their worst he thought of his feather, and what do you think? Quick as a flash, he turned into a feather and, caught by a playful breath of wind, was wafted back up the side of the precipice.

At the top he was blown against a rock and clung there until he turned again into a boy. Upon looking for the old man he saw nothing of him, so he continued up the mountain side.

When he was very hungry and tired he came to a house on the side of the mountain. On going in he found an old woman and her daughter there. These people pretended to make him welcome. They gave him food and bade him lie down and sleep. But he did not trust them much.

"They look like wicked people. I shall be very careful," he told himself, "for no one who has gone up the river has ever returned to his village."

He thought again of his feather, pebble and needle. That made him feel good, "for," he told himself, "the feather saved me from death. Who can tell what the pebble and needle will do?"

He had stayed with these people a short while, when the old woman said:

"Go up the mountain side a little way farther. My brother lives up there. He has prepared a bath for you."

"All right, I will go," said the boy.

In those days, when one wished a bath, he made a square box of walrus skins. Then he built a large fire beneath some rocks. When the rocks were hot he raked away the fire and set a stool over the rocks. Seating himself on this stool, he told a friend to put the walrus-skin box over him, then to pour water on the rocks. Since the rocks were still hot, steam rose from them and gave him a good, hot bath. But if his friend made a mistake and poured seal oil instead of water on the rocks, he was burned to death.

The old woman's brother did not make a mistake. He was a wicked man. It had been he who had killed all the others who had come that way. He meant to kill this boy as well. So, when the bath was ready, he poured oil on the rocks.

When Iyokok knew what had been done he was so frightened that he could not move.

"Now surely I shall be killed," he whispered in agony.

Just in time he thought of his pebble. As soon as he thought of it he was changed into a pebble and the boiling oil could not burn him.

As soon as the bath had cooled he changed back to a boy and stepped out of the box, saying, "I have had an excellent bath."

"Ah!" said the man, "I see you are not like the others."

Then he asked the boy to go with him up a very steep cliff. Just when he was preparing to push the boy off the cliff Iyokok's needle became a lance and, leaping at the man, he killed him.

So at last the wicked old man of the volcano was dead.

Iyokok made his way back to his own village. After the chief heard his story he gave him his daughter for his wife and he lived there happily for many years.

Trouble never came to those who went up the river after that.

From *Eskimo Legends* by Roy J. Snell. Copyright © 1925 by Little, Brown and Company, Boston.

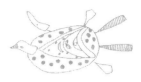

The Caribou Man

by Susan A. Kaplan

Caribou was a valuable resource for Western Alaskan Eskimos. Delicious meals of caribou meat and marrow were prepared by women and enjoyed by all. Women fashioned bedding and clothing out of the animal's warm fur, men carved implements out of its antlers, and both men and women used its sinew, which they twisted and braided, to sew clothes, lash together composite tools, and back bows. Caribou teeth were the chief ornaments on highly valued belts worn by women, and upon occasion caribou hooves were fashioned into snow goggles.

There was a settlement of Eskimos living at Cape Prince of Wales. Among them was a man with short legs named Nakasunaluk (Small Calves), who had a wife and two children. One day Nakasunaluk went caribou hunting and saw a herd of five or six animals. He stalked them and was about to shoot his arrow when one of the caribou pushed back the hood from its head and changed into a man dressed in a caribou skin parka. It called Nakasunaluk, telling him to come near. Nakasunaluk went over, and the caribou asked him if he would like to join the herd. He said he would, so the caribou removed Nakasunaluk's clothes and turned him into a caribou. Then they moved off together.

In their wanderings Nakasunaluk was always behind the rest of the caribou herd. The others asked him, "Why are you so slow?" He replied, "I keep stumbling all the time." They told him to look up at the stars as he walked along, for if he watched the ground he would always stumble. After this, by following their advice, Nakasunaluk was able to keep up with the herd. But when it came to feeding time, he could never find anything to eat, and in consequence became thin and weak. The caribou asked him, "How is it that you are so thin?" and he replied, "I cannot find anything to eat." So they taught him to eat their food.

Thus, Nakasunaluk lived a long time with the caribou, until one day they asked him if he would like to go back home. "Yes," he said, "my people will think that I am lost."

Once Upon a Story Knife
by Catherine Pessino

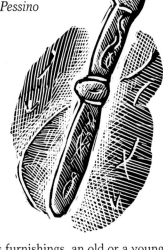

Years ago, I spent several summers with a friend in an Eskimo village, Bethel, in southwestern Alaska. My friend is a cousin of the doctor there, and we soon became known as "the cousins." Even with only two thousand people, Bethel was quite a population center, and in the summers, more Eskimos came up from the coast to set up their fishing camps on the banks of the Kuskokwim River.

An outsider in any small town is probably looked at with some suspicion, and I was no exception when I first came to Bethel. As I walked around the village, I would come upon groups of five or six girls giggling and talking. They seemed to be playing some mysterious game in the mud. The moment they saw me, they would stop what they were doing and wait for me to pass by before beginning again. I became more and more curious about their game. Finally, some grownups told me that the girls were telling stories and using story knives to draw pictures in the mud to illustrate them.

A story knife can be plain or elegant. A girl's father traditionally carves one for her of walrus tusk or bone, often shaping or decorating it to resemble a whale, walrus, or fish. A carved story knife is a special treasure, but girls also prize the table knives or other common tools they often use for drawing in mud or snow.

Eskimo girls play with story knives only in this part of Alaska, and they have their own set of shorthand symbols for drawing. With a few lines, they can quickly show the layout of a house and its furnishings, an old or a young person, an animal, or a river. Symbols allow the pictures to keep up with the story. Usually, each scene in the story is wiped out as the scene changes, and the next scene is drawn in the same spot. The firm mud is like a big, flat blackboard, and the story knife serves as both "chalk" and "eraser."

Like the Eskimos, you can tell stories outside in the firm mud or damp sand, or you can use clay or Play-Doh® that you can spread on a board to use inside. The kind of plastic knife that you take on a picnic makes an excellent story knife.

Eskimo girls tell stories they have learned from their grandmothers, mothers, or older sisters and from events in their own lives. Try creating your own version of a story and see how the pictures turn out. You and your friends can make up your own picture code or follow the Eskimo system. This game is just as much fun for boys as for girls.

For me, the story knife story had a happy ending. At the end of my third summer, I received a beautifully carved story knife of walrus ivory made just for me.

"Very well," said the animals, "we will take you home." Accordingly they started back. As they traveled the caribou said to Nakasunaluk, "While we sleep one of us is always watching with its head up; when that one sleeps another takes its place, for we are afraid of wolves and men. If you see a man or a wolf you will want to run away." At last they reached the place where they first encountered one another. There Nakasunaluk put on his clothes again and returned to his human shape, and went home. His people said to him, "Where have you been?" "The caribou," he said, "took me with them far away." "We watched for you a long time," they told him, "and when you did not come back we thought you were lost." Nakasunaluk said, "When I wanted to shoot a caribou one of them removed its hood, and taking a human shape, asked me whether I would like to become a caribou and go away with the herd. So they changed me into a caribou and taught me to eat their food and how I should look up at the stars when walking over the land." This man, Nakasunaluk, had very small legs (hence his name), and after his return home he was able to run very fast.

From *Spirit-Keepers of the North: Eskimos of Western Alaska* by Susan A. Kaplan. Copyright © 1983, The University Museum, University of Pennsylvania. Based on a myth told by a Cape Prince of Wales woman, collected by D. Jenness (1924).

An Old-Fashioned Eskimo Thanksgiving
by Helen Wieman Bledsoe

Thanksgiving brings to mind pictures of New England Pilgrims feasting on turkey, but for the Alaskan Eskimos, the scene was quite different. They gave thanks for a good harvest of whales, not grains, fruits, and vegetables. The time was spring, not fall. And instead of turkey, they dined on whale meat. Their favorite delicacy was mucktuck, inch-thick strips of whale skin with rich, fat blubber attached.

Imagine the entire population of a tiny village gathered on the beach of the Arctic Ocean or the Bering Sea. Think of music, dancing, feasting, and that most traditional of all Eskimo sports, the walrus-skin toss. Thanksgiving, or Nullakatuk* as they called it, lasted a night or a whole week and was the high point of the Eskimo year.

Whales were very important to the Eskimos because they were the primary source of food, oil for cooking and light, and even building materials. As soon as the hunters returned from the hunt, they hoisted gaily colored pennants on their overturned umiaks (skin-covered boats). This signified that it was time for Nullakatuk, and everyone dressed in fancy new clothes and headed for the beach.

The men hauled their long sleds loaded with whale meat onto the sand. The women then chopped the meat into chunks and cooked it in pots of oil right on the beach.

While the whale meat simmered, the men raised a windbreak of canvas or skins (they often used their overturned umiaks), then set up the twelve-foot-square walrus-skin trampoline. It was decorated with a fox tail or ermine skin.

The men and women danced separately. The men's dance was more vigorous, even violent. Their feet stamped, their bodies lurched, and they leaped high in the air, landing stiff-legged with a body-wrenching jar. Many dances had been handed down from generation to generation, and they often represented hunting or whaling exploits.

The women's dances were very different. They kept their eyes cast downward and never lifted their mukluks (skin moccasins) off the floor. Sometimes they even danced sitting down. Their movements from the waist up were quiet and graceful. Their arms fluttered like birds, as their bodies swayed gently back and forth. They sang:

Ayii, ayii, ayii,
My arms, they wave high in
the air,
My hands, they flutter
behind my back,
They wave above my head
Like the wings of a bird.
Let me move my feet.
Let me dance.
Let me shrug my shoulders.
Let me shake my body.
Let me crouch down.
My arms, let me fold them.
Let me hold my hands under
my chin.

Nullakatuk was a time for sport, feasting, and dancing. Just as other cultures celebrate a successful harvest, this was the Eskimos' way of giving thanks.

*It should be pointed out that in some places and with some people, Nullakatuk is still celebrated.

The Cranberry Feast

There are several kinds of bears in Alaska but the grizzlies are the fiercest. The myth on which "The Cranberry Feast" is based was recorded in English at Wrangell early in 1904. It was related by an old man named Kasank. It is curious that cranberries, which we associate with our Thanksgiving and Christmas dinners, should have been served at this feast of fellowship between the grizzlies and the old hunter.

To the raven clan belonged an old, old hunter who had outlived all his friends and family. He was so lonely that he often wished his days were at an end.

Early one morning, walking in the forest, the old man decided he would let the bears do away with him. He went to the mouth of a large salmon creek near his village and searched for a bear trail. When he found one, he lay down across the end of it.

Presently he heard the bushes breaking. A band of grizzly bears were coming his way. When the man saw how large was the leading bear and how white the tips of his hairs, he was overcome with fear. So when the leader approached him, he jumped up and, without knowing where the words came from, said:

"I am here to invite you to a feast."

The great bear's fur stood straight up. The man thought his last moment had come but he took a deep breath and repeated:

"I am here to invite you to a feast. I am lonely and would like your company at dinner."

At these words the leader turned and whined to the bears who were following him. Then, after bowing solemnly to the old man, he started to retrace his tracks. When the bears were out of sight, the man ran back to his village. Arriving home, he started to clean house. He put fresh sand around the fireplace, replenished the fuel pile, and looked to his supply of food.

The people in the village stopped to ask why he was making all these preparations. Since he had lost his family and friends, they had never known him to entertain anyone.

"I have asked some grizzlies to a feast," he answered.

His neighbors were amazed. "What made you do such a thing?" they asked. "They're our enemies."

He gave no answer.

Very early next morning the old hunter took off his shirt and painted himself with ceremonial stripes. He put marks of red across his upper arm muscles, a stripe over his heart, another across the upper part of his chest. With everything in order, he stood waiting outside his door.

When the village people saw the band of bears at the creek, they were so terrified that they shut themselves in their houses, but the old man hastened to receive his guests. The same big bear was leading the band and when they arrived at the house, the old man took them inside and gave them seats. The bear chief he placed in the rear surrounded by the others.

The old man served them big trays of cranberries preserved in grease. First, the biggest bear seemed to speak to his companions. Then, as soon as he started to eat, the rest started too. Whatever the biggest bear did, the others did also.

When the bears finished eating, the bear chief talked to the man for a long, long time. The old hunter did not understand the language but he gave his heart to listening. As the bear spoke, he paused every now and then to look up at the smoke hole as though deciding what to say next. After his talk, he left the house and the band followed him. At the door each licked a little paint from the host's arm and chest — a farewell salute.

The night after the feast the smallest bear returned in human form and spoke to the hunter. Whether he was awake at the time or dreaming, the old man himself could never say. The bear explained that he was a human being who had been captured and adopted by the grizzlies.

"Did you understand what the chief was saying yesterday?" he asked.

"No," answered the old man.

"He was telling you he has lost his friends and is lonely too. He wished you would think of him when you miss your companions."

So from that night, whenever the old man felt lonely, he gratefully remembered the visit of the solemn bear chief.

As for his neighbors, they were so astonished by the bears' civility that, now, when they give a feast, they invite strangers — even if they are enemies. They seek to become friends with them, just as the lonely old man did when he once served cranberries to the great white-tipped grizzly chief.

From *The Magic Calabash — Folk Tales From America's Isles and Alaska* edited by Jean Cothran, illustrated by Clifford N. Geary. Copyright © Jean Cothran. Reprinted with permission.

HAWAIIANS
Hawai'i

by Ellen Donohue Warwick and Walton Duryea

Wearily, the sailors rested their paddles. All they could hear was the sound of the waves beating against the canoe and the sail creaking in the wind. The drinking water in the gourds was getting low. Food they could always find. The sea was full of fish. But fresh water? Without it, they would die. They had been at sea for weeks without sight of land and had traveled farther across the empty water than any they knew had ever traveled before. Suddenly, one of the sailors gave a hoarse cry. There, over on the horizon — that black dot. The paddles flashed in the water, pulling the big double-hulled canoe toward the distant shore. The trip would soon be over. But coming ashore would not be the end. It would be the beginning.

Perhaps as long ago as fifteen hundred years, bands of Polynesians set sail in the southern Pacific Ocean seeking new islands to the north. They had neither compass nor sextant to guide them. Instead, they relied on their knowledge of wind, stars, ocean currents, and the paths of migratory birds to chart their course. This group of sailors journeyed more than two thousand miles to the north and settled the land that we now call Hawai'i.

For centuries, Polynesian sailors had explored and settled much of the South Pacific, settling most of Oceania, the thousands of islands scattered across the central and south Pacific. Now, perhaps motivated by a spirit of adventure and a desire to explore new lands or perhaps because their islands had become too crowded with not enough food for all, they were journeying farther north than any had gone before.

The first people to discover and settle Hawai'i probably sailed from the Marquesas Islands. Five hundred years later, historians believe, a second wave of migrants set out from Tahiti. After that, these long voyages seem to have stopped. No one else came across the sea to the islands for about seven hundred years.

The Polynesians traveled in long double-hulled canoes with sails. Platforms lashed between the two parts were packed with provisions. They brought plants to farm the new land — taro (a tropical plant that was an important part of their diet), sugar cane, sweet potatoes, breadfruit, bamboo, and gourds — as well as pigs, chickens, and dogs. They brought simple tools, bark cloth, and a few weapons. With these supplies, the Polynesians began a new life.

Most of the people were fishermen and farmers and lived in small villages near the seashore. The land was divided into pie-shaped wedges stretching from the mountains to the sea so that each group had all that it needed: forests for wood, land for crops, and the ocean for fishing. Each wedge was ruled by a chief, and the highest chief of each island was the king. The Hawaiians worshiped their king. Commoners could not look at him, and should the shadow of an ordinary man cross the king's path, the person suffered instant death.

The traditions established in this new land were much like those of other Pacific islands. Men obtained and prepared food. They fished with nets, spears, and hooks they made themselves. They planted taro, soaked its roots, and pounded them into poi, a thick paste that was the Hawaiians' daily bread. They cooked meals in huge underground ovens called *imu.*

Women tended the children and took care of the family's clothing. They softened the inner bark of the

mulberry tree in water, then pounded it into cloth called *kapa.* Sometimes they pressed designs into the kapa or colored it with dyes made from fruits and berries.

The Hawaiians believed that gods lived everywhere, including in rocks, plants, animals, and humans. There were special gods for war, the harvest, volcanoes, and the sea. The people prayed often and made offerings of food. Priests, or *kahuna,* presided over temples and made sure people obeyed the law. They also acted as healers, teachers, and advisors.

Life in early Hawai'i was well ordered and governed by laws called *kapu. Kapu* means "forbidden," and most of the kapu concerned things people could not do. Men and women could not eat together, nor could their food be prepared in the same oven. Certain fish could not be caught or eaten at specified times of the year. The home of a chief might be kapu to the common people.

Despite these many rules, the early Hawaiians enjoyed life. They liked to watch the hula, a sacred dance that told a story. Dancers trained for years and had a special god to whom they prayed. Hawaiians went swimming, canoeing, and surfing. Men wrestled, ran footraces, and boxed. Children used small, smooth stones to play games similar to jacks and button-button. People decorated themselves with leis, necklaces made of leaves and flowers, and gave them to special friends and honored guests. Each fall during the festival of Makahiki, all work stopped for four months, and the people feasted, played games, and took part in sports and contests.

Cut off from the rest of the world, this is how Hawaiians lived until 1778. That year, an English explorer discovered the islands. His ships were soon followed by others curious to see the island paradise he and his crew had described and

eager to trade with the people who lived there.

The foreigners introduced new ideas about religion and governing. Traders and whaling ships brought foreign goods and also disease. Christian missionaries changed many native customs but also taught the islanders to read and write. By the late 1800s, Honolulu on the island of O'ahu was an international harbor. Ships crossing the Pacific stopped for supplies; others were loaded there with sugar as Hawai'i began growing food crops to sell to the world.

Hawai'i's large sugar plantations were owned mostly by Americans. To protect their interests, the plantation owners worked to control the government as much as they could. Finally, in 1891, they took over the governing of the islands from the Hawaiian monarchy. Their goal was fulfilled when the United States annexed the island seven years later.

During that era, Hawai'i began to grow as a modern society. In the twentieth century, the money for development, which came first from trade and agriculture, also began to come from tourism. Modern transportation made it possible for many tourists to visit the islands. The United States opened military bases there, and the military became another important part of the islands' economy.

Today, as part of the United States, Hawai'i boasts modern cities with high-rise office buildings, shopping centers, residential developments, and three universities. Millions of tourists visit Hawai'i's hotels and beaches, and more residents work in the tourist industry than in any other. The U.S. military is the islands' second-largest employer. Hawai'i's sugar and pineapple plantations also continue to be important to its economy.

People of many races and nationalities live in Hawai'i. Only about one percent of the population is

pure Hawaiian, but the islands' traditions and history have not been forgotten. Royal palaces are now museums, and state holidays mark important dates in Hawaiian history. In addition, Polynesian traditions are still a big part of life in the islands, from Hawaiian words used in everyday language to the leis and hula with which visitors are greeted.

Pele

by Sondra Brooks

Chiefess Kapi'olani stood silently at the edge of the great crater Kilauea on Hawai'i. She had traveled to the volcano on foot, over more than one hundred miles of rugged lava. Fearful friends and followers had begged her not to defy the goddess Pele, who inhabited the volcano and could bring fiery destruction to the island. But the year was 1825, and Chiefess Kapi'olani had been converted to Christianity. She was ready to test the old ways and challenge the power of Pele.

Descending into the crater, she reached down and plucked some *'ohelo* berries from a bush. One of her friends gasped — eating them was *kapu* (taboo) according to Hawaiian legend.

"I defy you to punish me!" the proud woman called to the goddess. Her followers trembled. They knew that if someone made Pele angry, the earth would rumble and erupt into flames, with lava pouring out of the mighty mountain.

Kapiʻolani stood erect and placed a few berries in her mouth. A stillness fell over the group. All those present had memories of Pele's power. Many had lost loved ones and ancestors because of the volcano's activity.

Raising some large stones over her head, the queen hurled them into the pit below, calling out loudly, "God kindles these flames, not Pele!"

The volcano was quiet. Minutes ticked by. When the queen's followers heard no rumbling and saw neither steam nor fire, they rejoiced at what was to them the triumph of Christianity over Pele.

Who was this wild and powerful goddess? Was her power ended now that Kapiʻolani had tested her once, or would she strike again?

Legend tells us that most Hawaiians worshiped this goddess. Her brothers were the great gods of creation: Thunder-Maker, Earth-Shaker, Fire-Keeper, and Kamohoaliʻi, the god of steam. Kamohoaliʻi had asked his brother the fire god to teach Pele the art of fire making. She was a good student and soon learned to use her fire sticks to dig a pit and make fires that caused red lava to bubble and flow.

In one of her efforts, the lava reached the sea and destroyed many fish. Her sister, the sea goddess Namaka-o-kahaʻi, was furious and vowed to take revenge on Pele. "I demand that she be punished," Namaka-o-kahaʻi told her brother Kamohoaliʻi.

Knowing that these two powerful sisters could never live in harmony,

Kamohoaliʻi sent Pele away to find a home of her own. Arriving at Kauaʻi after a long canoe trip, Pele made another fire, but her sister saw it and sent huge waves to put it out. Pele fled to Maui and then Oʻahu, bringing fire to each spot. Each time, Namaka-o-kahaʻi's waves drowned the fire, but she never hurt her sister.

During her search to find a place of her own, Pele fell in love with a mortal, Lohiʻau. Changing herself into a beautiful young woman, Pele won his heart. The couple might have been happy together, but Pele soon grew restless. Leaving Lohiʻau behind, she canoed past many small islands until she spotted a great mountain on the large island of Hawaiʻi. Naming it Mauna Loa (Long Mountain), she paddled toward it for weeks, knowing that at last she had found a home.

All that remained was to send for Lohiʻau. This she did by asking her younger and very beautiful sister, Hiʻiaka, the goddess of lightning, to guide the handsome Lohiʻau to their new home. It took a very long time for them to arrive, and by then Pele was raging with jealousy. According to the *ka poe kahiko* (people of the past), Pele destroyed them both with

fiery lava when they arrived.

The islanders still tell many Pele stories today. Some tell of a goddess who walks among people, making dogs howl, cats hiss and spit, and horses rise up in fear. They say she can assume the form of an old woman begging, a beautiful young girl, or even a small white dog that appears on the barren lava slopes just before an eruption. Although there is no food or water for miles around, the dog appears to be healthy and well fed. It is also said that when all is very still on Kilauea, the goddess is pleased with those she meets. But if the earth trembles, someone has angered her, and an eruption will follow.

Poets have described the thin strands of volcanic glass that spin off the lava fountain as "Pele's hair." If the droplets of lava harden, they are called "Pele's tears." Many tourists who have visited Hawaiʻi and taken away pieces of lava rock have been known to have bad luck when they got home. Some have mailed packages of rocks back to the Volcano Post Office to rid themselves of Pele's spell. Perhaps these rocks are Pele's children, and Mother Pele puts an evil curse on those who kidnap them.

  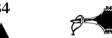 

Word Lore: Spoken Music

by Janeen R. Adil

Have you ever said *"Aloha!"* at a *lu'au,* where you danced the *hula,* wore a *mumu* and a *lei,* and played the *ukulele?* If you recognize these words, you already know something about the Hawaiian language. These are some of the more familiar words that English has borrowed from the islands.

Hawaiian did not become both a spoken and written language until the first missionaries arrived in the 1820s. Before that time, the Hawaiians preserved their history through songs, chants, and poems. The missionaries used the English alphabet to record the sounds they heard the natives speaking, using just twelve letters to write out these words.

The story is told that King Kamehameha II himself helped with this project. At one point, the missionaries had to decide whether to use an *r* or an *l* to signify a sound in Hawaiian that came approximately between them. They wrote down the king's personal name both ways and asked him to choose which one he preferred. The king liked Liholiho better than Rihoriho, so Hawaiian has the letter *l* in its alphabet but no *r.*

One of the Polynesian languages, Hawaiian is so pleasing to the ear that it has been called "spoken music." It is also a language that is full of surprises for someone learning to speak it. Some words in Hawaiian are simple to pronounce: *a, 'a'a,* and *'a'a'a* are all distinct words. More challenging is a word such as *humuhumunukunukuapua'a,* which is the name of a very small fish. But with a few rules of pronunciation to guide you, even this long word will roll off your tongue.

Hawaiian has five vowels, which are pronounced like this: *a* as in father; *e* as in obey; *i* as in machine; *o* as in so; and *u* as in rule. The seven consonants — *h, k, l, m, n, p, w* — sound like their counterparts in English, although the *w* sometimes sounds like a *v.* Every word and syllable ends in a vowel, and the next to last syllable is always the one that is accented, or stressed.

With these rules in mind, the word *humuhumunukunukuapua'a* turns out to be not too difficult after all. Just say hoo-moo-hoo-moo-noo-koo-noo-koo-ah-poo-ah-ah, remembering to accent the first *ah.* Now that you are warmed up, try *iwakaluakumamakahi,* the word for the number twenty-one.

Today Hawaiians speak mostly English. As any *malihini* (tourist or stranger) finds out quickly, though, many words from the Hawaiian language are used in everyday speech. No matter what their nationality, Hawaiians say *pa'u* (finished or all done), *hale* (house), *wahine* (woman or wife), *kane* (man or husband), and *haole* (Caucasian, especially an American).

As any *kama'aina* (long-time resident) can tell you, the Hawaiian language has other interesting features besides its pronunciation. For instance, the word *mahalo* (thank you) is used a great deal, but there's no real equivalent of "You're welcome." The islanders, known for their generosity, take this response for granted. And instead of referring to the compass when talking about directions, Hawaiians use *mauka,* meaning "toward the mountains," and *makai,* meaning "toward the sea."

Here are some more words and phrases that will help you sound like a kama'ai'na in no time!

mokupuni	island
'aina makua	mainland
kahaone	beach
moana	ocean
la	sun
halakahiki	pineapple
aloha	hello; good-bye; love or affection
Pehea 'oe?	How are you?
Maika'i no	I'm fine.
'olu'olu	please
Wiki	Hurry up.
Hau'oli la hanau	Happy Birthday
Mele Kalikimaka	Merry Christmas
'o wai kou inoa?	What's your name?
Kawika	David
Mika'ele	Michael
Kamaki	Thomas
Keoni	John
Kini	Jenny
Lahela	Rachel
Malia, Mele	Mary
Elikapeka	Elizabeth

PART III

Projects and

Creative projects draw us further into Earthmaker's lodge. Fun blends with learning in these artistic crafts of doll making, home building, weaving, beadwork, and more. From cave painting to Navajo sand painting to Eskimo drums, we explore native materials and designs and present projects and crafts based on natural objects and other art supplies.

ANCESTORS

by E. Barrie Kavasch

People have always been interested in where they came from, who their ancestors were, and where they lived. Knowing who and where we came from helps hold families and larger groups together and gives us a sense of who we are. These links with the past take unique forms for different tribal groups.

American Indians, whose ancestors lived here long before anyone else, take pride in their heritage as Native Americans. Long before written records, native peoples recalled their ancestors and traditions through spoken stories, ceremonies, and special ways of sharing by knowledgeable elders. These elders told the collected histories of the clans and tribes. When an elder died, it seemed that an entire library of special collective

Crafts

memories was lost. It is still that way, even though now we write things down.

In some Eskimo (Inupiat) villages, when an elder died, the first boy born afterward was often given the elder's name, both as an honor and in hopes of his carrying on ancient traditions. Some Northwest Coast Indian families look to a past when supernatural spirits gave a family ancestor exclusive privileges to valuable rights that remain in the family through many generations. Elaborate masks and rattles accompany these rights and rites.

The Iroquois and Algonquian peoples of the eastern woodlands depended on collective memories and memory aids, such as sacred wampum strings and belts, condolence canes, song sticks, story beads, and story baskets. Birch-bark scrolls of the Great Lakes Grand Medicine Lodge, or Midéwiwin, recorded ancestral wisdom of the people's origins and migrations and much more. Followers of this respected history evolved to become members of the ancient medicine society, which still functions today. Knowledge of the healing plants, songs, and formulas draws generations of new members.

The Yuchi of Georgia believe, through early legends, that one of their ancestors is tobacco, a sacred herb offered in their ceremonies, prayers, and hunting and healing rites. The Crow of Montana have numerous branches of their ancient tobacco society, and new members continue to be adopted into it.

Many American Indian tribal councils formed since 1934 have collected detailed enrollment records providing, in many cases, the Indian name, English name, age, family, and clan relationships of each member. Yet many old full-blood communities and pockets of native settlements in the eastern United States (and elsewhere) have resisted signing anything or being registered. They continue to blend the best of their new traditions with what they choose to retain from their past. Like their ancestors, they continue to break new ground and follow a different spirit.

Looking back over time helps us to look at our present and future with greater dimension. Ancestors — all of our relations — are part of who we are.

"The heyoka [holy man] presents the truth of his vision through comic actions, the idea being that the people should be put in a happy, jolly frame of mind before the great truth is presented."

Black Elk,
Oglala Lakota medicine man

Reaching for Your Roots

by E. Barrie Kavasch

Many years ago, while doing gravestone rubbings in an old cemetery in New Haven, Connecticut, I began to wonder about my early ancestors. Where did they come from? Where were they buried? Were they together? My curiosity grew as I visited other old cemeteries in Europe and the United States.

Sometimes it is hard to find information about your family, unless someone recorded it in the family Bible, in old quilts, or in beautifully stitched samplers. I have a dear friend whose uncle wrote the entire family history on a fine old window shade, which he brought with him when he went to visit relatives. What a lovely way to share this information!

Let's start small and make a four-generation family chart as a fan.

1. Fold an 8 1/2- by 11-inch piece of paper in half. Then fold it into quarters, eighths, and sixteenths.

2. Unfold the paper and then refold it like an accordion or fan.

3. Use the following numbering scheme: Begin with yourself as 1, then list your parents as 2 and 3, your grandparents as 4–7, and your great-grandparents as 8–15.

4. If you can add information such as birth date and birthplace (b), marriage date and place (m), and death date and place (d), you will gain a broad picture of your background.

Family History on a Window Shade

Now that you have researched your immediate family history, you can begin to add information about your aunts, uncles, and cousins. Follow the same general outline of your four-generation chart, but spread it out in a freeform, artistic layout. Use your imagination. Perhaps you will want to draw in lines, leaves, flowers, and roots between the names. Use pencil, lightly at first, because you are surely going to make additions and changes. This is a project in which your whole family can participate.

Many of my young friends are

Native American Toys

by Evelyn Wolfson

When European settlers first came to the New World, Native American children were playing with toys made out of natural materials. Because Native Americans lacked a written language, children learned by watching and listening very carefully to their elders. There was little difference between playing and learning, and it was always fun to imitate adult life using small tools, weapons, and utensils.

Boys and girls stayed with the women of the tribe until they were about six years old. They learned to help by gathering roots and berries in season, collecting firewood, and relaying messages from one home to another. The women of the tribe made toys for the children out of leftover materials. Children learned how to work grass, bark, clay, wood, bone, and antler while making toys of their own.

Some tribes encouraged boys and girls to play together until they were eleven or twelve years old. Most often, however, boys and girls played separately after their sixth birthday. This made sense because they had to learn and practice quite different skills.

Girls always stayed at home. They worked with the women of the tribe from the time they were six years old until they married. They learned to do everything their mothers did — to cook, weave, make pots, prepare animal hides, and take care of younger brothers and sisters. Their chores and responsibilities did not change much from the time they were young until they were adults. When they had time, young girls played with dolls and miniature utensils, and sometimes they even had small homes of their own.

On the Great Plains, where tribes followed herds of migrating buffalo, children set up small villages in which to play when the family made camp. Their toys were made out of the hide, bones, and organs of the buffalo. Plains children were allowed to play together until they were about ten years old. They played "house" in their small village during the day and returned to the family tipi at night. When families moved, children were responsible for their toys. Young girls from well-to-do families carried their small skin-covered tipis across their lap when they traveled by horse. Sometimes parents allowed them to tie their toys onto small travois (carriers made of poles) and hook them up to one of the family dogs. This was great fun and made the girls feel grown-up.

No one knows for sure whether Indian children played with dolls prior to European contact. Confusion about dolls has arisen because charms and amulets (small human or animal-like figures worn by adults to protect them against evil spirits) could be mistaken for toys. These charms were believed to possess magical powers, however, and were never used for play.

Chippewa girls, who lived around the Great Lakes,

adopted and do not know who their "birth parents" are. What do you do in this case? Each of us comes from two parents, four grandparents, eight great-grandparents, and so on. Perhaps you will never know all (or any) of their names. You may be more interested in their nationalities or professions (farmer, minister, midwife, ironworker, and so on). Use this project as a way to learn more about your background, whatever it may be.

played with dolls made of bunches of basswood leaves or grass. The head, arms, and legs of the dolls were tied together with fine pieces of bark to form a figure. Girls also played with dolls cleverly fashioned out of the long, thin needles of the long-needle pine. The pine dolls were set in a birch-bark container filled with water, then shaken back and forth to make them dance.

Blackfeet girls, living on the northern plains, had dolls made out of a thick birch limb about a foot long. The limb was rounded at one end, with eyes, nose, and mouth notched into it. The doll was not carved below the shoulders, but it was dressed in a traditional buckskin costume. When the girls were older, their grandmothers made them soft buckskin dolls stuffed with moss. These dolls were elaborately dressed in leggings, moccasins, and robes. They had beads sewn on for eyes, nose, and mouth, and their hair was braided out of horsehair. Tribal dolls dressed in traditional costume were popular with European children, too, and many Indian women made them to sell.

Boys enjoyed a great deal more freedom than girls. The most important part of a boy's education was learning to hunt and fish successfully, so boys were free to leave the campsite whenever they wished to practice their skills. They were given small bows and arrows as soon as they could walk. Fathers, grandfathers, and uncles continued to make larger pieces of gear for the boys as they grew up. Sometimes a boy had a special relationship with a maternal uncle who taught him how to fish and hunt and

brought him gifts. Young boys also learned from the older boys who went out to play with them.

Among tribes of the Montagnais, who lived along the northwestern shore of the St. Lawrence River, men watched their sons each spring during target practice, because a father whose son was skillful at hitting targets was expected to enjoy a prosperous hunting season of his own.

When boys traveled by river or stream to hunt, they usually went by canoe, so canoe construction was an important part of every boy's education. In New England, Native American boys learned to make pine dugout canoes. First, the builders packed mud around the base of a large tree, then set the tree on fire. The mud contained the fire, which was left to burn overnight. In the morning, the men and boys chipped away the charred portion of the tree with stone axes and shell scrapers. When all the charring was removed, they set a new fire. The process of burning and removing the charring continued until the tree fell to the ground. Once the tree was on the ground, the builders removed the lower limbs and packed mud along its length, leaving a large opening down the center. The central portion was then burned and scraped away until the log had taken the shape of a deep canoe with thin sides. The bow and stern were carved last.

Young boys sometimes made small pine dugout canoes of their own when they returned from hunting trips. They raced the canoes on nearby lakes and ponds.

Do-It-Yourself Cave Painting

by Tonia W. Falconer

How did prehistoric people paint and draw in caves? Remains of tiny stone lanterns have been found with traces of animal fat, which was used for fuel. These must have had a wick, possibly made of moss, that lit up the dark cave rooms. Ancient artists used mineral and clay deposits found in the cave walls to make their painting and drawing materials. They probably created brushes from moss and sticks to spread the color on the rock, and sometimes they painted their own hands and pressed them on the walls to make prints. Hollow bone tubes, through which artists blew paint, have been found with traces of color inside them. Many handprints were made by placing a hand on the cave wall and blowing paint around it, making a "negative" print.

To make your own "prehistoric" paintings, you need:

watercolor or tempera paints (These wash off easily.)

brushes or pieces of moss or wool

plastic straws

sticks (to stir paint or draw)

lots of paper (Brown paper is best because it is closer to the color of rock.)

newspaper to protect the floor

Try to use colors such as brown, yellow, dark red, and black — the colors prehistoric people used most often. Work outside or spread the newspaper all around so that you will not drip paint on the floor. Using the brushes, moss, or wool, paint pictures of animals that you think prehistoric people might have seen. Remember that there were many large animals such as bears, bison, mammoths, and deer.

You can make handprints in two ways. The first is to dip your hand in tempera paint and press it on the large piece of paper several times. Another way is to place your hand (this time with no paint on it) on the paper and blow paint with the plastic straw around it. When you take away your hand, you will have a "negative" print.

Prehistoric people also carved on rocks inside and outside caves. They often showed simple figures praying to the sun or chasing animals with large spears. Sometimes the artists carved animals such as deer, wolves, and horses into the rocks and afterward painted the engravings. Other times they carved war scenes with spears and other weapons, and sometimes even their own houses.

To make your own engravings, you need:

different-colored crayons

black crayon

thick sheet of paper

stick or broken pencil

Color the sheet of paper with different crayons, filling up the entire paper. Try to use colors that remind you of the earth. After you have filled the page, color over everything with the black crayon until the entire sheet is black. Then take your stick or pencil and draw figures or shapes on the black. The different colors from underneath will show up wherever you scratch away the black.

Making Cornhusk Dolls

by E. Barrie Kavasch

In the ancient Arawak language, *mahíz* means "life giver." European settlers in America called this plant "corn," the term for the people's most important food crop (in England, "corn" refers to wheat). Corn was an ancient, delicious, and versatile gift in Native American cultures. Archaeological evidence indicates that this very important food was first cultivated by early Indian farmers more than seven thousand years ago in the highland regions of what is now Mexico. From there it spread slowly to gardening peoples around the world.

Corn also is a useful, artistic plant. Native artists created mats, boots, bottles, and beautiful masks and dolls from cornhusks. They carved cornstalks into blowguns, whistles, and fiddles and worked cornstalk leaves into braided mats and other

items. They also used corn tassels and roots in various ways. Images of corn appear in sculpture, pottery, and other ancient tribal art forms.

Among their imaginative uses of corn, native artists made cornhusk dolls for their children, who learned to make the dolls for themselves and friends, often acting out stories and legends with these little figures. Continuing this ancient tradition, you can make some cornhusk people, birds, and animals. Perhaps you can create an early Indian village. Make a few other cornhusk characters who come to trade from another village. Use your imagination!

You Need

1-pound bag clean, ripe cornhusks

damp towel

Rit dye (several colors)

ball of string

scissors

handful of dry corn silk

crayons or markers (optional)

2 cornstalks

small rocks

1. Dampen the cornhusks and roll them up in the towel.

2. Select a few choice cornhusks to use as trim, clothes, and accent items. Dye them for these special uses. (Ask an adult for help in using the dye.)

3. Roll one medium cornhusk into a small ball for the head of your first cornhusk doll. Cover the ball with a choice cornhusk and tie the husk at the neck with a short piece of string.

4. Roll up a medium cornhusk for the arms. Tie small cornhusk strips at each wrist (either end of the roll) and slide the roll up under the loose cornhusks below the head. Tie it in place, forming the waist of your doll.

5. Gather the remaining husks to form the legs (or skirt) of your doll.

Set it aside to dry.

6. Continue making men, women, and children dolls to populate your village. Also make some birds and animals.

7. When each doll is dry, glue or tie corn silk on its head. Braid the hair, cut it short, or leave it long according to your own design. Leave the faces blank so that each doll can change character several times. Or draw faces on the dolls with crayons or markers to give each one a unique personality.

8. Cut and fashion the colored husks into trim, clothes, and accent pieces, using corn silk and other items for decoration if you wish.

9. Use extra cornhusks to make little baskets, brooms, bundles, and tools for your cornhusk people to hold.

10. Cut off one cornstalk just above the base and roots to use as a big tree. Cut the remaining cornstalk to use as smaller trees, or split and hollow out the pith to use as houses, canoes, and other items. Use these and the rocks to create a village or natural landscape for your cornhusk people.

Making Corn Grow

"Corn" once meant a little particle of something, such as a seed or a grain of wheat. Then the meaning of the word grew until it also came to describe the most important grain crop in different parts of the world. The English who came to America saw the crops that the Indians were growing and called the most important one corn. But back in England, "corn" still meant wheat because wheat was the most important crop there, and our corn was — and is — known as Indian corn, or maize.

You can grow the row of **CORN** on this page by adding the proper letters before or after the word to make a new word that fits the given description.

__CORN	A great oak grows from it
__CORN	To despise or look down on
CORN__ __	You often turn it when you walk or ride
CORN__ __	First cousin to a trumpet
__ __ __CORN	A famous one-horned animal that does not exist
__ __ __CORN	Our Founding Fathers wore this hat
CORN__ __ __	It projects from a building roof
__ __ __ __ __ __CORN	This animal "lives" in the sky
CORN__ __ __ __ __ __	An overflowing horn that stands for plenty
__ __ __ __ __ __CORN	It goes with salt
CORN__ __ __ __ __ __	A blue summer bloom
CORN__ __ __ __ __ __ __	Laying it makes a building official

If you have raised a good **CORN** crop, this one should be easy: add H to STARVE, scramble the letters, and make a new word.

__ __ __ __ __ __ __ __   The gathering of a crop

Answers on page 154.

Bullroarers

*by E. Barrie Kavasch
and Celia A. Daniels*

One of the oldest musical instruments, the bullroarer, is also one of the more mysterious. Many American Indian tribes made and used them, as did other primal groups in Africa and Australia. The bullroarers of our desert Southwest were unique wind instruments used in ceremonial curing rites.

Hopi medicine men spun bullroarers over their heads in ceremonial dances and at special gatherings to gain visions and insight into particular problems. These delicate, often beautifully designed and painted wind instruments were made of thin wooden slats. A cord was securely fastened through a hole or groove in one end of the bullroarer so that it could be twirled somewhat like a propeller on a helicopter or airplane. When whirled overhead or in front of the body, it made a roaring or buzzing sound, depending on how fast you whirled it. Different-size bullroarers created very different music.

As with kachinas, sacred spirits of the Hopi, Zuni, and other Pueblo peoples, bullroarers were sometimes made to teach young people about special aspects of Pueblo life. You can make a bullroarer by following these directions.

You Need

drill or ice pick

tongue depressor, large wooden craft stick, or piece of heavy cardboard

piece of string about 1 yard long

1. Ask an adult to drill or punch a hole about 1/2 inch from one end of the wooden stick or cardboard.
2. Thread the string through the hole and tie it loosely to the stick.
3. In an open space (make sure no one is standing too close), spin the bullroarer over your head as fast as you can. You may have to spin it for a minute or two before it starts to make a whirring or buzzing sound.
4. You may want to decorate your bullroarer with brightly colored designs, such as lightning bolts, clouds, or flowers. See whether it sounds any different to you after you decorate it.

Clay Storyteller Dolls

by Judith A. Brundin

The Pueblo people have lived along the Rio Grande and atop high mesas in New Mexico and Arizona for more than two thousand years. Pottery making has long been a part of their culture. For many centuries, they have made small human forms from clay, probably images of themselves. In this century, native artists are creating new types of clay figures.

Pueblo artist Helen Cordero molded her first clay storyteller doll in 1964, introducing a new art form. Now many artists create similar storyteller dolls.

Cordero is from Cochiti Pueblo in New Mexico. Her dolls are meant to represent her grandfather, who was a great storyteller. Children loved to listen to him. The dolls have an unusual face. Cordero explains, "His eyes are closed because he's thinking; his mouth is open because he's singing." Storytellers are important to Indian children because they keep and share the stories of history, important dreams, and special events. Stories also are a way of teaching children how to behave and how to live properly.

The first clay storytellers Cordero made included a few attached children, but now they have ten or more. The dolls have become so popular that other Pueblo artists are using storyteller designs in pottery, woven objects, and paintings.

You Need

newspaper

clay (available at art stores)

tools for making designs (pencils, sticks, toothpicks, etc.)

cups of water

acrylic or tempera paints and paintbrushes

1. Cover your work area with newspaper.
2. Roll small pieces of clay between your hands to make sausage-shaped objects. These will be the storyteller's children. Using the tools, carve a face in each one.
3. Make a clay ball about the size of a large walnut. Using the tools, press a rounded mouth into the face area. Pinch a small nose into the face above the mouth. More parts of

the face will be painted on later. Set the head aside.

4. Roll a large piece of clay into a ball the size of an orange. Push, pull, and squeeze the clay to form a body with two arms and two legs.

5. Attach the head to the body by scratching the clay at the neck area. Add a bit of water to the scratched area. Put the storyteller's head on the scratched area and press it in place. Attach the storyteller's children to the arms and legs, using scratched areas to help hold the clay in place. Let everything dry and harden in a dry, shaded place.

6. After the doll has dried, paint it.

Make a Net Market Bag

by E. Barrie Kavasch

Net making is probably one of the oldest forms of weaving. People almost everywhere in the world made many types of nets: fishing nets, hunting and game nets, hammocks, market bags, and many other types. Net bags were, and still are, convenient for carrying things to and from markets.

People usually made nets by knotting or finger-weaving native fibers twisted into string or cords. They created these practical bags in a great variety of shapes, colors, and sizes. Plant and animal fibers could be easily twisted, twined, rolled, or braided into strong cords to weave, knot, or braid into many kinds of articles.

American Indians created nets of plant fibers from dogbane, milkweed, nettle, inner tree bark, fine tree roots, reeds, rushes, strong grasses, and wild cotton. Fragments of fine plant fiber nets thousands of years old have been found at archaeological sites in the southwestern United States. People in Africa and the South Pacific made very similar net sacks. South American Indians invented hammocks.

Macramé (pronounced MAK-ramay) is a method of tying string with various knots to create designs. This French word comes from the Arabic *miqramah,* meaning "striped cloth." The technique dates back more than seven hundred years. Beautifully tied fringes of Oriental carpets and exotic shawls and fabrics were traded in markets and carried around the world. Industrious sailors with nimble fingers would fill long hours at sea tying and creating lovely functional knotted items, from huge fishing nets to simple net bags, fancy knotted purses, and other imaginative items that they could trade, sell, or bring home as gifts to loved ones.

Using basic macramé, you can make a simple knotted market bag. If you make it carefully and strong, you might be able to use it as a lunch or book bag.

You Need

ruler or yardstick

medium ball of cotton cord or sisal, jute, or rug yarn

scissors

chair

1. Measure out eleven lengths of cord 2 yards long, two lengths 6 inches long, and one length 12 inches long. Cut them carefully and evenly.

2. Tie the ends of one 2-yard cord

Overhand knot

Slipknot

together in an overhand knot. This will be the top (or mouth) of the bag.

3. Tie the two 6-inch cords onto this doubled cord. Slide them to opposite ends and hitch them over the back of a chair.

4. Find the exact middle of each of the ten remaining 2-yard cords. Tie five cords onto one side of the doubled cord with simple slipknots; tie the other five cords onto the other side. **Note:** Careful measuring and tying are very important!

5. Take one strand from each of two doubled cords that are side by side. Tie them together with a simple overhand knot 2 to 3 inches below the top. Do this all the way around to create "diamonds."

6. Repeat step 5 eight or nine times to make your net. It should look a little like a basketball net.

7. Gather all the cords together at the bottom and tie them securely together with the 12-inch cord. Your bag is ready to use.

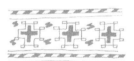

Navajo Sand Paintings

by Florence Temko

According to the lore of the Navajo Indians of the southwestern United States, the gods taught medicine men to make pictures in the sand to help cure illness. Some tribes believe that sand paintings should be kept secret, but in recent years, some Indian artists have shared them with the outside world without exactly copying the sacred designs.

A Navajo sand painting is traditionally made in the medicine lodge, where a large group assembles for the event. The medicine man and his assistants begin by spreading a layer of desert sand on the floor as a base. For the design, they trickle colored sand between their fingers as they slowly move their hands. A tightly stretched piece of string might serve as a guide for a long time. It takes at least three years of practice to be able to make straight lines and perfect circles freehand. Pictures vary in size from three to thirty-five feet.

The designs illustrate Indian legends about male and female gods, mountain spirits, thunder and lightning, and animals and plants. Colors have special meanings: white for east, black for north, blue for south, yellow for west, and red for sunshine. The colors are all ground from natural materials. For instance, limestone provides white, wood and charcoal produce black, and sandstone makes red and brown.

When the picture is completed, the patient to be cured is seated in the middle. While the sand painting is being made and throughout the healing ceremony, tribal members sing and pray for the help of the Great Spirit. The paintings are made and destroyed in one day or one night; otherwise, the Navajo believe, they will bring bad luck.

Instead of using loose sand, Indian painters now sometimes work on wooden boards. The artist mixes sand with dry glue and creates a design. The picture is left outside at night, and the morning dew moistens the glue enough for the sand to stick to the board.

The following instructions tell you how to make a sand painting using materials available in your neighborhood.

How to Make a Sand Painting

You can use sand from a sandbox, a sand pit, the beach, or the desert. Most kinds of sand, except construction sand, can be colored with fabric dyes. Prepare deep dye colors, such as black, red, royal blue, yellow, brown, and aqua.

For each color sand, you need:

1 tablespoon liquid fabric dye *or* 1 teaspoon powdered dye

3/4 cup hot tap water

plastic cup or container

1/2 cup sifted sand

newspaper or paper towels

paper plate

1. Mix the dye with the hot water in the cup. Add the sand and stir. Let the sand soak at the bottom of the cup for at least two hours. Slowly pour off the colored water.

2. Spread the sand on newspaper or paper towels and let it dry. When the sand is dry, pour it onto the paper plate.

To make the painting, you need:

12-inch-square piece of cardboard

felt-tip pen

white glue

colored sand on paper plates

newspaper

clear acrylic spray (Krylon or similar; optional)

1. Draw the design on the cardboard with a felt-tip pen. Spread glue on the areas where sand of one color — such as red — will go. Sprinkle the sand carefully over these areas and let it dry for a few minutes.

2. Tilt the painting and let any loose sand drop onto a sheet of newspaper. Bend the newspaper and let the extra sand run back onto the plate.

3. Continue gluing and sprinkling sand for each color until the picture is complete. When the painting is dry, spray with acrylic or cover with clear varnish or another craft finish.

Build a Navajo Hogan

*H*ogan (ho-ghún) is the Navajo word for house, dwelling, or living place. Hogans are well-insulated, secure places made of logs, poles, or stone masonry. The construction of the male and female hogans are prescribed in detail, following the instructions given to First Man by Talking God in Navajo house-building songs.

You Need

tracing paper

oak tag or construction paper

scissors

colored markers or crayons

glue

1. Copy pages 96–97 (use tracing paper if necessary) onto the oak tag. Cut out each shape along the outside lines. Color the sides of the house brown and the roof earth color.

2. Fold each piece on the broken lines.

3. Glue or tape tabs A to the inside of edges B. Be sure to match up the designs on the front side (see Diagram 1).

4. Attach the roof of the hogan to the walls by lining up the fold lines on the roof and the fold lines on the wall. Tape the roof in place.

5. Color the landscape and sheep scenes.

6. Overlap and glue tabs A and B of the sheep scene.

7. Place the landscape inside the band and behind the sheep scene (see Diagram 2).

Courtesy of The Heard Museum, Education & Public Program Division, Phoenix, Arizona.

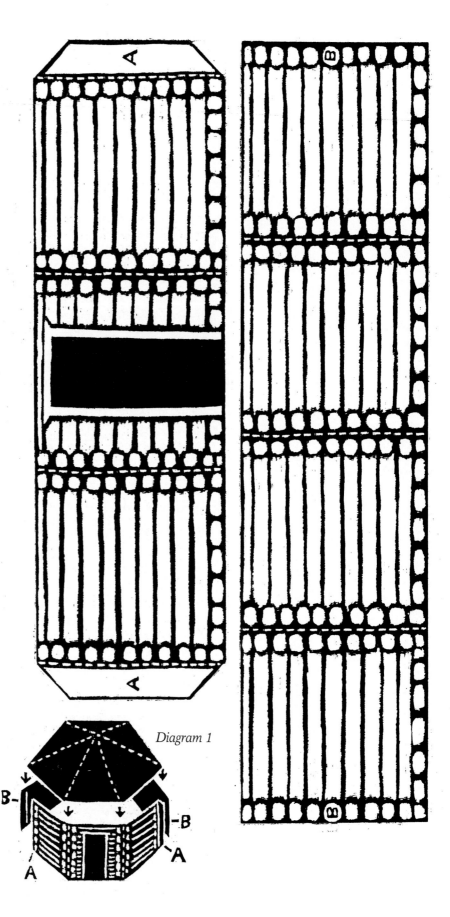

Diagram 1

  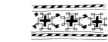

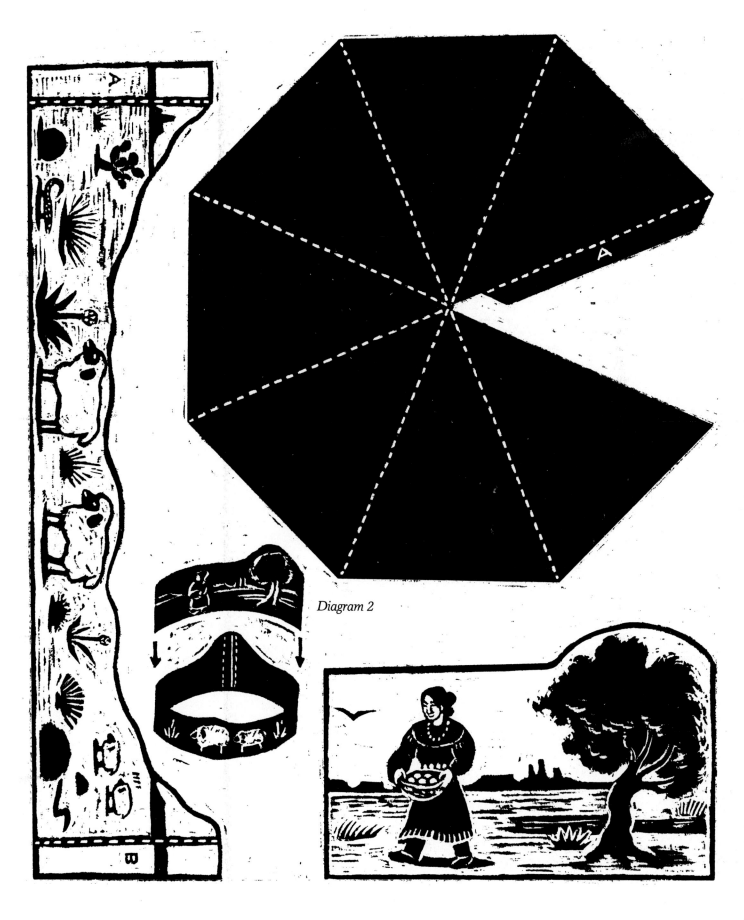

Diagram 2

Seneca Stone Reading

by Annie Moonsong

Yehwehnode (Twylah Hurd Nitsch) teaches stone reading as a life vision. Seneca elder and daughter of a Seneca mother and an Oneida-Scottish father, she lives on the Cattaraugus Indian Reservation in Irving, New York. She learned much from her mother, her Wolf Clan grandmother, and her grandfather, Moses Shongo, a Seneca medicine man. In her book *Language of the Stones,* Yehwehnode relates the origin of the stone reading tradition (see page 101).

If you want to follow this long-standing Seneca tradition, first find a stone that grabs your attention or seems to say, "Pick me up." It is best if it is larger than a pebble, can fit comfortably in your hand, and is found in your neighborhood. These are called environmental stones and reflect your home surroundings in relation to your personality.

If you have a collection of stones, they have been talking to you already! Although it may be difficult, choose your favorite stone from the collection. Holding each stone in your hand will help. The stone you choose should not have been bought in a store, polished, or received as a gift because such a stone will already have responded to another person's energy. The energy used in selecting your personal stone is important in the reading. You can read your stone in five different ways.

1. Determine how many sides your stone has. Put your stone on a flat surface. That counts as one side. (Your stone may be round or oval, which means it will not lie flat on any other side.) Now turn your stone; each time it lies flat on a different side, add one. The total amount of times the stone lies flat can tell you something about your personality.

Shape	Meaning
Round	You are flexible.
Oval	You are seeking a better life.
Two-sided	You are easily influenced by others or learn by watching them.
Three-sided	You know how you feel inside, are a good listener, tend to be quiet, like reading, and dislike noise and confusion.
Four-sided	You have self-respect and love nature. You are self-disciplined, are not easily talked into things, and make lasting friends.
Five-sided	You are very creative, appreciate beauty, show affection, and respect nature.
Six-sided	You have talents and can develop them. You are trusted and true, can see what other people need, and can make good decisions.
Seven-sided	You always say "thanks" for things in your life. You can be a good spiritual leader.

2. Check your stone's colors.

Color	Meaning
Sparkles	This is called a star rock. It means you have lofty ideals, charm, and charisma.
Brown	You are earthy, and you love nature and animals.
Gray	You are friendly.
Black	You are seeking the light (understanding).
Red	You are faithful.
Yellow	You are loving.
Blue	You are a good listener. You make good decisions by intuition (what feels right).
Green	You are dependable and responsible, and you like respect.

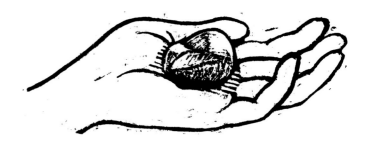

Pastel (any light color not mentioned)	You are creative and use this ability in your work.
White	You enjoy doing for others.
Purple	You are grateful for every moment and are spiritual.

3. Check the stone's texture and weight. If it has a hole through it, it is a protector stone. Make a necklace by putting it on a piece of leather, string, or yarn and wear it to remind you of the stone's spirit energy.

Texture/Weight	Meaning
Smooth and light	You are gentle.
Rough	You follow creative ideas or have scientific views.
Rough and heavy	You have many growth experiences.

4. Look for faces, animals, or plants in your stone. Use your imagination when doing this. You may see something no one else does!

Figure	Meaning
Dog or horse	You are devoted.
Bird	You have lofty ideals and bring messages of peace and goodwill.
Fish	Your problems are easily overcome.
Butterfly	You are surrounded by beauty and have a gentle personality.
Flowers, plants, or trees	You are growing and are dependable.
Large animals	You have strength of character and health.
Shells, snails, or other crustaceans	You stick to an idea or project.
Wolf	You are a trailblazer.
Human face	You are a teacher. If you are a male, you are gentle. If you are a female, you have strength and endurance.

5. Hold the stone in your left hand so that it feels comfortable, then transfer it to a flat surface with your open fingers pointing north. Read the following symbols on the side of the stone that is facing up.

Symbol	Meaning
	A large circle symbolizes the sun; it is the power of love and represents the male gender.
	A small circle means lessons of growth and changes; it symbolizes the moon, the guardian of the night, and the power of growth.
	A circle within a circle indicates relatives or relationships.
	A large equilateral triangle is the shape of equality, the symbol of wisdom and sensitivity, and the gift of inner knowledge.
	A small equilateral triangle is a symbol of gifts and talents to be developed; it represents the power of creativity.
	A left acute angle is a symbol of respect; it represents the power of accepting responsibility.
	A right acute angle is the symbol and power of accepting honor for achievements.
	A wide, shallow X means a new friend.
	Two parallel horizontal lines mean you are faithful to any cause.
	A vertical line represents the power of the spirit.
	A bird represents a free spirit with high ideals.

wood splints for as long as twelve hours. To obtain dark tones, the bark, husks, and roots of butternut and walnut trees were used, and to obtain red or orange tones, yellow-root and bloodroot were used.

Once wood or cane splints had been boiled with the desired plant products, the process of weaving could begin. But it was important to learn patience. Skill in the art of basketry could take years to acquire. Once this skill was acquired, an experienced basket weaver could make eight or more baskets in a week.

Clay pots were a part of every Cherokee household. Cherokee girls again depended on the older women to teach them to make clay pots. Young girls and their grandmothers would go to a place near a river to dig white clay. Fine-grained clay was used for making pipes, and coarser, sandy clay was used for pottery.

Young Cherokee girls learned that clay had to be molded until it had the consistency of putty before it was ready to shape. Next the clay had to be kneaded until it was soft and free of lumps. Then a small amount of clay was flattened to form the bottom of a piece of pottery. After this process was completed, a design could be created.

Carefully, clay was rolled into long, thin strips that were coiled around and on top of the base piece of clay. Layer after layer, more clay was added. Finally, when the pot had taken its final shape, the clay was smoothed and decorated with a Cherokee symbol or design. Sometimes designs were drawn on the clay with a sharp piece of bone. Often they were stamped on with a carved wooden paddle known as a *gastoti*. A favorite symbol was "Noonday Sun."

Before a clay pot could be used, it was set in the shade to dry for one to three days. Then it was placed near a hot fire. After about an hour, the pot began to turn brown all over.

Once it had turned brown, it could be safely rolled into the embers, mouth down, with a long stick.

If the pot survived this process without cracking, it was made waterproof by placing a handful of dried corncobs inside. The corncobs were set ablaze, and the pot was turned upside down to be certain that all the material inside was burned. Then the pot was ready for use.

Today Cherokee crafts are highly prized. Thousands of people visit Cherokee villages every year to watch and admire as craftspeople carry on the traditions of their ancestors.

Plaited Place Mats

by Annie Moonsong

Traditionally, the native people of the southern states saw their everyday utensils as works of art, and they took from their environment to create them. By making these useful items beautiful, they kept the beauty of nature close to them. Also, because nature (their ecological habitat) was their "God" or Great Spirit, using nature's bounty satisfied a need to be spiritually connected with their surroundings.

The Cherokee of Tennessee, Alabama, Georgia, and North Carolina and the Catawba of South Carolina usually used oak splints for making baskets and mats, although they also used some cane, cedar bark, palm fronds, and strips of yucca leaves. They created a checkerboard pattern with a plain plaiting technique and more intricate geometric designs and textures by dying splints several colors and twill-plaiting them. You can weave a similar mat by using strips of construction paper.

You Need

construction paper, at least two colors (more if you are doing twill plaiting)

pencil

ruler (with metal edge if you are using an X-Acto knife)

X-Acto knife or scissors

tape or glue

Plain Plaiting

1. Cut a piece of construction paper 18 by 12 inches. Lightly draw eleven lines with a pencil and ruler — 1 inch apart, 16 inches long, beginning 1 inch from the end.

2. Cut the "warp" lines you have drawn (eleven cuts) with the ruler and X-Acto knife (or scissors). Be careful when using the knife.

3. Cut sixteen strips, 15/16 inch wide and 14 inches long, from the second color of construction paper. These are called the "weft."

4. Weave one weft strip in and out of every other warp.

5. Tape or glue the end of the strip that is even with the edge of the sheet to the back of the warp. The strip will extend beyond the other side of the sheet. Fold the strip over to the back of the warp and tape or glue it in place.

6. Weave the second strip in and out in a pattern opposite that of the first (that is, over and under alternate warps). The end that folds over also will be opposite.

7. Continue by alternating the weaving pattern of the weft strips.

Twill Plaiting

Follow steps 1 and 2 as in plain plaiting, then continue with step 3 below.

3. Cut eight strips, 15/16 inch wide and 14 inches long, out of each of two different colors of construction paper, making a total of sixteen strips.

4. When weaving in the second color (first color strip), alternate every two warps (that is, two warps under, then two warps over the weft). Cut off the overhang of the strip and tape or glue both ends to the back of the warp.

5. Weave in the third color (second color strip) every two warps, up one warp from the second color. Tape or glue the end of the strip that is even with the edge of the sheet to the back of the warp. Fold the other end over to the back and tape or glue it in place.

6. Continue the pattern with the second color, again moving up one warp from the weft previously woven. Alternate the second and third colors until the strips are all woven in.

You can experiment with different weaving patterns. For instance, weave two wefts in the second color, then weave in the third color at every third weft. Or move the second color weft up one warp and the next weft down one warp. Whatever you do, follow your creative instincts to make a useful and beautiful place mat.

Tennessee Grasshopper Tent

by E. Barrie Kavasch

American Indian children were clever at making countless objects out of plant parts. Some items might have lasted only a day or two. Many were collected for museums, but many others were simply given back to nature.

As a child on my grandparents' farm in the Tennessee Valley, I was very aware of how different animals and plants come and go through the seasons and of their changing activities. Many of these activities were integral parts of special farm stories. Some of the stories were down-to-earth, and others took off into the rich world of imagination.

One day my grandmother taught me to make what she called a grasshopper tent. We sat in the summer grass and picked the tall, slim flower stalks of the ribbed (narrow-leaved) plantain. Plantain is common and considered a weed in many areas. Grasshoppers, too, are common and often considered pests in farm and garden regions, where they can destroy crops by eating the plants' leaves. Grasshoppers can destroy whole crops of cotton, clover, alfalfa, corn, and other grains.

As children, we would catch grasshoppers and hold them until they "spit" a juice we called "tobacco." They made this by chewing plants. Research shows that this liquid may help protect the grasshopper from predators such as ants, spiders, birds, mice, snakes, and other insects.

Grasshoppers often seek shade during the hottest hours of the long summer days. This activity took us out under shady trees, where we gathered ten long plant stems and sat weaving a bug-size tent in which grasshoppers, crickets, or spiders might find shade. Although it's hard to know whether any grasshoppers actually moved in, the fun of weaving the little tents often kept me busy making a whole encampment. And the more grasshopper tents I created, the more it pleased my grandmother, who liked having me pick the plantain — to her, an unwelcome weed. In some small way, I was doing something to benefit my farm's ecology. I began to learn more about this as I grew more interested.

You Need

10 flexible stems or paper straws 8 to 10 inches long

twist tie or 6-inch piece of string

1. Lay the stems along your middle finger, one by one, from base to tip, until you can fit no more. Each new stem lies on top of and across the ends of the one below it. The other's ends are then folded over its ends to hold it snug. (See the figure.)

2. Repeat these steps until your grasshopper tent is finished. Gather and hold together all the loose ends as you carefully slip the tent off your finger. Tie the gathered ends securely together, as in the figure. Then set your tent in the grass so a grasshopper can find it.

Story Beads

by E. Barrie Kavasch

When my mother was growing up on a farm in Tennessee, her mother and grandmothers made colorful braided rugs and warm quilts out of the family's worn-out clothes. These useful household items told stories about earlier outfits and the people who wore them, and they continue to tell us about an era of thriftiness and fine craftsmanship. Some of these family heirlooms are now in a museum, but we still use the homier pieces, which are three and four

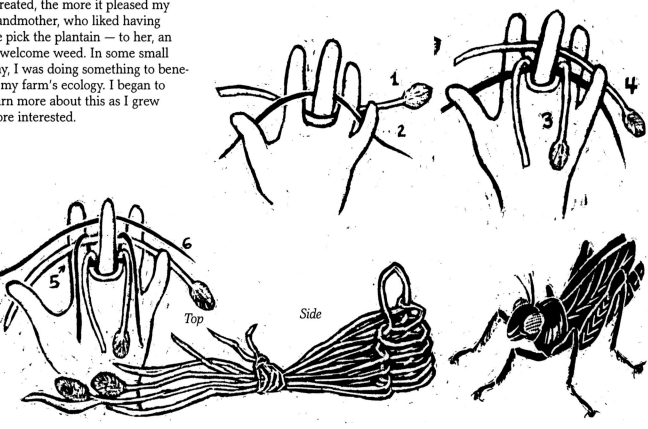

Top   *Side*

generations old. The same tradition of creative recycling inspires story beads.

Beads made from many different kinds of paper have stories to tell. You can make bracelets, necklaces, earrings, hair ties, fancy Indian beads, and trade beads from discarded paper. Use different papers to create different types of beads. Magazine and catalog pages result in gay, multicolored beads. Brown paper bags and old manila envelopes make beads that resemble wood. White paper bags and deli paper make bonelike Indian hair pipe beads. Newspaper and tissue paper make fine chinalike beads. And peeled corrugated cardboard makes large, geometric ornamental beads. These can be painted with bright acrylic paints and decorated to match special outfits or be used for special occasions. Plain, undecorated beads can be left as is or sprayed with enamel or shellac to add a protective, glossy sheen.

You Need

pencil and ruler

white paper bag or deli paper

brown paper bag

scissors

pencil, straw, or toothpick

3 feet of string, colored yarn, twine, or leather cord

small, soft paintbrush

1 tablespoon white glue mixed well with 1/2 teaspoon water in a shallow cup or dish

small bottles of colored enamel paint or spray varnish (optional)

1. Each bead is made from a long, thin triangle or rectangle of paper. Use the pencil and ruler to draw the patterns on the appropriate paper.

2. Cut out the paper shapes carefully.

3. Roll each bead snugly, starting at the broad end, around a smooth pencil, straw, or toothpick, depending on the thickness of the string, yarn, twine, or cord you plan to use for stringing the finished beads.

4. Brush the last 2 inches of the paper strip with the glue mixture. Then roll the bead snugly to the end of the strip, pressing it gently to secure the end.

5. Hold the paper firmly and slide it off the pencil. Allow the bead to dry completely.

6. Repeat this process until you have as many beads as you wish.

7. When the beads are completely dry, you can sand and trim them if necessary, then paint and shellac them if desired.

8. String the beads on the string, yarn, twine, or cord.

Practical Presents

by E. Barrie Kavasch

Regional thriftiness is remembered in Knoxville knots, paper pretzels, and Cape Cod oysters. These fire starters are important to people who use wood stoves, cast-iron cook stoves, fireplaces, and campfires. They are made from old magazine and catalog pages.

To make a knot, hold three or four magazine pages together in the center (lengthwise). Roll them up snugly, then tie them in a single overhand knot. Repeat this process until you have a pile of knots.

Fill a small brown paper bag or shopping bag with the knots. Take them on your next camping trip or give them to someone you know who can use them.

Hands Only: Plains Indian Sign Language

by Stanley Freed

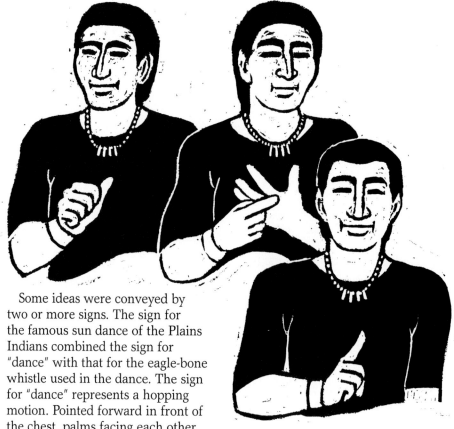

For many centuries, American Indians of the Great Plains roamed from Canada to Texas over the vast open grassland between the Rocky Mountains and the Mississippi River. Living chiefly by hunting the immense migratory buffalo herds, the twenty-seven tribes of Plains Indians followed a nomadic lifestyle, which led to frequent contact among tribes, both friendly and hostile. Because the Plains Indians speak many different languages, difficulties in understanding one another led them to develop an effective sign language that is understood by all tribes.

Anything but clumsy and slow, Indian sign language is fluid, graceful, and almost as rapid as spoken language — and it is done with the hands alone. Indians keep their faces almost motionless when they use sign language, drawing all attention to the lively hand motions.

The Indians generally related signs to the activities or objects they symbolized by imitating typical movements or illustrating particular features. The sign for "bear," hands near the head, palms to front, suggests a position of the bear's front paws when scouting or the animal's ears.

The sign for the Mandan Indians, who lived in North Dakota and practiced tattooing, represents a woman tattooing her chin. The sign is made by bringing the tip of the thumb to the compressed fingertips and then tapping the chin and lower part of the face several times.

Some ideas were conveyed by two or more signs. The sign for the famous sun dance of the Plains Indians combined the sign for "dance" with that for the eagle-bone whistle used in the dance. The sign for "dance" represents a hopping motion. Pointed forward in front of the chest, palms facing each other about six inches apart, the hands are moved a few inches up and down several times. The sign for "whistle" is made by holding up the right hand, thumb in front of the mouth, index finger extended and pointing up and forward. The hand is moved a few inches back and forth in the direction the finger is pointing.

The Gros Ventre, who live on the northern plains along the Canadian border, were named "big bellies" by early French explorers because, in Indian sign language, they were designated by a sweeping pass with both hands in front of the abdomen, meaning "always hungry."

To make a sentence in Indian sign language, the signer strings together signs for the basic idea. "I arrived here today" needs four signs: I — arrived here — now — day. "Today" uses two signs for a single English word, yet one sign expresses "arrive here."

The sign for "I" is to touch the chest with the thumb of the right hand, fingers closed, back of hand to the right.

"Arrive here" is represented by holding the extended left hand before the chest, fingers pointing right. Bring the closed right hand, index finger extended and pointing up, briskly against the back of the left hand.

"Now" is made by bringing the closed right hand, index finger extended and pointing up, about eight inches in front of the face and then, without stopping, moving it a little forward, stopping with a slight rebound.

The sign for "day" calls for extending the arms and hands in front of the chest, then sweeping the hands upward, to the right and left, and then downward in a graceful curve, the two hands moving simultaneously and ending when the hands are opposite the shoulders.

"Our tipis were round like the nests of birds, and these were always set in a circle, the nation's hoop, a nest of many nests, where the Great Spirit meant for us to hatch our children."
Black Elk, Oglala Lakota medicine man

Plains Indian Tipis

by E. Barrie Kavasch

North American Indians built many different kinds of houses, depending on the environment. For hundreds, perhaps thousands, of years, most Indian houses had a wooden frame with various types of covering. Only a few of these were movable.

The tipis of the Plains Indians were the most portable structures. More than twenty tribes that hunted and traveled across the Great Plains, an area of almost eight hundred thousand square miles, lived in tipis. These people moved quickly and often to follow the buffalo (bison) herds, which were their primary source of food, medicine, clothing, robes, tipi covers, and much more. For them, the tipi (from a Sioux word) was an ideal dwelling.

Traditionally, the Plains Indians made their conical tipis out of buffalo hides stitched together to form secure covers. Sometimes they used elk or deer hides, and in some regions, tree bark and mats covered the tipis. The buffalo was, however, the center of Plains Indian life, and the Indians used every part of it: the skins for robes, clothing, tipi covers, storage containers (parfleches), dew cloths, drums, riding gear, and war shields; the bones and horns for tools, utensils, ornaments, and glue; the sinew for thread, bowstrings, and small hunting snares; the brains for tanning the hides; the stomach for containers and cooking vessels; the hoofs for rattles and hunting charms; and the dung for fuel.

The women and girls tanned and prepared the buffalo skins, which was a long process. Generally, the women also made and owned the tipis, although the men helped throughout the process. Summer hides were preferred because they were thinner than winter hides, and when fine-tanned, they would let more light into the tipi's interior. Hides were smoked to make the tipi cover water repellent and to keep it from hardening after repeated rain and snow.

The Plains Indians invented a unique frame system that would allow them to pitch (set up) and strike (take down) their tipis quickly. The placement of the poles with a slight backward tilt increased the usable interior space and braced the tipi against the high winds and occasional twisters of the Great Plains. The tipi was always pitched with the door facing east into the rising sun and opposite the prevailing westerly winds. The central hearth fire was placed toward the center-front of the lodge, allowing for more headroom and family space in the rear.

A large family tipi might require more than twenty-five poles and twenty buffalo hides, with each hide weighing about twelve pounds. This would make an eighteen-foot lodge.

The Indians originally used dogs to help move their tipis from one campsite to another. The dogs pulled the tipi poles, which were lashed into a harnessed frame called a travois. Once the horse was introduced, the plains tribes were able to travel farther and faster and to carry more possessions, so the tipi poles increased in size. Each tribe adopted its own tipi design. For instance, the Crow Indians had very long tipi poles, often topped with feathers or streamers to show which way the wind was blowing. This allowed them to adjust the smoke flaps, or "ears," at the top of the tipi to make the fire inside draw well and to keep the interior of the lodge smoke free.

The destruction of the buffalo by the 1880s forced the Plains Indians to switch to canvas for their tipi covers. The disappearance of the herds also changed their tribal lifestyles. But the tipi has become one of the universal symbols of the North American Indians, and you can still see tipis at powwows, museums, and environmental centers.

Painted Tipis

by E. Barrie Kavasch

"A beautiful tipi is like a good mother. She hugs her children to her and protects them from heat and cold."

Sioux proverb

Painted tipis were the homes of special individuals within each Plains Indian tribe. An encampment of many tipis might have had only a few painted ones, which would be located in the most honored places. The Indians usually grouped their tipis in a large circle opening to the east (as each tipi also faced east into the rising sun). Privileged locations for the painted tipis of medicine people and warrior societies were usually pitched on the south side of the circle near the eastern opening.

The Plains Indians decorated their tipis for religious and ceremonial reasons and to preserve tribal histories. Gifted people guided by visions or dreams created "medicine tipis," which were believed to have the power to protect the people within. Some designs were considered to have supernatural strength, so the tipi upon which they were painted became a sanctuary, much like our churches or synagogues.

The Indians prepared special earth pigments to use in painting tipis and other objects such as parfleches, medicine bundles, war shields, dew cloths, and even dancers' bodies. Before commercial paints were available, the best earth pigments were found in the northern plains, and some tribes, such as the Kiowa, used twelve different pigments. The basic colors were black from charred wood, blue from blue clay or mud, green from pond scum (algae) and certain plants, yellow from buffalo gallstones, and red from hematite (a form of iron ore) and pipestone (a red stone). Hide scrapings, horns, and bones were boiled to make a kind of glue, which bound these powders into a paint that would stay on the hides. Buffalo-tail brushes or porous bones were used to paint the tipi covers. A medicine person, or shaman, or a special tribal member usually did the painting.

Painted tipis were the largest form of Plains Indian art. Symbols are very important in any type of art, and this is especially true in that of the Plains Indians. Large white circles might represent stars, mushrooms, or buffalo dung; dark triangles separated by lines might indicate mountains divided by the plains; buffalo hoofs, buffalo heads, and bear paws were usually good hunting and strong medicine symbols. Some Blackfeet tipi designs represented the cosmos, or world view. The bottom band was the earth, the large middle band represented the living world, and the top (usually painted blue or black) symbolized the night sky, with white circles for constellations such as the Pleiades and the Great Bear (Big Dipper).

Some special examples of painted tipis include the following:

Blackfeet All Star Tipi In this design, the large white circles on the tipi usually represent stars and sometimes fallen stars or mushrooms. Some tribes believed that mushrooms were actually fallen stars come down to earth for the people's benefit. Mushrooms, especially large white puffballs, were important foods and medicines throughout the plains. These circles also might represent buffalo dung, which was a source of fuel. This, too, was a good-luck symbol, indicating that the people who lived within would always be able to find enough buffalo and fuel.

Sioux Medicine Tipi This design shows a large buffalo facing east, like the tipi door, open to the rising sun, the source of warmth and spiritual power. It was a symbol that would provide for all the family's needs.

Comanche Bear Paw Tipi Animals were thought to be important sources of help and protection. The bear was a valuable food resource, and bear images were symbolic of strength and good medicine. The Bear Medicine Society was one of the more sacred in many tribes. Bear paws were a ceremonial symbol copied from Comanche war shields and were thought to protect the people who lived within this tipi.

Although many tipi paintings have been lost over the years, some still remain to remind us of this special art form.

Erecting a Tipi

by E. Barrie Kavasch

As the primary shelter for the Plains Indian tribes, the tipi was warm in winter and cool in summer and was able to withstand the severe winds and rains of the Great Plains. A team of five or six people could pitch a large tipi in less than thirty minutes. You can make your own tipi by following the directions on page 110.

a. *A tripod of three or four poles, lashed together near their tops, is raised up. Tipi poles are usually thirty feet long and are made of lodgepole pine or red cedar. The tipi is always positioned so that it faces east looking into the sun, which signifies the renewal of all life.*

b. *The tipi frame is balanced, with the first pole marking the north doorpost. The long end of the tying rope is used as a guy to help guide, and eventually to wrap around, all the poles at the top and to anchor them to the ground.*

c. *The next five poles are added counterclockwise on the north side of the doorway. Poles are placed in the top crotch of the frame with their bases secured in the ground in a large circle determined by the size of the tipi cover. On the average, twenty-five tipi poles are used.*

d. *The rolled tipi cover, tied to the last (lifting) pole, is raised into place, usually at the back of the frame. Today Plains Indians make their tipi covers of canvas, although traditionally the covers were made from tanned buffalo hides.*

e. *Stretching (or unfurling) the tipi cover around the framework of poles was usually done by women. Plains Indian women generally made and owned the tipis, and they were responsible for pitching and striking them when they moved camp.*

f. *The two sides of the tipi cover meeting in the front are pinned together with wooden lacing pins, usually carved from Rocky Mountain birch. Then the flap poles are inserted into the upper corners of the smoke flaps, or "ears," of the tipi cover. The bottom edge of the tipi cover is fastened down with short tipi stakes.*

Captions elaborated from pages 12-13 in "Painted Tipis by Contemporary Plains Indian Artists," an exhibition organized by the Indian Arts & Crafts Board of the USDEP, catalogue of the exhibit published by the Oklahoma Indian Arts & Crafts Cooperative, Anadarko, Oklahoma, 1973.

You Need

8 chopsticks, long pencils, or straws

3 toothpicks

yarn or string

tracing paper

pencil

heavy paper or felt

scissors

paper punch or awl

colored markers

1. Cut eight sticks 10 inches long for poles.

2. Use three toothpicks 2 to 3 inches long for fasteners.

3. Take a 9-inch piece of yarn or string and tie the long sticks near their tops. Stand them up and balance them for your frame.

4. Copy the pattern for your tipi cover from this design (enlarge it 2 1/2 times).

5. Place the pattern on the heavy paper or felt and cut it out carefully. Punch out the lacing holes with the paper punch or awl.

6. Spread out your tipi cover and decorate it with colored markers.

7. Fit the tipi cover around the sticks and fasten the front together, lacing sticks in and out.

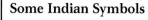

Some Indian Symbols

1. Bear paw, 2. Buffalo hoof, 3. Buffalo head, 4. Stars or mushrooms, 5. Mountains and plains, 6. Water or lightning

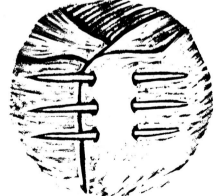

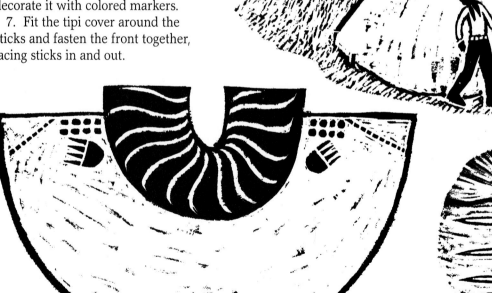

Beadwork

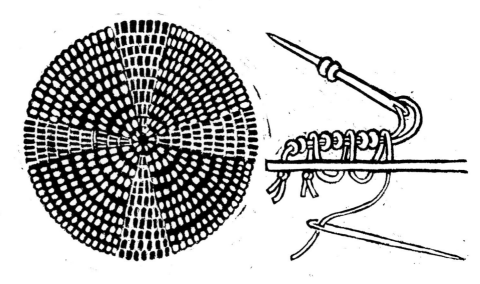

In the long-ago time before the coming of people, it is said that Bobolink wore a necklace of shell and bone beads. These were perhaps the first beads used in what later became home to the Nez Perce.

Old-time Nez Perce artists gathered elk and deer teeth, salmon backbones, and turkey bones and fashioned them into necklaces, bracelets, and earrings. They traded for materials with peoples along the Pacific coast. Shells from the coast — iridescent blue abalone and white tusk-shaped dentalium — were traded by Nez Perce as far as the Mississippi River valley.

The first glass beads to reach Nez Perce artists followed the same route. By the late 1700s, maritime merchants were trading European goods to coastal peoples for sea otter pelts. Faceted Russian and Italian glass beads were traded upriver to Nez Perce artists, who worked the new materials into their existing art forms.

When white traders came overland and began supplying Nez Perce artists with a steady supply of beads, the classic style of Nez Perce beadwork bloomed. Based on designs originally worked in porcupine-quill embroidery, rawhide painting, and cornhusk basketry, beadwork became an art form. By the late 1870s, Nez Perce artists were famous for their work.

Traditionally, the Nez Perce used beaded rosettes, worked in many colors, to decorate moccasins, women's saddle pommels, and blanket strips and as forehead ornaments for horses. Today rosettes also are used to make earrings, necklaces, bolo ties, barrettes, braided ties, and belt buckles. You can make your own beaded rosette by following these directions.

You Need

piece of canvas 3 inches square

pencil

silver or brass paper fastener or small pronged disk from a hobby shop

common pins

brown paper 3 inches square

thread

2 sewing needles

small glass beads

scissors

white glue

felt, cotton calico, or buckskin for backing (cut to size of finished rosette)

1. On the canvas, draw a circle the size you would like the finished rosette to be (1 1/2 to 2 inches is a good size to work with). Draw one line across the circle and another at a ninety-degree angle to the first, dividing the circle into four equal parts. Push the prongs of the fastener or disk through the center of the circle and flatten them on the back to attach it. Pin the brown paper to the back of the canvas to keep it flat as you stitch.

2. Thread the needles, one with a double thread and the other with a single thread. String beads for the cross lines on the double thread and, beginning at the center, sew the beads along the pencil line by anchoring their thread with the single thread.

3. Once the cross lines are done, bead the quarters. Start at the center and sew in curved rows following the edge of the disk in the center. You can create designs with different-colored beads. Finish the rosette with a row of beads in a contrasting color to outline the design.

4. Remove the brown paper and trim the canvas 3/8 inch from the edge of the beadwork. Tuck under the remaining canvas edge and glue the felt, calico, or buckskin to the back of the rosette to finish it and protect the stitching.

You can make jewelry by poking a necklace or earring wire through the top edge of the rosette, or you can stitch the backing to a belt buckle or jacket.

Adapted from Beginner's Beading Kit, Nez Perce National Historical Park, National Park Service, Spalding, Idaho.

Make a Parfleche

by Janet Buell Dresser

The Sioux made many types of storage containers out of buffalo hides. The French explorers who first encountered the Sioux in the early seventeenth century called these containers *parfleches* (PAHR flesh).

To the Sioux, parfleches were like our drawers and closets. They put pemmican and other foods, clothing, and camp accessories in them. Women used parfleches as sewing bags, keeping paint, sinew thread, beads, quills, and decorative grasses in them. When it was time to break camp, the parfleches were already packed and ready to go.

Nature's rich palette of colors was used to decorate the parfleches. Dried duck manure produced the color blue. Yellow came from bullberries or buffalo gallstones, black from burnt wood, green from plants, and white from certain light-colored clays. The colors were mixed with natural glues to help them adhere to the untanned hides.

You Need

piece of awning canvas 28 by 34 inches*

ruler

pencil

scissors

paper

acrylic paints

brushes

paper punch or awl

4 split cowhide strips or rawhide laces approximately 8 inches long

1. Using the dimensions shown in the diagram, draw the parfleche on the canvas. Use scissors to cut out the pattern.

2. Make a rough draft of your design on a piece of paper. Use a pencil to copy the design on the *untreated* side of the canvas. Paint the design with acrylic paints. Limit your palette to three colors, allowing each color to dry before using the next one.

3. To close your parfleche, fold sides A and B to the center, then fold in sides C and D. Punch holes where illustrated on the diagram. Make sure the holes line up when the parfleche is folded. Put the holes at least 1/2 inch from the edges of the canvas to keep it from tearing. Use split cowhide strips or rawhide laces to tie the parfleche as shown in the diagram.

4. Use the parfleche to store items that will remind you of special memories.

*Awning canvas is available at most fabric stores. One side of it has been treated with a coating to which paint will not stick. Ask the salesclerk to show you which is the *untreated* side.

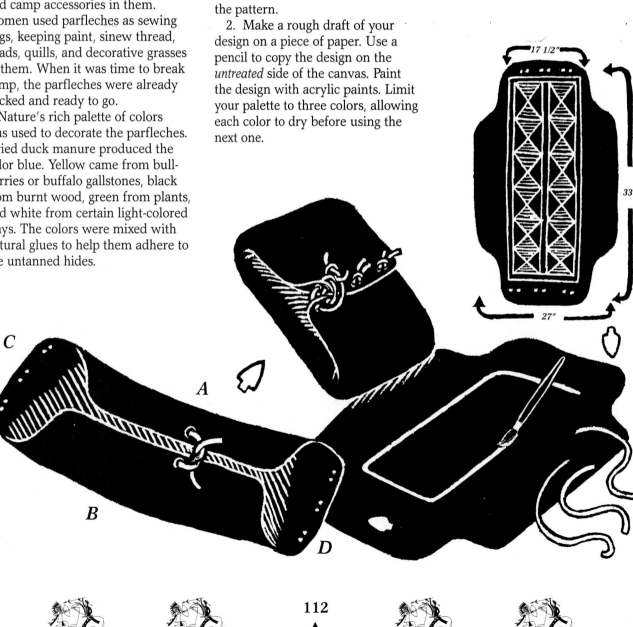

Soapstone Carving

by E. Barrie Kavasch

Eskimo peoples and other native peoples carved figures out of a common native stone called soapstone (steatite). This is one of the softest stones, easily quarried out of rich veins that run throughout our country. Soapstone quarries were noted gathering places for native peoples, who would travel to these locations periodically to harvest this material for bowls, pots, beads, and other objects. Easily carved with simple tools, the stone yields a powdery talc that feels soapy. This, too, was used in various ways by native peoples.

Imaginative, stylized figures of animals, birds, and people were carved out of soapstone. Eastern woodland Indians carved beautiful bowls, effigy pipes, symbolic animals, and totem symbols. Northwest Coast peoples and Eskimos carved killer whales, seals, bears, wolves, and other fascinating creatures. Sometimes these were magic hunting amulets, fashioned to bring good luck to those who carried them.

You Need

large cake of soap, such as Ivory

short, sturdy, dull knife with a point

1. Turn the soap in your hands until you decide what to carve — perhaps a wolf, bear, buffalo, whale, or person. Remember to keep your design simple.
2. Carefully trace the outline of your design on the soap. Begin to carve off corners and whittle curves and angles. Then begin to add details.
3. Keep turning your sculpture around in your hands to get the feel of it. Carve carefully as you add the fine details. Smooth the form with your hands to give it a finished look.

Make an Eskimo Drum

by Susan T. Maupin

Traditionally, Eskimos have played only one musical instrument, the *ayayut,* which is a member of the frame drum family and is similar to a tambourine. The ayayut consists of a thin, circular frame made of bent wood or bone with a single piece of material (such as walrus stomach) stretched over one end. The drum is held in one hand by a handle attached to the frame, with the covered side facing away from the body. A short, thick stick, usually held in the other hand, is used to beat a rhythm on the wood. Ayayuts are never beaten on the skin, only the frame. They often span more than two feet in diameter, so it takes skill and stamina to manage one. You can make a miniature ayayut.

You Need

wooden embroidery hoop 8 to 10 inches in diameter

plastic wrap or wax paper (Saran Wrap works best)

scissors

spring-type clothespin

rubber band

stick or dowel about 1 foot long

1. Separate the hoop and place a piece of plastic wrap over the inner hoop.
2. Ease the outer hoop over the plastic membrane and inner hoop.
3. Tighten the adjustment screw on the outer hoop and pull the plastic gently to make a smooth, snug membrane.
4. Trim any excess plastic.
5. Place the clothespin handle on the outer hoop screw, securing the handle to the frame with a rubber band.
6. To play your ayayut, grasp the handle and hold the drum like a giant lollipop, with the plastic side away from your body. Bring the stick in your other hand up *under* the drum so that it hits only the wooden frame. Now beat your own rhythm.

For a variety of sounds, try using different kinds of paper and plastic membranes such as newspaper, a shopping bag, wrapping paper, or a trash bag.

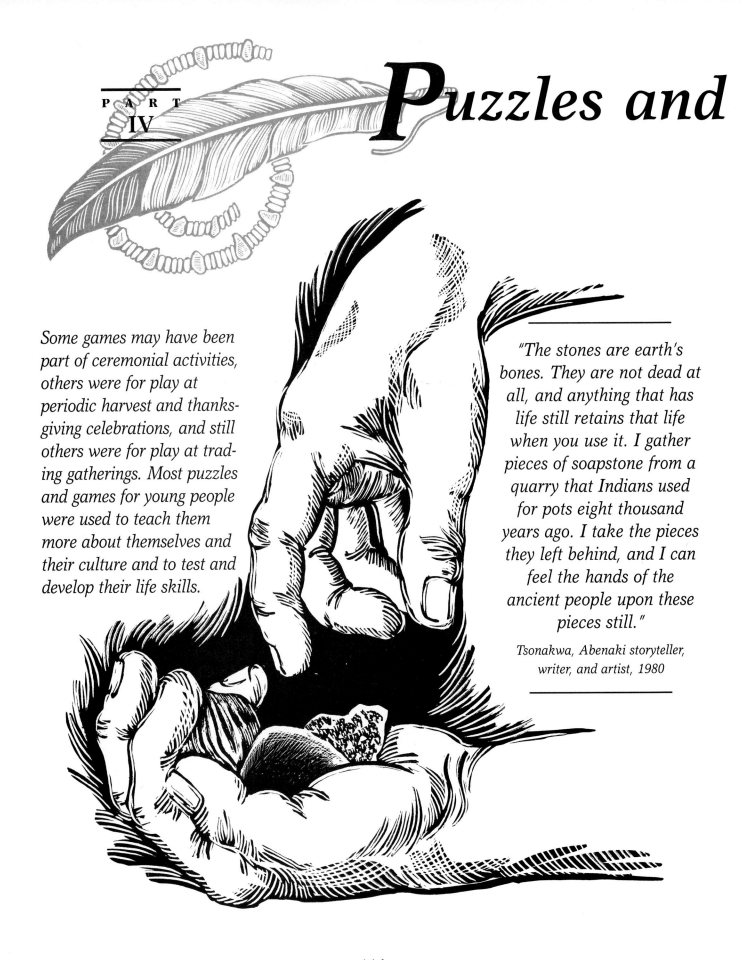

Puzzles and

Some games may have been part of ceremonial activities, others were for play at periodic harvest and thanksgiving celebrations, and still others were for play at trading gatherings. Most puzzles and games for young people were used to teach them more about themselves and their culture and to test and develop their life skills.

"The stones are earth's bones. They are not dead at all, and anything that has life still retains that life when you use it. I gather pieces of soapstone from a quarry that Indians used for pots eight thousand years ago. I take the pieces they left behind, and I can feel the hands of the ancient people upon these pieces still."

Tsonakwa, Abenaki storyteller, writer, and artist, 1980

Games

Chunkey: Ancient America's Game

Lynn E. McElfresh

Chunkey was a game prehistoric Americans seemed to enjoy watching as much as playing. It is believed that groups of fans cheered along the sidelines and bet on the outcome of competitions held in plazas during tribal celebrations.

Chunkey was a contest between two players, each of whom had a spear. One player rolled a polished, concave stone disk down a flat, grassy stretch of land. Then each player would throw a spear after the rolling disk in the hope of landing the spear closest to the disk once it stopped rolling.

The Equipment

The ancient game required two spears, a flat, grassy stretch of land, and a polished, concave stone disk. In our twentieth-century version, you can replace the spears with 5-foot-long, 1/2-inch-diameter dowels or PVC tubing or with heavy cardboard tubes from bolts of fabric. All make fine "spears" and are not as dangerous, but players should be careful not to hit anyone. Substitute a tennis ball for the chunkey stone disk.

The Players

Play the game with three people. One person acts as the ball roller and referee, and the other two are the spear tossers.

The Game

1. Make sure everyone is ready. On the count of three, the ball roller

rolls the tennis ball as the spear throwers toss their spears.

2. As the ball keeps rolling and the spears are in the air, try to imagine how the ancient Americans might have raced along after their spears, using body language and cheers of encouragement.

3. The winner is the one whose spear lands closest to the ball when it stops. The referee can use his or her feet to measure which spear is closest if it is too hard to judge by sight.

4. The winner then competes against the referee, and the loser becomes the referee.

Digging Up Artifacts

by Lynn E. McElfresh

Artifacts are pieces to a puzzle. Archaeologists learn about past peoples by studying the artifacts (human-made objects) left behind. Buried in the lower half of this puzzle are some artifacts. Unscramble the letters in each column into the boxes directly above them to form answers to the clues. Once a letter is used, cross it off and do not use it again. When all the answers are in place, you will be able to see which artifacts belong in the six Indian periods listed to the right of the puzzle.

1. Prehistoric carrying devices
2. Solar calendar parts
3. Cliff dweller plumbing
4. Prehistoric hockey puck
5. Hunter's tip
6. Music maker
7. Farm implement
8. Spear thrower
9. Old megafauna slayer
10. Older megafauna slayer

Answers on page 154.

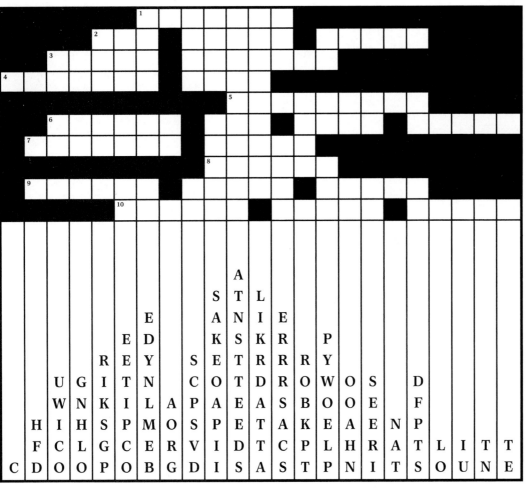

WOODLAND
MISSISSIPPIAN
CLIFF DWELLERS
MISSISSIPPIAN
WOODLAND
HOPEWELL
ADENA

PALEO-INDIAN

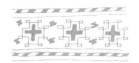

Navajo Code Talkers

*by Harry Gardiner
and Rena V. Buser*

When Japanese planes attacked Pearl Harbor on the morning of December 7, 1941, most members of the United States' largest Indian tribe were isolated from the problems of the day. When they heard the news, though, they picked up their guns and headed for the nearest recruiting station.

More than three thousand Navajo would eventually serve their country in World War II. Those who did not enter military service contributed in a variety of ways at home by working in ports building ships, in munitions plants, for the Red Cross, or for the Bureau of Indian Affairs. Many Navajo women served in the Women's Army Corps as cooks, weather forecasters, nurses, and nutritionists.

One man, Philip Johnston, a civil engineer from Los Angeles, changed the lives of many young Navajo men in a unique way. The son of a missionary father, Johnston had spent a large part of his early life living among the Navajo and spoke their language fluently. This was not easy to do, since the language is extremely complex, very difficult to learn, and nearly impossible to imitate. Johnston proposed that the Marine Corps use a code based on the Navajo language to prevent Japanese and German cryptographers from decoding U.S. messages. His plan was approved, and during the next five years, he helped turn more than four hundred Navajo into Marine "code talkers" and the Navajo language into one of the United States' more successful secret weapons.

The Navajo Code
by Harry Gardiner

In selecting words for their code, the Navajo recruits agreed on words that had clearly defined meanings, were not too long, and could be easily memorized. Many words came from the Navajo's experiences with nature. Words for letters of the alphabet were mostly names of animals — for example, ant for A, bear for B, goat for G, rabbit for R, and weasel for W.

Military Term	Navajo Word	Navajo Meaning
Corps	*Din-neh-ih*	Clan
Squad	*Debeh-li-zini*	Black sheet
Colonel	*Atsah-besh-le-gai*	Silver eagle
Dive bomber	*Gini*	Chicken hawk
Observation plane	*Ne-as-jah*	Owl
Battleship	*Lo-tso*	Whale
Submarine	*Besh-lo*	Iron fish
Mine sweeper	*Cha*	Beaver
January	*Yas-nil-tes*	Crusted snow
Bombs	*A-ye-shi*	Eggs
Engineer	*Day-dil-jah-hi*	Fire builder
Grenades	*Ni-ma-si*	Potatoes

To test the usefulness of the code, Navajo not in the code program were sent into the field to try to decipher messages sent with these words. Even though all the words were part of their native language, without knowing the special meanings, they were unsuccessful.

The Navajo were chosen for several reasons. First, Johnston had an intimate knowledge of their language and culture. Second, the tribe was big enough to provide a large number of speakers. Third, only twenty-eight non-Navajo, mainly missionaries and anthropologists, could speak the language — and none of these was Japanese or German.

The Navajo language developed over many centuries, making it very complex. For example, the same word spoken with four different alterations in pitch or tone of voice has four different meanings. Depending on how you pronounce the Navajo word written *ni´á,* it can have meanings as different as "A set of round objects extends off in a

horizontal line" and "I bought it." This complexity, combined with fluent speakers who could transmit the code more quickly than an artificial code, made it difficult to decode.

Because it might fall into enemy hands, this new code was to be spoken only over the radio or telephone and never to be put into writing. Since the plan was to develop a code of Indian words, not merely to use translations of Indian words, there had to be complete agreement on the meanings of all words used. Any variation in interpretation could spell disaster. The code talkers had to memorize the entire vocabulary of 411 terms. The code was so successful that the Japanese and Germans failed to decipher a single syllable of the thousands of messages sent with it.

After the war, some of the code talkers went to work for the Bureau of Indian Affairs. Others found work as interpreters, engineers, and construction supervisors. Still others continued their education and became teachers, lawyers, and doctors.

Navajo code remained a secret until 1965. In March 1989, the surviving code talkers were reunited in Phoenix, Arizona, and honored by the commandant of the Marine Corps. A statue was unveiled at the ceremony.

Code Talker Cryptogram

Try your hand at the following cryptogram, which describes an important event in Navajo and U.S. history. In a cryptogram, each letter stands for another letter — for example, in the puzzle, the letter A stands for the letter D. To solve the cryptogram, you must decipher this pattern. Hint: The term "code talkers" appears somewhere in this puzzle.

Answer on page 154.

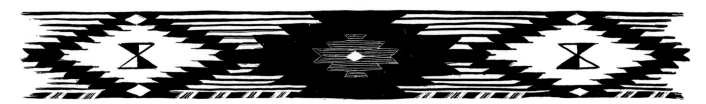

ABCDEF GHCIA GJC KGH, KLM EJNJOH

DEADJEP GMCM JQHEF KLM QHPK

KCMJPBCMA HR HBC RDFLKDEF QME.

SEHGE JP KLM "THAM KJISMCP," KLMU

THBIA PMEA JEA AMTDVLMC QMP-

PJFMP DE KLMDC EJKDNM KHEFBM

KLJK GMCM BEAMTDVLMCJWIM WU

HBC MEMQDMP.

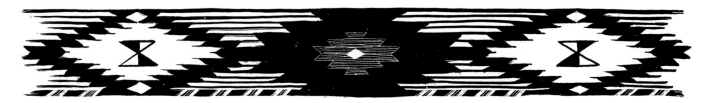

The Sacred Bowl Game

by E. Barrie Kavasch

The inventive Iroquois had many games. At ceremonial times during the year, they played games of skill and chance. Some of their games, such as lacrosse, have become classic American sports. Others, such as snow snake, ring toss, moccasin game, and various stick and dice games, continue to be enjoyed by Iroquois people and many others. Different versions of one of their most enjoyable games of chance are played by many Indian tribes. This game was called hubbub (because of the noise created when playing it) or peach-stone, plum-stone, dice, basket, or bowl game. The Iroquois called it *gus-ká-eh*, or "sacred bowl game."

The Iroquois Midwinter ceremony celebrates the end of one cycle in nature and Iroquois life and the beginning of another. During this ceremony, many rituals take place. Playing gus-ká-eh is an important part of this celebration. The game symbolizes the struggle between the Twin Boys, who represent good and evil in the Iroquois creation legend, to win control over the earth. The contest between creative and destructive forces reminds the Iroquois to maintain a balance within the life-giving forces of nature and to honor the Creator with pleasure.

The game was first played with plum-stone dice made from the woody pits of wild plums. After European settlers introduced peaches, peach stones became the favored dice. Players tossed the dice into a shallow wooden bowl or tray or a shallow wood-splint basket.

Two teams usually competed against each other to win all the game counters.

You Need

medium-grit sandpaper

6 clean plum or peach stones

wooden bowl or tray

black felt-tip marker or quick-drying paint

20 dried beans or tally sticks, used as counters

1. Hold the sandpaper securely in one hand and carefully sand off any sharp points, edges, and rough spots on the clean, dry plum or peach stones. Also sand the top and bottom so that the stones rest evenly on a flat surface. (Do not sand too much, as you want some irregularities to remain.)

2. Gently toss each die as you finish it to see how it lands. Then toss them all together in your cupped hands or in a bowl or tray.

3. Color one side of each die with the marker or paint. Leave the other side natural.

4. Divide the counters evenly between the two players or teams, who should sit facing each other. Place the six dice in the game bowl and decide who will begin.

5. Players take turns tapping the bowl on the floor to make the dice jump and flip over. If five of the six dice land with the same color up, the player scores one point and takes one counter from the opponent. If all six dice show the same color, the player scores five points and takes five counters from the opponent. Other combinations do not count as a score. The player keeps tossing until he or she fails to score. The toss then goes to the opponent.

6. The game ends when one player has won all the counters.

Akwesasne Longhouse Maze

by Annie Moonsong

Canada has many native nations, including the Cree, Micmac, Inuit (Eskimos), and Mohawk, to name just a few. Some of these communities are divided by the boundary between Canada and the United States. The Mohawk, who call themselves Ganiengehaka, "people of the flint country," are one such nation. The Mohawk, along with the Seneca, Cayuga, Onondaga, Oneida, and Tuscarora (who joined in 1711), make up the Six Nations of the Iroquois. These nations are also called the Haudenosaunee, "people of the longhouse."

The Mohawk and descendants of various Indian tribes live on the Akwesasne Indian Reservation, also called the St. Regis Reservation, and their population of six thousand is equally divided between the two countries. While the Mohawk in the United States have the Akwesasne Tribal Council as a governing body, the Mohawk in Canada have the St. Regis Band Council. The Akwesasne Longhouse serves all the Mohawk people and links the communities in the United States and Canada together.*

It is prior to 1700, and the Five Nations of the Iroquois are planning to meet. Help each nation find the way to its designated campfire in the longhouse. Pathways cannot cross or be shared except on waterways (including lakes).

Answer on page 154.

*Traditionally, the longhouse is an association for mutual assistance or service to reach a common goal. A longhouse is also a dwelling consisting of a wooden, bark-covered framework often as long as one hundred feet.

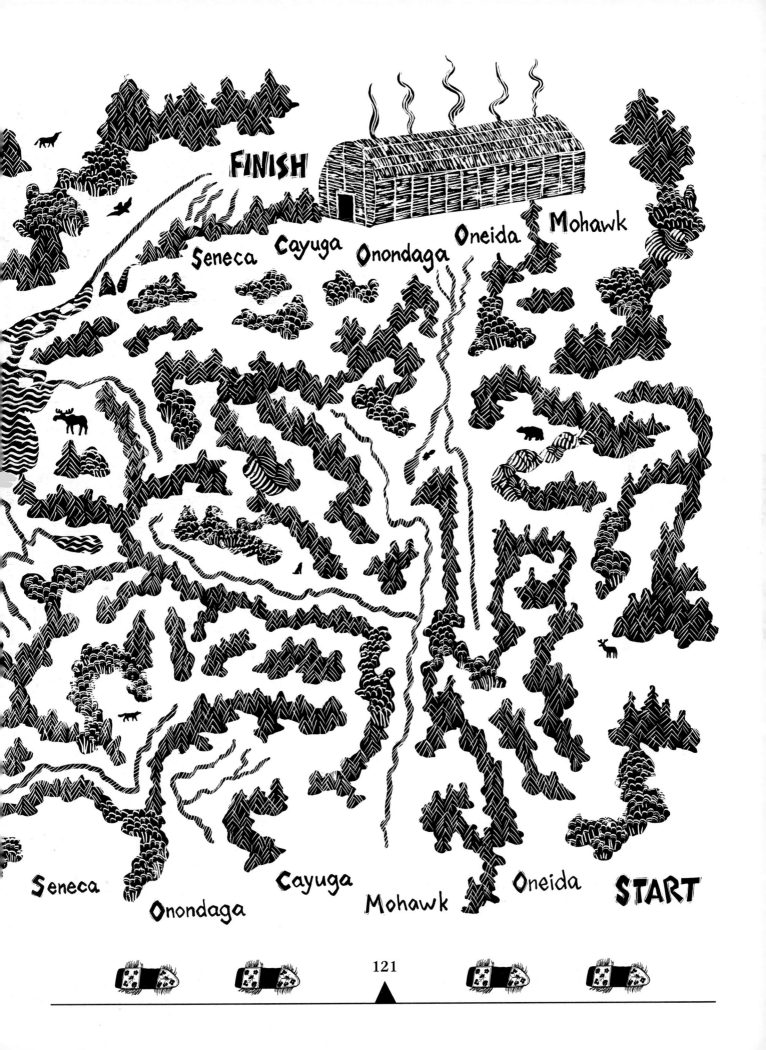

FINISH

Seneca Cayuga Onondaga Oneida Mohawk

Seneca Onondaga Cayuga Mohawk Oneida START

Cherokee Basket Game

This basket game is played by Cherokee children in North Carolina today, but it originated long ago, before the arrival of Europeans. Traditionally, the basket was constructed of white oak splints a foot square with sides about three inches high. Six "dice" used in the game were made of butter beans or wood, and each had a burned design on one side and was white on the other. Two or more people may play.

You Need

Felt-tip marker.

Dice. You can use six flat beans, such as lima or butter beans, or six identical buttons, preferably made of wood.

Basket. It should have a flat bottom and be approximately 1 foot square with 3-inch sides. If a basket is not available, a cardboard box of similar dimensions may be used instead.

1. Using your marker, draw a design on one side of each of the six dice.

2. The first player holds the basket containing the six dice in both hands. He or she then tosses the dice into the air by flicking the basket and catches them again.

3. If all the dice land with the marked side up, the player scores three points. If all white sides are up, two points are scored. If five out of six of the dice have the same side up, one point is scored. Otherwise, no points are scored.

4. The same player plays until he or she fails to score. Then the basket is passed to the next player. The first

player to score twelve points wins the game.

You might wish to create your own scoring rules using different color combinations than those given above. For instance, four of one color and two of another might have a point value. Before beginning the game, practice tossing the dice into the air and catching them again until you master the technique.

Corncob Darts

by E. Barrie Kavasch

Like the whole corn plant, corncobs were valuable to many Indian tribes. They were a plentiful source of fuel and were used as stoppers, light tools, handles, pipes, and game objects. Plains Indians enjoyed games of skill and chance and often showed considerable imagination and artistry in their many activities. This game will remind you of badminton, although the manner of play is somewhat different.

You Need

1 clean, dried corncob per player or team

knife (optional)

small nail or sharp pencil

1 to 3 feathers per player or team

thick glue

different-colored ribbon (or cloth torn into strips about 12 inches long)

colored markers

large square of oak tag or cardboard

1. The stem (or butt) end of the corncob is heavier than the tip, and

when the cob is tossed, the stem end will land first. Break or cut about 1 inch off the tip and pierce the cob pith (center) 1/2 inch deep with the nail or pencil. Make a hole for each feather you plan to use. (The feather or feathers adorn the cob and help it to fly well.)

2. Choose your feather(s) and dip 1/4 inch of the quill tip into the glue. Allow the glue to dry slightly, then insert the tip into the small hole in the cob. Push in each feather securely.

3. Securely tie a piece of ribbon or cloth around the cob about 1 inch below the feather(s). Cut the ends into fringe if you wish.

4. Repeat steps 1 through 3 with different-colored ribbon for each player or team.

5. Allow the glue holding the feather(s) in place to dry completely while you make your target.

6. Use the markers to decorate the oak tag or cardboard with your own or tribal designs. Place the target on open ground with no obstacles around it. Establish a line 10 to 15 feet away from it. Also decide what the winning score will be, perhaps twenty or twenty-five points.

7. To play, take turns tossing the corncobs at the target while standing behind the line. Each toss that hits the target earns one point. Each player or team accumulates points until one of them reaches the winning score.

122

The Seven Lakota Council Fires

by Craig Gingold

The Teton Sioux are the seven tribes, or "council fires," of the Lakota Nation, each with its own distinctive personality. Stories of how they came by their names have been passed on for generations, sometimes in different versions. Some of the stories hint at the Lakota's wry sense of humor, while others suggest tribal character traits.

The **Miniconjou,** considered the most traditional of Lakota, were probably still living in the lake and river region to the east when they acquired their name, a Lakota term that means "planters by the water."

The **Brulé** (French for "burned") are known in Lakota as the Sichangu, or "burned thighs." One account says that their legs were scorched when they ran through burning grass that had been set on fire by their enemies, the Pawnee.

The **Blackfeet,** or Sihasapa (in Lakota), got their name after walking across miles of charred prairie, which blackened their moccasins.

The **Sans Arcs** (French for "without bows"), known in Lakota as the Itazipcho, are the keepers of the Sacred Buffalo Calf Pipe. Their name is said to refer to a time when a hunting party discovered that it was without bows.

The **Two Kettles,** known in Lakota as the Oonenunpa, were so named because they once were saved from starvation by finding a rawhide bundle that held enough meat for two kettles.

As for the fierce **Oglala,** one story says that two brothers were having a quarrel when one threw a handful of dirt at the other. Somehow the whole tribe got the name Oglala, which signifies a gesture of throwing something (at someone).

The proud **Hunkpapa,** "those who camp at the head of the circle," had the honor of setting up their tipis at the opening of the great camp circle when the tribes were gathered in one place. Considered the best warriors, they were chosen to guard the entrance.

For the Lakota, the circle is the most powerful and sacred of symbols. It represents Wakan Tanka, the Great Mystery, which has no beginning and no end. The Lakota see the world as circles within circles: the sun, moon, earth, stars, and rainbows are all circles within the great circle of the universe. The Lakota sit in a circle inside a tipi, which stands in a tribe's camp circle. And the seven Lakota council fires are held within a sacred hoop.

The answer to each of the following questions is the name of one of the seven Lakota "council fires." Write each name on the correct line in the answer grid. The word spelled out in row G in the grid is the answer to the following question: What Teton Sioux word means "the allies"?

1. Things got a little too hot for this tribe.

2. These people were named for their blackened moccasins.

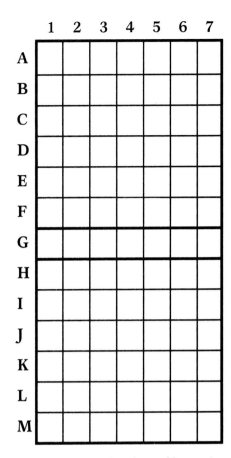

3. This tribe had a place of honor in the camp circle.

4. These people had plenty of water for their crops.

5. This lucky tribe did not go hungry.

6. Members of this tribe were known for their hot tempers.

7. This tribe guarded the peace pipe.

When you have written all the answers in the correct positions in the grid, you are ready for the second part of the puzzle. Each box in the circle that surrounds the picture at left corresponds to one square in the grid. When you have transferred all the letters from the grid to the boxes, you will have a special message. You will have another special message in the middle—the Lakota name for the Black Hills!

Answers on page 154.

Games of Family, Games of Fun

by Nancy Day

"My bones are flying,"
*one man says in his native
Makah language.*
**"Playing bone game with
you,"**
the others chant.

Inside each closed hand, the man holds a bone. One bone has a line, carved and painted, around the middle. The other is unmarked. The man moves his hands with the sound of the drums, crisscrossing them to confuse the other team's pointer, who will have to point to the hand that holds the unmarked bone. The pointer watches the man's face carefully, looking for clues. The man's team tries to distract the pointer, singing, waving, and making bets on whether he will guess correctly.

The bone game, or *slahal,* is the most widespread Native American game. Slahal requires only gestures, so people who speak different languages can play it. This allowed it to spread easily from one area to another. Some version of the bone game has been found among eighty-one different tribes. Both men and women play this game, which is one of several Indian gambling games. Players may bet on the outcome of each round or the whole game.

Helma Ward has played the bone game only a few times. "I tried, but I wasn't good at it," she says. "I don't know whether it showed on my face, which side the unmarked bone was on. I think it becomes a

second sense after you've played it. Some of the people get really good at guessing which side."

Now in her seventies, Ward remembers many games from her childhood. "We had a game similar to hockey," she recalls. "We called it shinny. We made little balls out of kelp [seaweed]." The balls were about the size of a golf ball. "We all used to go up into the woods to get our own sticks, which were curved," Ward continues. "We would play that on the beach — bury the ball in the sand to start the game, choose up sides, and then score just like the pucks [hockey]. We used to play that game quite a bit."

While Ward was growing up, she often saw her mother playing the beaver-tooth dice game, a gambling game played mainly by women. "My mother had her own dice made out of beaver teeth," Ward says. "She and her friends used to play the beaver dice game all the time. In the summertime, when they'd go hop picking, they'd just spread their blanket and play on the ground." (Hop is a plant used to flavor beer.) The dice Ward's mother used once belonged to her grandmother and are at least one hundred years old. Bones and dice are often passed down from parent to child for several generations.

Families pass down something even more important than lucky bones or specially carved dice. They pass down games that have particular significance. These games are *tu pot,* or part of a family's personal tradition, and are considered their property. Special songs or stories may be part of the games. The family might invite others to play, but members of other families cannot play the games at any other time. To take another family's tradition would be stealing something very valuable and personal from them. Family members keep the games secret

and carefully protect them.

Ward has a difficult time explaining how important these games are to her people. "It's more than a game," she says. "It's a family privilege, a ritual."

Ward's family has a feather game and two whale games. They play the games only on special occasions, such as weddings or birthdays. She will not say very much about them, but she does say that the feather game, which uses an eagle feather, is played mostly for engagements. The whale games can be played only after the couple is married.

Ward remembers how she felt when her family played the feather game on the day she was married. "You're worried for a while," she says. "You're sitting there, and you're worried. Then pretty soon it changes, and you're not worried anymore. That's all I can tell you." The family plays these games not only to make the couple happy but also to make their future children happy.

Family games are passed down as part of the family heritage. At the Makah Cultural and Research Center in Neah Bay, Washington, games are passed along as part of the Makah's cultural heritage. The bone game club is very popular, and games are an important part of the annual Makah Days festival. Members of the center travel to area schools to teach the beaver-tooth dice game. They use it to help preserve the Makah language and to teach counting skills. Games are taught along with tribal stories and legends and the history of the Makah people.

Players often take games like the bone game very seriously, but family games are at the center of what it means to be part of a family and what it means to be Makah. They can change the way people think, feel, and behave. They are more than games; they are tu pot.

Frog Race

by E. Barrie Kavasch

Frogs are important symbols in Northwest Coast Indian art and legends. They are usually associated with rain, dampness, fertility, and renewal. Frogs also reflect a sense of serenity and fun. Haida artists carved frogs on house poles to prevent them from falling over.

This is a funny jumping game in which players imitate frogs jumping, while trying to keep their balance and remember the goals of the game. This classic game comes from the Northwest Coast, where young Native American athletes enjoyed competing in games of skill and chance.

1. The chief (or teacher) in charge of this activity marks a long, straight line on the ground (the starting line) and another, parallel line 30 to 50 feet away (the finish line).

2. All the players line up at the starting line, a good space apart, and squat down facing the finish line. They wrap their arms around their legs, clasping their hands just above the ankles. The object of the game is not to let go and to try to keep your balance without standing up.

3. When the chief shouts, "Ready! Jump!" the players begin to hop, froglike, across the ground to the finish line. If a player loses his balance and falls over, he is not disqualified unless he loses his grip around his legs. If he can right himself without letting go, he can continue the race. The first frog to reach the finish line counts coup and wins. As the frogs get better at this sport, the game can be extended to jumping back across the starting line.

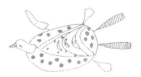

The World Eskimo/Indian Olympics

by Judith K. Jones

A heavy stillness hangs in the auditorium. The audience watches a contestant wipe his sweaty palms, place his feet against his opponent's, and seat himself on the floor. Both men flex their fingers to grip a small, round stick between them. The referee signals to begin. Each man strains to knock the other off balance. The World Eskimo/Indian Olympics have begun.

Tribes of Eskimos and Indians from all over the Arctic come to Fairbanks, Alaska, to compete in these Olympics. The games are traditional contests that have been practiced by the natives for centuries. There are nearly forty categories that demand skill, speed, strength, and endurance.

One of the most popular competitions is the *nalukatuk*, or blanket toss. The nalukatuk evolved from ancient contests for entertainment and amusement. For this event, forty natives, called pullers, hold a tough reindeer-hide "blanket" by heavy rope loops sewn around the edges. The contestant balances himself in the center. As the leader calls "Go!" all the pullers jerk backward, stretching the hide taut. The contestant sails fifty or sixty feet in the air. He must land on the nalukatuk balanced on both feet and is judged for height and form.

The *knuckle hop* is a contest that originated as part of the northern way of life. It requires that the participant assume a push-up position. Then, balancing on the knuckles of his toes and fingers, he hops as far as he can. The seal hunters of the village used a similar method to approach their prey. By imitating the seals' movements, hunters could advance on the nearsighted seals.

The *two-foot-high kick* is related to hunting also. For this contest, the athlete must use both feet together to kick a sealskin ball suspended in midair. He must land in a standing position. This game recalls when whalers would do high kicks on the beach as signals to the villagers of their good fortune.

Another kick, the *toe kick*, evolved

from the Eskimos' need to be sure-footed on the Arctic ice. The object of the toe kick is to jump forward, kick a target backward, and follow through with the jump, landing on both feet. Developing foot agility and dexterity is crucial to the Eskimos, who live in a land of ice fields and glaciers.

These historic competitions have endured for hundreds of years. The games highlight Indian celebrations called *potlatches.* The host village provides food and lodging, and each village shares a performance of original dances.

These dances are now a part of the Olympic competition, and native judges choose the most authentic and most artistic presentations.

Dressed in native costume, performers act out their motion dances accompanied by a drum. The Eskimo dances, performed by one person or a small group, tell stories of whaling trips, great storms, and wise animals. Adults set the drumming rhythm by beating a stick of bone or wood upon a piece of whale or walrus intestine stretched over a large circle of hardwood.

The Indian dances, on the other hand, tell stories about ravens, crows, and wolves, and they are performed in large groups. The Indian costumes are adorned with unique designs and intricate bead patterns.

The songs and dances are not recorded on paper, but must be handed down by word of mouth from adult to child. Unfortunately, the modern world threatens to extinguish these timeless traditions. In defense, World Eskimo/Indian Olympic organizers gather native participants from northern communities of Canada, the United States, and the countries of the former Soviet Union. By keeping these games very much alive, the organizers hope to strengthen the histories of these Arctic peoples and preserve their cultures.

The Spiral Quest for the North Pole

by Annie Moonsong

Although other explorers have tried getting to the North Pole by the straightest possible route, you will go by spiral. Before beginning your trip, make copies of, color, and cut out the dogsled found at the top of the next page. Fold along the dotted lines and glue the A tabs to the other side of the drawing of the dogsled driver.

Begin your quest with two or more players. Use a die to see who goes first and for each movement around the spiral. When you land on a space, follow the instructions of the corresponding number below. Do not follow the directions on the second space you advance to during your turn.

1. From Frobisher Bay, fly 1,400 miles to Ellesmere Island. Move ahead 2 spaces.

2. Inuit help procure and pack 1,300 pounds of food and equipment per dogsled. This helps save you time. Go ahead 3 spaces.

3. Leave Ellesmere Island prepared and enthused. Go ahead 2 spaces.

4. Reach open water; leads too big to cross. Go back to beginning.

5. The weight of your equipment causes a delay in travel. Lose a turn.

6. Pemmican (dried beef and lard) gives you energy. Go ahead 1 space.

7. You successfully cross the first polynyas (open areas in frozen seas). Move ahead 1 space.

8. Pressure ridges form, forcing you to go around them. Go back 1 space.

9. Waterway will freeze over in 2 hours. Go ahead 2 spaces.

10. The thought of Robert E. Peary's trip to the pole in 1909 gives you energy to go on. Move ahead 1 space.

11. You wear out a pair of mukluks on "corn" snow and rubble ice. Lose a turn.

12. Perspiration builds up in your sleeping bag, which now weighs 50 pounds. Discard. Go ahead 1 space.

13. Use ice floe to cross water. Go ahead 2 spaces.

14. Polar bear on ice floe. Go back 1 space.

15. Temperature minus 70°F; slight wind freezes eyelids shut. Lose a turn.

16. You strain to get the dogsled over a large crack in the ice. Throw the die again. If it's even, you succeed and move ahead 1 space. If it's odd, you get hurt and lose a turn.

17. The ice becomes jumbled, and you must use levers to pull sled over it. Skip a turn during the delay.

18. As food is used up, the sled becomes lighter and the pace quickens. Move ahead 1 space.

19. Your chronometer and sextant show you are going in the right direction. Skip ahead 2 spaces.

20. Patch mukluks with a piece of your nylon sled cover and dental floss. Move ahead 1 space.

21. The temperature warms to minus 20°F. The leads don't freeze, and you must detour. Go back 1 space.

22. Your lead dog gets injured and must rest. Miss a turn.

23. A team member gets frostbite and must be airlifted out. Toss the die again. If it's even, go ahead 1 space because load is lighter. If it's odd, go back 3 spaces because of the delay.

24. Go to the pole. You win.

25. You hit the worst storm of the trip. Skip 2 turns.

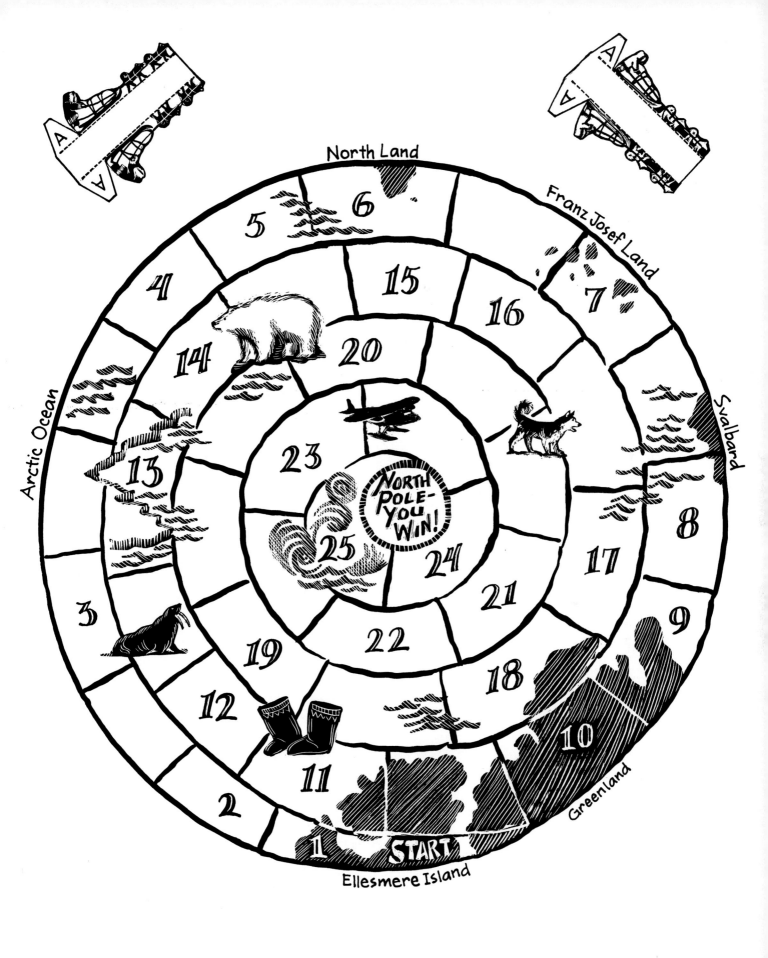

North Land

Franz Josef Land

Arctic Ocean

Svalbard

Greenland

Ellesmere Island

1 START
2
3
4
5
6
7
8
9
10
11
12
13
14
15
16
17
18
19
20
21
22
23
24 NORTH POLE - YOU WIN!
25

Makahiki

by Marsha L. Davidson

The people of old Hawai‘i greeted the high winds and heavy rains of October with glee. The rule of Ku, the war god, was over. The rainy season belonged to Lono, the prankster god, and for four months, Hawaiians celebrated Makahiki, the New Year, with sports and games. After the *kahuna* (priests) collected taxes, the fun began.

Warriors who fought each other the rest of the year now competed in boxing or wrestling matches. The object was to knock your opponent off balance. These matches were a popular spectator sport.

Other sports were more fun to play than to watch. Sledding does not require snow; any steep, slick surface will do. Commoners rode bundles of leaves down hillsides, but the chiefs had real sleds with wooden runners. They built long, grass-covered sled runs and sprinkled them with nut oil. When the sun heated the oil, the slope got slippery, and the sleds flew down the hill.

"Surf's up!" That call to play in the waves is centuries old. Polynesians invented surfing, and almost every Hawaiian over the age of eight had a surfboard to match his or her size and skill. The old Hawaiians' boards were made of solid wood and could weigh as much as one hundred fifty pounds. Surfing techniques have changed somewhat with modern lightweight fiberglass boards, but the islanders still love the sport.

No‘a

After a day full of sports, Hawaiians would relax with quieter games. *No‘a* was a favorite pastime requiring two teams. The Hawaiians played no‘a using five pieces of crumpled *kapa,* or bark cloth, but you could use bath towels. The no‘a is a small stone about the size of a quarter. A person on one team hides the no‘a by holding it in his or her fist and placing his or her arm up to the elbow under first one cloth and then another. The player leaves the no‘a under one of the five cloths, and the second team must decide where it is. Once the players agree, the cloth they choose is removed. If the no‘a is there, that team wins a point. If the players are wrong, the other team wins a point. The first team to get ten points wins.

This may seem like a children's guessing game, but that is not the way the Hawaiians played it. They would watch the person hiding the no‘a very carefully, noting any changes in facial expression or movement of the arm that might indicate when the no‘a was dropped. Sometimes they would try to trick the hider into revealing the stone's location.

‘Ulu Maika

‘Ulu maika is a type of lawn bowling. The Hawaiians used a stone disk about three inches in diameter and an inch thick. You could use a baseball. You need a smooth, level playing field. At one end, set two sticks into the ground six inches part. From the opposite end of the field, try to roll the ball between the two sticks. Start with the sticks six to eight feet away, then move back as you improve. The Hawaiians played ‘ulu maika with the sticks thirty to forty yards away.

Recipes

Food is a necessity that nourishes us. It also can be nurturing to our bodies, minds, and spirits. Food, like music, dance, and games, overcomes language barriers and ethnic differences. North American foods have gone around the world many times during the past five centuries and have come back to us as vital ingredients in the foods of other ethnic groups. Our modern Native American foods embrace trail snacks, ceremonial foods, "soul foods," and powwow and tribal festival foods. More than sixty percent of the food that we eat today was originally developed to some degree by Native Americans. Most of the recipes included here were inspired by creative native cooks.

A CELEBRATION OF AMERICAN INDIAN FOOD WAYS

by E. Barrie Kavasch

We walked here once,
   Grandfather.
These trees, ponds, these
   springs and streams,
and that big flat rock across
   the water over there.
We used to meet with you over
   there.
Remember, Grandfather? And
   we would
dream, dance, and sing, and
after a while, make offerings.
Then we would sing the
   traveling song
and would go our ways, and
sometimes we would see your
   signs
on the way to our lodges.

But something happened,
   Grandfather.
We lost our way somewhere,
   and
everything is going away.
The four-legged, the trees,
   springs, and streams,
even the big water, where the
   laughing
whitefish goes, and the big sky
   of many eagles
are saying good-bye.
Come back, Grandfather, come
   back!

Thank you, O Great Spirit, for
   all
the things that Mother Earth
   gives!

This Narragansett Indian prayer of thanksgiving eloquently interweaves the tribe's world-view with their appreciation of all living things. Its timelessness speaks to us as it carries us forward into the future.

Giving thanks for rich, seasonal harvests reflects the fact that American Indians were practiced connoisseurs of what we call gourmet foods today. America's seasonal larder is harvested from raw materials of land and sea. American Indian foods are interwoven intimately within the contemporary American culture. We continue to enjoy this continent's indigenous cuisine.

Trail Snack

by E. Barrie Kavasch

This delicious modern recipe is developed from many different ancient ones. The easiest way to preserve earlier fruit harvests was by drying. Sometimes the ripe fruit was pounded into a pulp with animal fat and shaped into little cakes, then laid out on clean, flat rocks to dry in the sun.

Before European settlers brought apple, pear, apricot, and peach trees to North America, Native Americans in various parts of the country made an early, wild version of this concentrated, high-energy trail snack. Depending on where they lived, Indians harvested and dried fruits such as persimmons, cactus fruits, wild plums, cherries, strawberries, blueberries, cranberries, buffalo berries, bearberries, and salmonberries.

Apple Leather

This snack is very sweet, chewy, and simple to make. Drying takes about 2 days, or 6 to 8 hours in a slow oven (about 150°F) with the door open a crack.

You Need

1 quart chopped apples (remove the cores but not the skins)

water

2 tablespoons lemon juice

2 teaspoons mixed spices (such as cinnamon, cloves, and nutmeg)

1/4 cup honey (or to taste)

vegetable cooking spray

blender, 11- by 16-inch cookie sheet

1. Place the chopped apples in the blender, a few at a time, with just enough water to start the blending action. Continue adding the apples slowly until the blender has turned them into a thick applesauce. Then add the lemon juice, mixed spices, and honey. Blend well.

2. Coat the cookie sheet with vegetable cooking spray. Spread the applesauce evenly onto the cookie sheet, about 1/4 inch thick. The layer will get thinner as it dries.

3. Place the sheet in a warm, dry place that has good air circulation, or put it in the oven. When the sauce has dried, it will be barely sticky to the touch and pliable.

4. Peel the apple leather from the cookie sheet, gently rolling it up with your hands along the length of the sheet. Slice the roll into eight smaller rolls. Store them in a large, airtight container until you are ready to eat them. Each roll of apple leather is equal to about 1/2 cup of fruit.

Southwestern Foods You Can Bake

by Caroline Bates

Corn Chili Bread

When Pueblo women bake corn chili bread, they often use cornmeal made from blue corn, one of the many colors of corn they have been planting for centuries. The Hopi match a color of corn to each of their main directions: blue corn stands for southwest, for example. Directions are important as the sources of the needed weather — hard rain to help seeds germinate, gentle rain to help the young corn grow, or a cooling wind in the heat of summer. You may not find blue cornmeal in your supermarket, but yellow or white will do fine for this traditional Pueblo bread, made nice and spicy with chili powder.

Read the complete recipe before you begin so that you will be sure to have everything you need.

To sift in a big bowl, you need:

1 1/2 cups white or yellow cornmeal

1 1/2 cups flour

1/4 cup sugar

4 teaspoons baking powder

1 teaspoon salt

Combine all these items in a strainer or flour sifter over the bowl and sift them in.

To mix in a smaller bowl, you need:

3/4 stick (6 tablespoons) butter or margarine

2 eggs

1 1/2 cups milk

4 teaspoons chili powder

Melt the butter over very low heat in a little pan. Do not let it burn. Break the eggs into the bowl and beat them well with an eggbeater. Add the melted butter, milk, and chili powder and beat some more.

To add at the end, you need:

1/2 green pepper, seeds removed

1 small onion, outer peel removed

1/2 cup shredded Cheddar cheese

Chop the pepper and the onion into very small dice. If you are not used to handling a sharp knife, ask somebody to help.

Preheat the oven to 400°F.

To put everything together:

Pour the egg mixture in the smaller bowl into the sifted mixture in the big bowl and stir well with a wooden spoon. Add the cheese,

 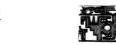

green pepper, and onion and stir again to mix them in.

To bake the bread:

Grease a 9-inch-square baking pan. Pour in the batter and bake the bread at 400°F for about 30 minutes. When a toothpick inserted in the middle comes out clean, it is done. The top should be lightly browned. Serve it hot, cut into squares.

Pumpkin Pie Pockets

Big, fat, and luscious, the pumpkin tastes as good as it looks. Long before the first Europeans came to America, Indians from New England to New Mexico were growing this native American plant as an important food. The Spanish who settled in the Southwest learned to appreciate the pumpkin and made it part of one of their own favorites, the little pie pockets called *empanaditas*. The mix of New World pumpkin and Old World empanaditas makes a very special dessert — good any day of the year and perfect for Thanksgiving.

For the pumpkin filling, you need:

1/2 cup raisins

3/4 cup canned pumpkin

1/3 cup brown sugar

2 teaspoons whole aniseed

pinch of salt

Begin by putting the raisins in a cup with 1 to 2 tablespoons water. Let them soak.

For the pie pockets, you need:

packaged pie dough mix

shortening

ice water

While the raisins soak, make the pie dough. Cut it in half, wrap each half in plastic or wax paper, and set both halves in the refrigerator to chill.

Preheat the oven to 400°F.

To make the filling:

While the dough chills, put the soaked raisins, pumpkin, brown sugar, aniseed, and salt into a heavy-bottomed pan. Heat the mixture until it just bubbles. Cook it slowly over low heat, stirring all the time, until the brown sugar melts completely and there are no more lumps — about 5 minutes.

To make the pie pockets:

Roll out half the chilled dough on a lightly floured board. It should be rolled thin. Cut 3-inch circles with a round cookie cutter or the rim of a glass. Cut the circles as close together as possible.

Put 1 teaspoon of the filling in the middle of each circle.

Dip a finger in water and run it around the edge of each circle. Fold each in half to make a pocket that covers the filling. Pinch the edges of each folded pocket to seal it tight.

Use the other half of the dough to make more pie pockets the same way.

Gather up the unused parts of the dough and freeze it to use some other time.

To bake the pie pockets:

Put the pie pockets on ungreased cookie sheets and bake them at 400°F for about 20 minutes. They should be lightly browned. Take them out of the oven and immediately sprinkle white sugar on top of each. Let them cool on a rack.

Fish Baked in Clay

by E. Barrie Kavasch

Campfire cookery is fun and fascinating. Many different people enjoy cooking over an open fire. Earlier peoples often wrapped raw foods in big, edible leaves or packed them in mud or clay, then put the "packages" around the edges of a fire to cook. Cornmeal, wild mushrooms, bits of meat, and wild vegetables were cooked in this way. This tradition has evolved in various elegant ways. Here is an easy, delicious favorite. You will need help from an adult with this recipe.

You Need

small 2-pound fish (sunny, bluegill, or small trout or bass) or equal amount of raw chicken

enough fresh clay or mud to pack it 2 to 3 inches thick all around

medium campfire or hearth fire*

1. Clean and gut the fish, or have the fish market do it. Pack the fresh fish in a 2- to 3-inch blanket of clay or mud. Poke one or two tiny holes in the clay to allow steam to escape. Allow the clay to dry slightly for a few minutes.

2. Carefully place this natural package at the edge of the fire (or wrap it in heavy foil and place it in a 350°F oven). Cook for 30 to 40 minutes. Carefully turn the clay package with tongs or a heavy stick once or twice during the baking. Push it deeper into the fire so that it will cook evenly.

3. Remove the package from the fire and cool slightly. Crack the clay (using heavy oven mitts) on a rock or brick. If you strike the spine ridge of the package, it should crack open nicely into two halves. The scales and skin will stick to the clay. You can eat your fish right out of this dish! Afterward, brush out the clay-fired dish and save this "fossil print" of your fish.

*This might be done in a home fireplace *with supervision* or in an oven if the clay is wrapped in heavy foil.

Sweet Southern Popcorn

by E. Barrie Kavasch

Popcorn was grown in every color by early American Indian gardeners. Ancient pottery popcorn pots have been found at some South American prehistoric sites. Large golden peanuts have been found at similar sites. These objects suggest that these two early vegetables were very important to the native peoples who grew them. Today we know that people gain the maximum protein and nutrition from corn and peanuts when they are eaten together rather than separately. Evidently, prehistoric people knew or sensed this, too, as these two vegetables are usually found together at ancient sites.

Popcorn is one of the most popular varieties of maize. It is easy to grow and a lovely ornamental crop. But whether you pop strawberry red, black jewel, Hopi blue, Narragansett white, or yellow popcorn, all are creamy white after they explode. Try this elegant southern-style recipe.

You Need

1/2 cup pecans

1 cup peanuts

1/2 cup raisins

1/2 cup maple syrup or molasses

1/2 cup popcorn (any color)

salt and pepper (optional)

measuring cups, shallow baking pan, mixing spoon, hot-air popper

1. Combine the pecans and peanuts in a shallow baking pan and bake in a 325°F oven for 20 minutes.

2. Soak the raisins in the maple syrup or molasses for 10 minutes, then pour this mixture over the hot roasted nuts. Blend well.

3. Pop the corn in the hot-air popper.

4. Sprinkle the pecans, peanuts, and raisins on the popcorn and add the salt and pepper (if using). Blend well.

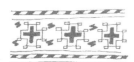

Navajo Foods

by Joan Ennis

Imagine entering a Navajo hogan. The rounded earth-and-log house has an opening at the top for smoke. Inside, a woman stirs stew over a hot flame and adds a final touch of chili. She throws a tiny amount into the fire. When the family begins to eat, they toss a pinch of bread in the direction of each of the four winds. Navajo Indians feed the spirit world when they cook and eat. They believe that spirits helped the food grow and that food heals both body and mind.

The Navajo consider corn a blessing from the gods. They prepare it in more than two hundred fifty ways, including mush, pancakes, breads, dumplings, and cakes. Squash, melons, pumpkins, chilies, beans, and yucca bananas also are important. Green and red chilies are eaten fresh or sun dried for later use. Roasted chili peppers are added to meats, soups, and stews. Chili paste is added to other foods. The Navajo use piñon nuts in soups, stews, and baked goods. Eggplant-shaped yucca bananas taste bitter raw but sweet when cooked. Dried banana can be used as sugar.

Corn and wheat flour are the main ingredients in breads and cakes. The Navajo eat flat fry bread by itself or covered with chili paste or taco filling. Cakes, traditionally baked over a fire in the ground, contain blue and yellow cornmeal.

Navajo ceremonies emphasize the sacredness of food. The bride's grandmother gives the couple a basket of cornmeal at the wedding. The bride and groom exchange a pinch of the cornmeal and receive the blessing and strength of the

spirit world through the corn.

Soon after the birth of a baby, parents hold the child's head toward the fire to thank the spirits and pray for a healthy life. They wait for the baby's first laugh to celebrate. The person who made the baby laugh brings a large basket filled with food for the festivity. The mother holds the baby and basket while friends admire the infant and take food. The tradition ensures that the child will be kind and generous.

Navajo Taco
A Navajo taco is made by covering fry bread with layers of fried hamburger meat, shredded lettuce, cheddar cheese, chopped onions, and diced tomatoes. Cover the top with red or green chili sauce according to taste.

Navajo Fry Bread
Navajos use this bread as a base for tacos, and for other spreads such as chili paste. They also enjoy it plain, freshly cooked when it is hot and chewy.

2 lbs. lard or 2 quarts oil

3 cups sifted flour

1 tablespoon baking powder

1/2 teaspoon salt

1 cup warm water

Melt lard in 5 quart deep pot.

Combine flour, baking powder, and salt in a large mixing bowl.

Add warm water in small amounts and knead dough until soft but not sticky. Sometimes more flour or water will be needed. Cover bowl and let stand for about 15 minutes.

Pull off large egg-sized balls of dough and roll out into rounds about 1/4 inch thick. Punch hole in center of each round, piercing several times with fork, to allow dough to puff.

In a heavy skillet fry rounds in lard or other shortening until bubbles appear on dough, turn over and fry on other side until golden.

Recipes from *Southwest Indian Cookbook*, Marcia Keegan, Clear Light Publishers, Santa Fe, New Mexico.

The Three Sisters: Corn, Beans, and Squash

by Ron LaFrance
and E. Barrie Kavasch

The Iroquois people believe that corn, beans, and squash are sacred, life-giving foods. They call these vegetables The Three Sisters, and their ceremonies often center on the planting, hoeing, and harvesting of these vital foods.

Whenever the Iroquois gather, an opening address acknowledges every living and life-giving entity in the universe. The speech is divided into many sections, one of which is devoted to The Three Sisters.

The speaker also explains what is happening at the present time. For example, he will say that even though we are trying hard to maintain our tradition of The Three Sisters, the environment, our Mother Earth, is going through many changes. The speaker warns the people of the growing air pollution we experience and how we must work so that The Three Sisters can continue as we and our ancestors have enjoyed them.

Long ago and today, in the months of July and August, most Iroquois communities hold ceremonies celebrating the coming of The Three Sisters. The people celebrate with feasts and dances in their honor. The Iroquois have continued this tradition for as long as the oldest living person can remember. The speeches and songs that go with the ceremonies have been passed down to the different clan members of the Iroquois.

The Iroquois do not worship The Three Sisters; they give thanks to them. In Iroquois belief, corn, beans, and squash are gifts from the first Sky Woman who came to Turtle Island, the Iroquois name for earth. The Three Sisters are the major sustainers of life.

The Iroquois were farmers long before Christopher Columbus came to America. The hilling of corn and the planting of beans and squash alongside are traditional practices. Today scientists who study different methods of planting are beginning to understand why the Iroquois planted this way. When grouped together, these three vegetables exchange important nutrients within the soil that help them to grow. Above the ground, the cornstalks serve as "poles" for the climbing beans, while the large spreading leaves of the squash plant shade the ground. Their shade smothers the weeds and cuts down moisture loss in the soil. These three crops can all be raised with simple wooden tools.

Corn has many uses. It can be roasted, dried, and stored for many years and made into bread, soup, and mush. Corn is shelled and boiled in hardwood ashes, then put in a hulling basket and taken to a brook or large tub where it is thoroughly rinsed, removing the ashes, hulls, and skins. Often, depending on the time of year, people mix corn with different types of berries and meat to bring out a different flavor. Adding maple syrup to corn is one of the oldest Iroquois customs.

Corn, along with beans and squash, provides all the protein needed for a healthy diet.

Succotash

Iroquois succotash — Ogonsaga-nonda — is a favorite dish inspired by generous gardens at harvest time. Numerous Iroquois recipes form the basis of this one, a modern classic with a balance of nutrition, color, and tradition. The combination of tasty vegetables is a fine addition to any meal, and for many Iroquois children, it is a meal in itself. If you want a heartier dish, you can add a cup or two of diced meat such as turkey or bacon — or bear!

You Need

4 tablespoons butter

1 medium onion, diced

1 medium green pepper, diced

2 cups whole-kernel corn

1 cup cut green beans or lima beans

1 cup red kidney beans

1 cup water or chicken broth

1 zucchini squash, cubed

1 yellow squash, cubed

salt and pepper

squash blossoms (optional)

chopping knife, large pot, large serving bowl

1. In a large pot or kettle, melt the butter over medium-low heat. Add the diced onions and green peppers. Sauté for 5 minutes. Stir carefully and often.

2. Add the corn, green or lima beans, kidney beans, water or broth, zucchini, and yellow squash. Stir well. Add salt and pepper to taste.

3. Cover and simmer on low heat for 20 to 30 minutes. Stir occasionally.

4. Ladle into a large serving bowl and top with fresh washed squash blossoms if desired. Serves 6 to 8.

Johnnycakes

by E. Barrie Kavasch

Algonquian Indians believed that corn was a gift from the Creator to be respected and honored with periodic celebrations throughout the year. The Green Corn Festival, with its special dances, songs, and prayers, continues to be one of the many annual American Indian thanksgiving celebrations, honored by many different tribes throughout North America. One early legend tells of Crow bringing the first seeds of corn from the southwestern tribes to native peoples in the East, long before the Colonial era. The corn kernels were Crow's gift of life. Many other tribal histories contain corn origination stories.

This valuable grain has become the real "gold" of America. Corn, always a versatile crop, was the major grain used to make bread in prehistoric America, before Europeans brought wheat, oats, and rye to these shores. Cornmeal was worked into countless types of bread and cooked in every conceivable way. These johnnycakes* are sure to please.

You Need

1 cup white or yellow cornmeal

3/4 teaspoon salt

2 teaspoons sugar

2 tablespoons maple syrup or honey

1 cup water

2 tablespoons butter

1/4 cup milk

measuring cups and spoons, medium bowl, mixing spoon, small saucepan, griddle, metal spatula

1. Combine the cornmeal, salt, and sugar in the bowl.
2. Put the maple syrup or honey, water, and butter in the saucepan and bring to a boil over high heat. Add to the dry ingredients.
3. Add the milk (the batter will be stiff).
4. Heat the griddle; grease well with butter or oil.
5. Drop the batter from a large tablespoon onto the hot griddle and form 4-inch cakes.
6. When the cakes are golden brown on the underside, turn them over with the spatula. Cook until golden brown on the other side.
7. Serve hot with maple syrup and butter.

*Also called journeycakes.

Clam (Quahog) Chowder

by E. Barrie Kavasch

Many types of clams are delicious to eat. Soft-shell or littleneck clams, butter clams, razor clams, and surf clams are all tasty. But the best chowder clam is the hard-shell quahog of the northeastern Atlantic Ocean. This is also the wampum shell of American Indian fame (see page 139). In its younger form, it is known as the cherrystone clam.

Chowder is usually a fish or vegetable stew made thick with meat and potatoes. Salt pork, bacon, or milk (or tomatoes) may be added. This recipe was inspired by creative Shinnecock, Narragansett, and Wampanoag cooks. Countless generations of coastal Algonquians gathered the seasonal wild foods that filled their ancestral pots. Smoked clams, oysters, mussels, scallops, and conches also were cooked at the same time.

You Need

10 to 12 medium quahogs, or 2 cups canned clams, diced and drained; reserve all clam liquid*

1 thick celery stalk

2 bay leaves

2-inch cube of salt pork, diced, or 4 slices of bacon, cut in half

1 large onion, diced

1 cup diced celery

1/2 cup diced green pepper

2 tablespoons cornmeal

salt and pepper to taste (optional)

3 potatoes, peeled and diced

chopping knife, measuring cups and spoons, deep pot, tongs, wooden spoon

*If you are using canned clams, omit steps 1–3 of the recipe.

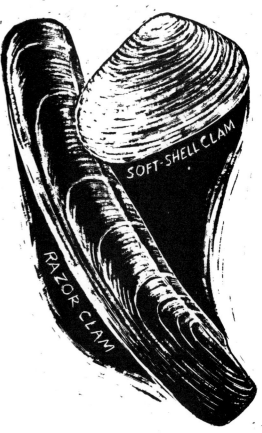

SOFT-SHELL CLAM

RAZOR CLAM

1. Carefully scrub and clean the clams under cold running water. Place them in the pot and cover with lightly salted cold water to about 2 inches above the clams. Add the celery stalk, cut into four pieces, and the bay leaves. Cover, bring to a boil, and simmer over medium heat for 20 minutes.

2. Remove from the heat and cool slightly. Remove the clams with tongs and reserve the broth.

3. Remove the clams from the shells. (Save the shells for another use.) Coarsely chop the clam meat.

4. In a medium skillet over medium heat, sauté the salt pork or bacon slowly for 3 to 5 minutes. Add the onions and stir. Add the diced celery and green pepper, stirring well. Sprinkle the cornmeal over all and add salt and pepper to taste (if using). Simmer for 5 to 10 minutes.

5. Add the diced clams and potatoes and cover with 4 to 6 cups of the reserved clam broth (use water if necessary). Cover and simmer until the potatoes are done, about 25 minutes.

Feeding Clams

If you dig (or gather) your clams a day before cooking, scrub them well in cold water and place them in a large, deep bucket. Cover with clean, cold seawater. Sprinkle 1/2 cup fine cornmeal over the surface and keep in a cool, dark place overnight. The cornmeal "feeds" the clams and helps them to "flush" the fine sand and internal wastes out of their stomachs. They will taste sweeter and be cleaner. Native American cooks also use this technique with turtles and other shellfish.

6. Adjust the seasonings and thickness to taste. Chowder always tastes better the following day, so if you can wait, or if there is any left over, store it in the refrigerator and reheat.

A Native American Clambake

by E. Barrie Kavasch

The Wampanoag and Narragansett Indians probably taught English settlers to steam native coastal foods in deep beds of seaweed over hot stones on the beach. Nothing can match the fragrance and succulence of these delicious foods mingled together and cooked in a deep pit. Tribal gatherings such as festivals and powwows often revolve around events such as a clambake.

You Need

3 to 4 bushels fresh, wet seaweed

3 dozen ears fresh sweet corn

50 to 100 quahogs or other hard-shell clams

20 sweet or white potatoes

10 to 15 small sweet onions

200 soft-shell clams, mussels, scallops, or crabs

20 lobsters (1 1/2 to 2 pounds each)

2 pounds butter (approximately)

10 lemons (approximately)

watermelon and other seasonal fruits

2 long-handled garden shovels, 2 metal rakes, 20 to 40 large, smooth rocks (avoid sandstone, as it crumbles when hot, and quartz or flint, which can explode in high heat), firewood and kindling, buckets, burlap bags (optional), large canvas tarp, long-handled tongs, large platters, pot, paring knife

1. Select a spot about 10 yards back from the high-tide mark. It is easier if the sand is hard packed.

2. Dig a pit about 2 feet deep and 4 feet in diameter. A flat bottom and steep, straight sides work best. Clear and rake at least a 3-foot area around the pit.

3. Line the bottom of the pit with rocks.

4. Build a big fire on top of the rocks. Tend the fire, feeding it continuously, for 1 1/2 hours, while others wash the seaweed and remove the tough outer husks (leave two or three layers of inner husks) and silk from the corn and soak it in buckets of clean water.

5. After about 2 hours, let the fire die down a bit and rake the coals evenly over the bottom of the pit. Quickly spread wet seaweed about 3 inches deep over the hot rocks using the metal rakes.

6. On top of the seaweed, layer the hard-shell clams, all but three potatoes, the onions, and the corn.* You may place these ingredients inside loosely tied wet burlap bags if you want to keep them together.

7. Layer the soft-shell clams, mussels, scallops, or crabs; lobsters; and about 3 inches of wet seaweed. Place the reserved potatoes on top and cover the pit with a wet canvas tarp. Weight it down securely with large rocks.

8. Steam the foods for about 1 hour. The tarp should puff up a little; that is a sign of a good bake.

9. Lift one corner of the tarp and test the potatoes on top. When they are done, the bake is done. Remove the tarp and let the bake cool down slightly. Then lift out the foods with long-handled tongs, clean shovels, or rakes. Have large platters waiting to hold these treasures.

10. Melt the butter in a pot. Cut the lemons into wedges. Serve the feast with the melted butter and lemon wedges on the side.

11. For dessert, serve the watermelon and other seasonal fruits.

*If you have plenty of seaweed, you may want to place thin layers between the different foods. Soaked cornhusks also work well.

Wampum

by E. Barrie Kavasch

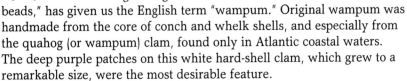

Wampumpeag, an Algonquian word meaning "string of shell beads," has given us the English term "wampum." Original wampum was handmade from the core of conch and whelk shells, and especially from the quahog (or wampum) clam, found only in Atlantic coastal waters. The deep purple patches on this white hard-shell clam, which grew to a remarkable size, were the most desirable feature.

Distinctive, cylindrical beads were cut from the hard shells, ground, and polished. A hole was bored through the center with a small hand drill. These precious beads were then strung on natural thread made from the twisted, twined inner bark of the elm or linden tree or native Indian hemp (dogbane). Of the many different types of native twine made, these three were the most decay resistant.

The coastal Indian tribes of southern New England and Long Island were the major wampum makers, and other tribes traded with them for the beads. The Narragansett, Pequot, and Montauk tribes were among those who dominated the trade. They established vital trade networks with many interior tribes, especially the powerful Iroquois League. Wampum was used to record important events and agreements. Although it was often taken in tribute from one tribe by another, it generally symbolized truth, friendship, and harmony.

Wampum strings represented the authority of the Iroquois League and its council. In the seventeenth century, the Dutch used wampum as a means of exchange in the fur trade. The English also used wampum as a magnet "to draw the beaver out of the interior forests," increasing its demand and weakening native trading relationships. During the eighteenth century, the colonists began to use wampum as an early form of money and tribute. It was demanded as payment from tribes when they were judged to have violated Colonial laws or failed to pay taxes. Many treaties between Indian nations and the Colonies (later the U.S. government) were commemorated with special wampum belts.

Native wampum artists continue the tradition today. Tall Oak, a Narragansett artist and wampum maker, has taught generations of artists. Courtney Murray is a Nanticoke wampum maker, sculptor, and jeweler. Judy Chrisjohn, an Oneida artist and teaching specialist, has completed a museum copy of a famous Iroquois wampum treaty belt.

Wampum reflects the beauty of enduring traditions in the tribal Northeast. Sometimes called quahog jewelry, it is the ultimate in artistic recycling of natural resources. On the Shinnecock Reservation in Southampton, New York, the tribe has established a successful clam and oyster project, raising these two valuable native shellfish in rich marine beds.

Today wampum is sold for ever-increasing prices to people fascinated by its long tradition and loveliness. Much like the abalone jewelry and artwork of western tribal traditions, quahog wampum work continues to evolve.

Potato Bargain

by E. Barrie Kavasch

This thrifty New England recipe from generations of talented Wampanoag cooks is just one of many delicious classics. Warmth and generosity surround Wampanoag foods, which are always served with good humor. Laughter is a valuable ingredient! I first enjoyed this dish at the Flume, an outstanding American Indian restaurant in Mashpee, Massachusetts. Chief Earle Mills, Sr., celebrated for his culinary talent, owns and runs the restaurant.

You Need

6 slices of bacon or 3-inch cube of salt pork, diced

1 medium onion, thinly sliced

6 large potatoes, sliced

2 cups chicken, vegetable, or beef broth

salt and pepper to taste

large iron skillet with lid, measuring cup, wooden spoon

1. In the skillet, fry the bacon slices or diced salt pork over medium heat until golden brown. Add the onion slices, stirring well. After 5 minutes, add the potatoes, broth, and salt and pepper. Stir well.

2. Cover and cook over medium heat for about 30 minutes, or until the potatoes are tender. Serve hot. This is an excellent side or main dish to enjoy with good friends.

Corn to Eat and to Drink

by E. Barrie Kavasch

One of the tastiest and most nutritious discoveries made five hundred years ago was corn, which the Taino Indians of the Caribbean called *maíz,* "life giver." Indian corn was the real gold of the Americas, and it has traveled around the world nourishing hungry people and animals.

First grown by Indians in what is now central Mexico more than seven thousand years ago, corn was developed from a wild grass. Indian peoples throughout the Americas grew it in many varieties and colors. The types of corn grown included popcorn, flour corn, flint corn, dent corn, and sweet corn, as well as an early form of pod corn. Corn was believed to be a gift from the Creator, and the Maya Indians believed that the Creator made them from corn.

Corn is a major part of our diet today, from corn flakes and corn on the cob to popcorn and corn chips. Corn syrup sweetens and flavors soda, tea, and other beverages, as well as ice cream, pudding, baby food, candy, and syrup. From corn-starch, corn oil, grits, corn bread, and corn crackers to glucose and dextrose products and feed for live-stock, we use corn daily. We also use corn to make methyl alcohol, which may fuel our cars and machines in the future.

Some authorities estimate that Americans consume three pounds of corn a week. Following are two recipes that use some form of corn. The first, *soffkee (sofkey),* is based on a traditional Indian preparation that was sometimes eaten as a soup or cereal and sometimes drunk by peoples who lived in what is now the southern United States, especially the Cherokee, Creek, Choctaw, Catawba, Seminole, and other tribes.

Soffkee*
You Need

1 gallon water

1 quart hominy grits

1 cup maple syrup, molasses, or corn syrup

1 cup chopped hickory nuts (optional)

large kettle, long-handled wooden spoon, mugs or soup bowls

1. Combine the water with the grits in the large kettle over medium heat.
2. Bring the mixture to a boil. Lower the heat and simmer for 2 to 3 hours, stirring occasionally, until the mixture has a milky appearance.
3. Stir in the maple syrup, molasses, or corn syrup. Add the nuts if desired.
4. Spoon the soffkee into mugs or bowls when hot or let it cool first. Refrigerate the leftovers. Soffkee is even better the next day.

*Adapted from *Corn Recipes From the Indians* compiled by Frances Gwaltney. Published by Cherokee Publications, Cherokee, North Carolina, 1988.

Cornmeal Biscuits
You Need

1 1/2 cups all-purpose flour

1/2 cup fine yellow cornmeal

1/2 teaspoon salt (optional)

1/4 teaspoon pepper (optional)

1 tablespoon sugar or honey

4 teaspoons baking powder

7 tablespoons cold butter or margarine

1 large egg, lightly beaten

1/2 cup milk, buttermilk, or soffkee

baking sheet; medium bowl; mixing spoon; fork, table knife, or pastry blender; lightly floured board; rolling pin; 1 1/2-inch biscuit cutter

1. Preheat the oven to 450°F. Lightly grease the baking sheet.
2. Combine the flour, cornmeal, salt (if using), pepper (if using), sugar or honey, and baking powder in the bowl.
3. Cut the butter or margarine into the dry ingredients with the fork, table knife, or pastry blender until the dough is crumbly.
4. Stir in the beaten egg and milk or soffkee, blending well until the dough can be gathered into a ball. Turn the dough out onto the board.
5. Pat the dough into a large circle, then roll it out to a 1/2-inch thickness. Cut out the biscuits, then place them on the baking sheet. Gather and reshape the dough scraps and cut out more biscuits. Repeat until you have used all the dough. You should have about 16 biscuits.
6. Bake the biscuits for about 15 minutes, or until they are lightly browned. Serve them warm with soffkee.

Mississippi Mud Pie

*by E. Barrie Kavasch
and Jane Scherer*

Two fragrant, aromatic "beans" flavor countless foods and beverages that we enjoy today. These are just two of the many gifts from prehistoric Indians in Central America and northern South America that have gone around the world many times. Here we enjoy them in a delicious, earthy dessert that honors one of America's great rivers — the "Big Muddy," or Mississippi.

The Aztec Indians considered chocolate the food of the gods. They introduced Spanish explorers to this noble wealth, which they called *xocolatl* — from *xococ,* meaning bitter, and *atl,* meaning water. Cacao seeds come from large beans with thick husks, which are attached to the trunks of cacao trees. In some regions of Central America and Mexico, they are still gathered as they were prehistorically. The beans are husked and the seeds spread out to dry in the sun. Then they are roasted and fermented to develop the distinctive, familiar flavor.

Vanilla beans come from the dried seedpods of several wild South American orchids, but principally *Vanilla planifolia.* The long, thin pods are dried in the sun, then stored for six months to a year to develop their aromatic quality. Vanilla comes from the Spanish word *vanilla,* meaning "little sheath," which refers to the appearance of the ripe bean pods.

Today these special plant gifts are common commercial foods, but their roots are truly ancient. "Discovered" and named by the Spanish five hundred years ago, chocolate and vanilla are only two of the countless native plant treasures we enjoy and take for granted.

The following pie looks like a real mud pie that has dried in the sun: crunchy on top but soft and luscious inside. If you love chocolate, you will love this recipe.

You Need

pie crust (ready-to-use dough from the dairy case or frozen pie shell)

1/4 cup (1/2 stick) margarine

3 squares baking chocolate

3 eggs

3 tablespoons corn syrup

1 1/2 cups sugar

1 teaspoon vanilla extract

pie plate, small saucepan, stirring spoons, fork, small bowl, measuring cups and spoons

1. Preheat the oven to 350°F.
2. Line a pie plate with the dough or use the frozen pie shell in its own pan.
3. Melt the margarine and chocolate in the small saucepan over low heat, stirring constantly.
4. Beat the eggs with a fork in the small bowl. Stir in the corn syrup, sugar, and vanilla extract. Pour this mixture into the saucepan and mix well with the chocolate.
5. Pour the filling into the pie crust. Bake for 35 to 40 minutes, or until the filling is set. It should be firm on top but soft inside.
6. Serve warm with vanilla yogurt or ice cream.

The Mississippi River: Father of Waters

Algonquian-speaking Indians gave the river its name, *misi sipi,* which means "big water." The Indians called it "great river" and "father of waters." These names describe this mighty river well. Flowing from northern Minnesota to the Gulf of Mexico, the Mississippi River drains forty percent of the United States and is a mile wide in some places. Thirty-one states and two Canadian provinces contribute water to its flow as it reaches to within 500 miles of the Pacific Ocean and 225 miles of the Atlantic Ocean. The 300 billion gallons of water that reach the Gulf of Mexico each day make the river's volume among the greatest in the world.

The river runs approximately 2,300 miles from its source to its mouth. Because the river meanders and sometimes changes course, it is difficult to measure it exactly. Many claim that the Missouri River, the Mississippi's largest tributary, is longer, depending on how the former is measured.

The Mississippi River was not always as long as it is now. Millions of years ago, it flowed only as far as a point just south of what is now Cairo, Illinois. There it emptied into an inlet of what is now the Gulf of Mexico, 600 miles north of its mouth today. The river itself filled in the long, shallow bay. Sediment was dropped as the river flowed out and created a low valley and much of the land that we now call Louisiana. Where the river now enters the Gulf of Mexico 100 miles downstream from New Orleans, a large delta has formed. Because 500 million tons of sediment are dropped there every year, the Louisiana shoreline grows by about 300 feet each year.

As well as influencing the shape of our country, the Mississippi River has influenced much of its history. Indians built their villages in its valley because the river provided transportation, food, and fertile land. American settlers stayed for the same reasons. Today modern cities have grown from those settlements.

Pemmican Patties

by E. Barrie Kavasch

One of many American Indian words that has been accepted for common use in the English language is *pemmican,* originally from the Cree Indians. For hundreds of years, many different tribes prepared this high-energy food mixture. Pemmican was originally made from lean, dried strips of wild meat pounded into a paste and mixed with animal fat (tallow), bone marrow, and wild berries. This mixture was then pressed into small cakes.

Some food historians think that pemmican is one of the ancestors of chili, as it could be eaten plain or mixed with boiling liquid to make soups and stews. Certainly, early chili stews began with pemmican and developed into the modern versions we know today, or into sweet *wasna,* a choice pudding-like sauce or dessert.

Sun-dried and smoked (jerked) slices of buffalo meat were pounded into tart wild plums or acidic chokecherries, along with buffalo tallow and bone marrow, to create pemmican. Shaped into small cakes or balls, this concentrated, delicious food was highly valued on long journeys or hunting trips and during ceremonies. Quantities of choice pemmican would fill a special pouch given to respected people.

You Need

1 1/2 cups yellow cornmeal

1/2 cup sunflower seeds

1/2 cup chopped peanuts or hazelnuts

1 cup dried currants or raisins

1 cup vegetable oil

1/2 cup maple syrup

measuring cups, shallow baking pan or cookie sheet, medium bowl, wooden spoon (optional), serving tray or plate, plastic wrap (optional)

1. Preheat the oven to 325°F.
2. Spread the cornmeal, sunflower seeds, and nuts evenly in the pan and toast them in the oven for 20 to 30 minutes, or until they are golden brown and fragrant. Shake the pan gently once or twice while toasting.
3. Remove the pan from the oven and cool the mixture slightly. Combine it with the remaining ingredients in the bowl. Mix well with your hands or a wooden spoon.
4. Form the pemmican into 1 1/2-inch-thick patties (like hamburgers). Arrange the patties on the serving tray or plate.
5. If you don't eat all the pemmican patties, wrap them tightly in plastic wrap and store them right away in the freezer. They'll make a nutritious snack for your next hiking trip.

Plum Raisin Bread

by E. Barrie Kavasch

Wild plums and cherries grow in many places throughout this country, especially in North and South Dakota. The Sioux harvested great quantities of each. They pounded the fruit into pemmican or used it to make cakes and other traditional foods. The Sioux also used dried wild grapes (raisins) in many foods. These two recipes were inspired by my stay at the Cheyenne River Sioux Reservation in Eagle Butte, South Dakota.

To make the plum raisin bread, you need:

1/2 cup raisins

1/4 cup boiling water

1 can (30 ounces) purple plums, drained and pitted*

1/2 cup (about 2 ounces) chopped toasted pecans or toasted hazelnuts

1/2 cup (1 stick) butter, melted

2 teaspoons baking soda

1 teaspoon salt

1 teaspoon cinnamon

1/2 teaspoon ground cloves

1/2 cup honey

1/2 cup maple syrup

2 cups all-purpose flour

additional cinnamon

measuring cups and spoons, small and medium bowls, 5- by 9-inch loaf pan, potato masher, mixing spoon, wire rack

1. Place the raisins in the small bowl. Add the boiling water and let the raisins soak for 30 minutes.

WILD PLUM

Salmon Cakes

by E. Barrie Kavasch

O Supernatural Ones!
O Swimmers!
I thank you that you are
willing to come to us.
Protect us from danger that
nothing evil may happen to
us when we eat you.

The Kwakiutl people offer this prayer each year at the beginning of the first salmon run. According to tradition, five species of Pacific Coast salmon are considered supernatural beings who live in their own villages beneath the sea. Each summer, disguised as fish, they take turns swimming up the rivers and streams to offer themselves as food to the Northwest Coast peoples. Salmon caught during these seasonal migrations receive ritual respect before they are eaten or stored.

Each tribe has its own traditions, ceremonies, and prayers for honoring, cleaning, and cooking the salmon, directed through legends given to them by the salmon people. The native people believe that ignoring these traditions will stop the salmon run.

Five salmon runs occur each year. The king, or Chinook, salmon swim up the Alaskan and Columbia rivers to spawn. Then the sockeye, coho, dog, and humpback salmon, each in its own season, migrate up coastal streams. Many people and animals prize the eggs of mature salmon as a food item. According to the traditions of some tribes, it is important to place the bones of the first salmon caught and eaten back in the river or stream.

2. Preheat the oven to 350°F. Butter and flour the loaf pan.

3. Mash the plums in the medium bowl. Add the raisins with their soaking liquid and the pecans or hazelnuts. Mix in the melted butter, baking soda, salt, 1 teaspoon cinnamon, and cloves. (The mixture will bubble.) Then add the honey and maple syrup. Blend in the flour.

4. Pour the batter into the pan. Dust the top lightly with cinnamon. Bake for about 1 hour, or until a toothpick inserted in the center comes out clean.

5. Cool the bread in the pan on the wire rack for 10 minutes. Invert the bread onto the rack and cool completely. Serve with plum butter (recipe follows).

To make the plum butter, you need:

1 can (30 ounces) purple plums in juice

1 1/2 cups sugar

potato masher, small bowl, medium-size heavy saucepan, stirring spoon, blender or food processor, ladle, jars with covers

1. Pit the plums,* then mash them in their juice in the small bowl. Transfer the fruit and juice to the saucepan and bring to a boil. Reduce the heat and simmer for about 10 minutes, stirring occasionally, until the fruit is tender. Cool slightly.

2. Purée the fruit in the blender or food processor. Return the fruit purée to the pan. Add the sugar and cook over low heat for about 1 1/4 hours, stirring frequently, until the mixture thickens to the consistency of molasses.

3. Ladle the mixture into hot jars. Be careful; the mixture will be very hot. Cover the jars and cool completely. Store them in the refrigerator. Makes about 2 1/2 cups.

*Save the pits to use as game stones for the sacred bowl game on page 119.

1 cup cooked or canned salmon, flaked

2 cups cooked, mashed white or sweet potato

1 egg, beaten

1/2 teaspoon celery seed

1/2 teaspoon dill weed

1 teaspoon chopped onions

1 teaspoon parsley

1/8 teaspoon paprika

1 cup cornmeal, crushed corn chips, or crushed corn flakes

1 cup corn oil

measuring cups and spoons, medium bowl, mixing spoon, shallow dish, frying pan, spatula

1. Combine the salmon, potato, egg, celery seed, dill weed, onions, parsley, and paprika in a medium bowl. Mix well.

2. Shape the mixture into six to eight cakes (like hamburgers). Put the cornmeal in a shallow dish and dredge each cake in it.

3. Heat the oil in the frying pan over medium heat. (Ask an adult for help with this step.) Cook the cakes for 10 minutes, or until nicely browned on the bottom. Turn the cakes with the spatula and cook for 10 minutes more, or until browned.

4. Serve the cakes hot or cold with salad, peas, corn bread, and baked potatoes.

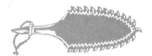

Island Ambrosia

by Doris C. Schulte

Ambrosia means food of the gods or anything with an especially delicious flavor. The main ingredient in Island Ambrosia is pineapple, which makes it an appropriate food for either Hawaiian gods or people.

A Spanish settler, Don Francisco de Paula Marin, wrote in 1813 of planting pineapple in Hawai'i. The fruit was not grown there for commercial purposes, however, until the 1880s. Next to sugar, pineapple is now Hawai'i's most important agricultural product. Pineapple plantations are found on Maui, O'ahu, and Lana'i. Much of the island of Lana'i, in fact, is one large pineapple plantation, making it the "Pineapple Island."

The coconut palm and banana plant were brought to Hawai'i by early Polynesian migrations. Bananas are still grown as a food crop, and coconuts are eaten in many ways. Island Ambrosia contains all three of these tropical fruits. The dish can be used as a salad or dessert.

You Need

1 1/2 cups fresh or canned pineapple chunks

1 cup fresh orange pieces

1 peeled and sliced banana

1 cup shredded coconut

1 cup miniature marshmallows

fresh strawberries or cherries (optional)

large bowl, wooden spoon

1. Combine all the ingredients except the strawberries or cherries in a large bowl. Mix them gently with a wooden spoon, being careful not to break the fruit.

2. Chill in the refrigerator for 1 hour or more. Serve on lettuce leaves for salad or in individual serving dishes for dessert. The ambrosia may be garnished with strawberries or cherries. Makes 6 to 8 servings.

The Life of a Salmon

by E. Barrie Kavasch

Hatched in fresh water, salmon spend much of their lives at sea, returning to fresh water only to spawn from November to January. Each salmon species has its own cycle and season. The king, or Chinook, salmon is the biggest, usually weighing around twenty pounds.

Eggs hatch in an underwater gravel nest, called a *redd,* in late April to early May. As tiny *fry,* the salmon remain in the nest area for three to five weeks, or until they have used up their rich egg sacs. As *parr,* they have become active, swimming and feeding in shoals (shallow water). After three to five years, the silvery parr, now about six inches long, begin their journey to the sea. Their bodies and skin undergo a series of changes in color, shape, and thickness from here on.

Salmon travel widely in the ocean, migrating to rich feeding grounds in some of the colder northern regions. Unfortunately, many of these isolated areas have been overharvested, which has caused a serious decline in the native salmon population.

Pacific salmon normally return to their native rivers or streams after two to four years at sea. After spawning, they usually die. Atlantic salmon also may die after spawning, but many of the smaller species make two or three more runs.

A Glossary of Native Peoples

by E. Barrie Kavasch

Some of the native peoples and culture groups noted in this book are described here. Most of these tribes predate current geopolitical boundaries, but we use these boundaries to help locate them more easily.

We have used a basic phonetic pronunciation guide for the Native American groups listed here, although most, in their own languages, do not lend themselves well to phonetics. Many native names and terms also can be said several different ways; for example, Abenaki can be said "Ab' en a kēē" or "Ab e na' kē," depending on your regional preference. The most important thing is to say them the best that you can and with respect.

— A —

Abenaki (Ab' en a kēē), "people of the dawn." Algonquian group of the northeast woodlands who lived in Vermont, New Hampshire, and southern Quebec. Many Abenaki people still live in these regions. Part of the great Wabenaki (Wa' ba na' kēē) Confederacy. (Wabenaki means "those living at the sunrise.") This confederacy, which lasted from about 1750 to 1850, also included the Penobscot, Passamaquoddy, Micmac, Maliseet, and Pennacook peoples.

Acoma (A' co ma). Pueblo people who are one of the oldest tribes in the Southwest. Acoma Pueblo also is one of the oldest inhabited settlements in New Mexico (and the United States).

Adena (A de' na). Ancient Mound Builder culture from approximately 1000 B.C. to A.D. 200 in what is now the Ohio River valley. Adena Indians constructed many impressive earth mounds, especially the Great Serpent Mound in Ohio, which is 1,330 feet long.

Alabama (Al' a bam' a), "plant gatherers." Early tribe of the powerful Creek Confederacy, for whom a state and a river are named in the Southeast.

Aleut (Al' e yōōt), "islanders." A branch of the Inuit who inhabit the chain of one hundred islands forming a "bridge" almost twelve hundred miles long between Alaska and Siberia. The Aleut fish and hunt in umiaks and kayaks, two unique types of skin-covered boats that they build.

Algonquian (Al gon' kē an); also **Algonquin** or **Algonkin.** A large group of tribes related by similar languages (dialects). Many Algonquian tribes lived in the eastern woodlands and Great Lakes regions. Eastern Algonquian tribes were among the earliest peoples to encounter European explorers and settlers.

Anasazi (Ańa saz' zē), "ancient ones." Prehistoric farmers and cliff dwellers of the Southwest who built huge planned towns at Pueblo Bonito and along Chaco Canyon in what is now northern New Mexico. The Anasazi lived between 900 B.C. and A.D. 1100 in the Four Corners region, where present-day New Mexico, Arizona, Utah, and Colorado come together. They were probably distant ancestors of the Hopi.

Anishinabé (Ah nish' ih na' bey), "first people"; also known as **Chippewa** (**Ojibway** in Canada). These Algonquian-speaking peoples of the Great Lakes region of North America originated in the Northeast and migrated west to the Great Lakes. *See also* Chippewa.

Apache (A patch' ēē). Numerous Apache bands (tribes) live in the Southwest, where they have adapted various ways of life. They are skilled basket makers and are especially noted for their ceremonial dances, ritual beliefs, and art.

Arapaho (A rap' a hō'). Various branches of Arapaho live across the Great Plains, from Oklahoma to the Wind River Reservation in Wyoming. Like many other Plains Indians, they are noted for their highly evolved social organizations, especially their warrior and medicine societies, and their art.

Arctic peoples (Ark' tik). Different from other Native American groups, the distinctive Inuit (Eskimos), Inupiat, and Aleut share many unique cultural traits that have helped them survive for thousands of years in some of the world's harshest and most beautiful environments.

A:shiwi, Áshiwi (A shē´ wē). *See* Zuni.

Assiniboin (As sin´ uh boin´), "those who cook with stones" (which refers to the early method of lifting hot stones from the fire and placing them in containers of water to heat it); also **Assiniboine.** Different bands of Assiniboin hunted broadly across the Great Plains to northern Canada. They are noted for their social organization, spirituality, and art. *See also* Sioux.

Aztec (Az´ tek). Native Nahuatl-speaking Indians of central Mexico (Mesoamerica). Aztec warriors conquered many neighboring tribes and built a great empire. They kept records in hieroglyphics, a traditional form of picture writing.

— B —

Bella Coola (Bel´ la Cool´ a). Distinctive group of the lower Northwest Coast. The Bella Coola live in British Columbia, where rich natural resources sustain one of the densest concentrations of native peoples.

Biloxi (Bi lox´ ē). A small southeastern tribe who have merged to some extent with the Tunica and have settlements in Louisiana, Oklahoma, and East Texas.

Blackfeet; also **Blackfoot.** Three closely allied tribes of the northern plains — the Blood, Piegan, and Siksika. Today they are centered in Browning, Montana, and in Canada. They were early buffalo hunters and noted warriors, as well as traders and artists.

Brulé Sioux (Brū le´ Sue´), "burned." Deeply traditional Lakota people who live on the Rosebud Reservation in southwestern South Dakota. The Brulé (Sichangu) are one of seven bands of the Teton Sioux. Originally woodland Indians of the upper Mississippi River region, they migrated west to the Black Hills.

— C —

California Indians. Diverse, bountiful environments sustained a great concentration of tribes. Some of them (north to south) are the Hoopa, Yurok, Pomo, Maidu, Miwok, Yokut, Chumash, and Mission Indians. *See* individual listings.

Catawba (Ca taw´ ba), "people of the river." Agricultural village Indians who settled in river valleys in the southeast region that became North and South Carolina. Since the late 1700s, they have centered mostly in South Carolina.

Cayuga (Kī yōō´ ga), "people of the marsh." One of the original five tribes of the Iroquois League who lived in the Finger Lakes region of central New York State. They now have settlements in New York and Canada.

Cayuse (Kī yōos´). Indians of northern Oregon and southeastern Washington. Hunters and gatherers, they became famous horsemen of the Columbia Plateau and Great Basin region. Today many live on the Umatilla Reservation in Pendleton, Oregon.

Cherokee (Chair´ o kēē). Largest of the southeastern tribes, the Cherokee originally settled broad homelands in the southern Appalachian Mountains, the Blue Ridge, the Great Smoky Mountains, and eastern Tennessee. Skilled hunters, traders, warriors, farmers, and medicine people, they were forced, through government removal, to walk the Trail of Tears in the fall and winter of 1838–39. More than four thousand Cherokee died along the way. Today tribal headquarters are located in Tahlequah, Oklahoma (in the West), and Cherokee, North Carolina (in the East).

Cheyenne (Shy ann´), "red talkers" or "people of a different speech." Originally village farmers of the Great Lakes region, the Cheyenne migrated to the Great Plains and have endured centuries of bloody conflict. Today most northern Cheyenne live on their reservation in Lame Deer, Montana. The southern Cheyenne share federal trust lands with the southern Arapaho in Concho, Oklahoma.

Chickasaw (Chick´ a saw). Southeastern and Mississippian people close to the Creek and Choctaw Indians in many respects. Chickasaw agricultural village settlements were noted for their hospitality. In the early 1800s, many Chickasaw relocated west of the Mississippi River, where they are today noted as one of the Five Civilized Tribes.

Chinook (Shi nook´); also **Tsinuk.** People of the Columbia River in Washington State, the Chinook were famous traders, fishermen, and artists. The word "chinook" also refers to the strong winds blowing from the western Pacific across the general area of the Chinook's tribal homelands and to the Chinook salmon.

Chippewa (Chip´ uh wa). Largest and most powerful Algonquian tribe of the Great Lakes, especially western Lake Superior, and noted farmers, fishermen, artists, and healers, famed for their Midéwiwin (Grand Medicine Society). Today they are located on reservations in Wisconsin, Minnesota, Michigan, Montana, North Dakota, Ontario, and Manitoba, as well as elsewhere. In Canada, they are called **Ojibway.** *See also* Anishinabé.

Chitimacha (Chit i ma´ cha). Southeastern tribe of the Mississippi Delta in what is now lower Louisiana. The Chitimacha were skilled hunters, fishermen, farmers, and artists noted for their blowguns and intricately plaited split river-cane baskets.

Choctaw (Choc´ taw). Skilled farmers, plant gatherers, fishermen, hunters, and artists, the Choctaw are descendants of the ancient Mound Builders. Though generally peaceful, the Choctaw were among the first to be relocated to the West in 1830, suffering great losses along the way. Today the western Choctaw hold trust lands in Durant, Oklahoma, and the eastern Choctaw have a reservation near Pearl River, Mississippi.

Chumash (Choo´ mash). Pacific Coast plant gatherers and fishermen noted for their cedar-plank boats. Their homelands were in central California, near present-day Santa Barbara. Disease and settlement pressure drove them to the edge of extinction.

Cochiti (Kō´ chi tī). Pueblo people on the Rio Grande south of Santa Fe, New Mexico. These southwestern people are noted farmers, jewelry makers, and potters. They are especially noted for their clay storyteller dolls.

Comanche (Cō man´ chee). Noted horsemen, buffalo hunters, and traders of the southern plains with a long and colorful tribal history. The tribe is now centered in Lawton, Oklahoma.

Coushatta (Cō sha´ ta); also **Koasati** (Kō a sat´ ē). Originally lived in what is now Alabama and were members of the Creek Confederacy. Village farmers, they were removed to Indian Territory (Oklahoma) in 1830, where many still live; other Coushatta live in Louisiana, Texas, and Alabama.

Cree. Canadian Algonquian hunters, scouts, fur traders, and artists of the subarctic region. Disease and conflicts reduced their numbers considerably, but they are widespread in Canada and share the Chippewa Reservation in Montana. They have garnered public support for their "Save James Bay" campaign against a Canadian hydroelectric project that they believe would destroy their homeland.

Creek. Village farmers, hunters, gatherers, and artists, the Creek were probably descendants of the Temple Mound Builders of the prehistoric Southeast. The Muskogee, Alabama, Coushatta, and many other bands were part of the Creek Confederacy. Their villages were located along rivers and creeks. Their forced removal from their homeland in 1836 caused many deaths. Today their tribal centers are in Alabama, and the Creek Confederacy is in Okmulgee, Oklahoma.

Crow; also Absaróke (Ab sar´ ōke), "bird people." Buffalo hunters, scouts, and plant gatherers of the Great Plains, the Crow were early relatives of the Hidatsa of the upper Missouri River. Today the Crow Reservation is in Montana, where the tribe is famous for its annual fair, rodeo, and sun dance.

— D —

Dakota (Da kō´ ta), "allies"; also **Lakota** or **Nakota.** The Santee Sioux and their four bands (Sisseton, Wahpeton, Wahpekute, and Mdewkanton) are the Dakota people, for whom two U.S. states are named. Eastern Sioux, they blend many woodland and prairie Indian traditions in their culture.

Delaware. Considered the "grandfather people" to many eastern tribes, the Delaware [many of whom prefer their own name, **Lenni Lenape** (Len´ni Le nap´ e), or "true men"] originally lived in the area that became New York, Delaware, New Jersey, and Pennsylvania, and many still do. Named for Lord De La Warr, the first governor of Virginia, this tribe suffered the early pressures of settlement period conflicts, which forced many to move to Canada and Oklahoma.

Desert people and **cliff dwellers.** Prehistoric Indians of the desert Southwest who lived during what is called the Formative Period, from about 1000 B.C. to A.D. 1500. These complex ancient cultures are noted for their artistic accomplishments and social organization. They were the ancestors of some of today's native tribes. We call them the ancient Mogollon, Hohokam, and Anasazi, among others. *See* individual listings.

Diné (Din eh´), "the people." Migrated from the North to the Southwest perhaps 1,000 years ago. Horsemen, farmers, weavers, jewelers, and noted healers and medicine people, the Diné (more commonly known as the **Navajo** or **Navaho**) have become our biggest tribal nation, with more than 250,000 members. They are centered on the Navajo Reservation, covering almost 16 million acres in the Four Corners region.

— E —

Erie (Ear´ ē), "wild cats" or "nation of the cat." Iroquois Indians living in southern Canada until the mid-1600s, when they were decimated by tribal conflicts over the rich fur trade.

Eskimo (Es´ ki mō). *See* Inuit, Inupiat.

— F —

Fox; also Mesquakie (Mes kwak´ ee), "red earth people." Prairie Algonquians of the western Great Lakes; also known as "people of the calumet" because of their sacred pipes (calumets), which they used in their ceremonies. They were close allies of the Sac, and they now have reservations and trust lands in Oklahoma, Iowa, and Kansas.

— G —

Ganiengehaka (Gon ie yeh´ ga), "people of the flint country." *See* Mohawk.

Great Lakes tribes. Algonquian Indians who lived around the Great Lakes include the Kickapoo, Sac (Sauk), Fox, Chippewa (Ojibway), Ottawa, Potawatomi, and Menominee. *See* individual listings.

Gros Ventre (Grōw Van´ tru), "big belly." Once members of the Blackfeet Confederacy, the Gros Ventre were skilled buffalo hunters of the plains. They now share the Fort Belknap Reservation in northern Montana with the Assiniboin. *See also* Hidatsa.

— H —

Haida (Hī´ da). Northwest Coast tribe of woodworkers, totem pole carvers, boat builders, and fishermen who lived on the Queen Charlotte Islands off the coast of British Columbia. They built huge plank houses of native cedar and spruce and were noted weavers, artists, and potlatch (ritual gift-giving) people. Today they live in Canadian villages near their original homelands.

Haudenosaunee (Hō´ dāy nō shōw´ nēē), "people of the longhouse." More commonly known as **Iroquois** (Iro quoy´), the League of the Six Nations: Oneida, Onondaga, Seneca, Cayuga, Mohawk, and Tuscarora. Village agriculturists, warriors, statesmen, medicine people, and artists, the Haudenosaunee maintain reserves in Quebec and Ontario and reservations in New York and Wisconsin. They are noted for their clans, longhouse traditions, and system of government, which influenced the formation of the U.S. government. *See* individual listings.

Havasupai (Ha va sōō´ pī), "people of the blue-green water." Canyon dwellers of the desert Southwest, these peaceful village agriculturists irrigated fields along the Colorado River and grew corn, squash, beans, sunflowers, melons, and tobacco. They continue to live in their homelands along the rim of the Grand Canyon.

Hawaiians. Polynesian and other Pacific islanders were prehistoric settlers of the eight Hawaiian Islands, earlier known as the Sandwich Islands. Fishermen, farmers, and village dwellers, Hawaiians established royal families and were ruled by a king and queen. More than two hundred years of settlement, exploitation, and disease have reduced the native population, but they remain strong in their traditions.

Hidatsa (He dot´ suh); also **Minitari** (Mi ni tar´ ēē), originally called **Gros Ventre** (Grōw Van´ tru) by French trappers and traders. Traders, hunters, artists, and village farmers who built earth lodges on bluffs overlooking the Missouri River. Today the Hidatsa share reservation life and enterprises with the Mandan and Arikara (Three Affiliated Tribes) near Fort Berthold, North Dakota. *See also* Gros Ventre.

Hohokam (Hō hō´ kam), "the vanished ones." Prehistoric desert farmers of the arid Southwest who lived in the Gila and Salt river valleys from 100 B.C. to A.D. 1500. They were noted for their extensive irrigation systems and ancient ball courts, which seem to reflect a close association with the ancient Mesoamerican cultures. Their etched shells, stylized pottery, weavings, and mounds have remained as striking reminders of this sophisticated early culture.

Hopewell Culture (Hopewellian). Ancient Mound Builder culture centered in the prehistoric Ohio, Illinois, and Mississippi river valleys from about 300 B.C. to A.D. 700. The Hopewell Indians were skilled craftspeople who established widespread trading networks and left us haunting, artistic reminders of their presence.

Hopi (Hō´ pēē), "peaceful ones." Westernmost of the Pueblo peoples in the desert Southwest, the Hopi were peaceful mesa villagers and arid farmers who lived along the Colorado Plateau. Their homeland has become part of northeastern Arizona. The Hopi are now famous for their masked kachina dances, religious festivals, and ceremonies.

Hualapai (Wah´ la pī), "pine tree people" (after the piñon pine); also **Walapai**. Hunter-gatherers in the Colorado River region, now northwest Arizona. Today their tribal center is near Peach Springs, Arizona, near the Grand Canyon.

Hunkpapa Sioux (Hunk´ pa pa Sue´). Westernmost band of Teton Sioux (Lakota) living in the Black Hills region of South Dakota, eastern Wyoming, and Montana. Skilled horsemen, buffalo hunters, statesmen, and artists, they followed their chief Sitting Bull in opposing the gold miners and U.S. Cavalry in the sacred Black Hills during the late 1800s. Many continue to live on reservation and trust lands in the Dakotas and surrounding regions.

Huron (Hur´ on), "rough"; also **Wyandot** (Wȳ´ un dot´), "islanders" or "peninsula dwellers." Northern Iroquoian hunters and traders of the Great Lakes region of Ontario. The Huron also were noted farmers who located their longhouse villages on river plateaus. They were nearly exterminated during the Fur Trading Wars in the 1600s. Today tribal members live in the United States and Canada.

148

— I —

Illinois (Ill in noi´). Woodland and prairie Algonquian buffalo hunters and traders who were decimated by Indian conflicts, disease, and westward expansion. They were removed to Indian Territory west of the Mississippi River in 1833, where they live today.

Inuit (In´ you it), "the real people." Subarctic and Arctic native peoples, often called Eskimos, who are closely related to the Inupiat, Kaladlît (of Greenland), and Aleut, who live in these broad circumpolar regions.

Inupiat (In you´ piat), "the real people"; also **Inupiaq.** People of Alaska and western Canada (where they are called Inuit). These dynamic Arctic and subarctic peoples, often called Eskimos, are hunters, fishermen, and skilled craftsmen. Their numerous villages are organized into six native corporations according to the Alaska Native Claims Settlement Act of 1971. Canada also has set aside considerable territory in the Northwest Territories for the Inuit.

Iowa (Ī´ ō wa); also **Ioway.** Buffalo hunters, horsemen, and farmers of the Mississippi and Missouri river valleys who suffered many of the same fates as the Illinois Indians and also were removed to Indian Territory in 1833, where many live today.

Iroquois (Iro quoy´). *See* Haudenosaunee.

— J —

Jicarilla Apache (Hē ca rēēl´ ya A patch´ ēē). Noted basket weavers, hunters, and gatherers of New Mexico and Colorado. One of numerous Apache groups, each with its own bands, living in the Southwest. Elaborate ceremonies, dances, and artwork are hallmarks of their culture.

— K —

Kaladlît (Kal ad´ lît). *See* Inuit.

Karok (Kar´ ok). Closely related to the Yurok and Hoopa, and fine basket makers, the Karok are one of the numerous California Indian tribes who were hunters and gatherers in their rich environments.

Kickapoo (Kick´ a pōō). Originally Great Lakes Algonquians of the Wisconsin River region, the Kickapoo tribe divided into different branches and, as warriors and hunter-gatherers, moved to other regions. Today their settlements are in Kansas, Oklahoma, and Mexico.

Kiowa (Kī´ ō wa), "the main people." Migratory hunters and warriors of the Great Plains and allies of the Apache and Comanche, with whom they share trust lands in Oklahoma. Today their tribal economies are enhanced by farming and oil leases. Their tribal headquarters is in Carnegie, Oklahoma.

Kittitas (Ki´ ti tas). *See* Northwest Coast Indians.

Klickitat (Klik´ i tat). *See* Northwest Coast Indians.

Koasati (Kō a sat´ ē). *See* Coushatta.

Kwakiutl (Kwah´ kēē ōō´ tel). Distinctive Northwest Coast tribe of northern Vancouver Island. The Kwakiutl were hunters, fishermen, skilled woodcarvers, totem pole carvers, and craftsmen. They were most noted for their potlatches (feasts of giving) and mystical religious societies, with elaborate rites, masks, and rituals. Today there are ten Kwakiutl bands in British Columbia, and the salmon industry is of central importance.

— L —

Lakota (La kō´ tah), "allies." Principally the Teton Sioux. Dynamic western plains tribes of the Black Hills, the Lakota bands are the Brulé (Sichangu), Oglala, Hunkpapa, Two Kettles, Blackfeet, Miniconjou, and Sans Arcs. They continue to be centered on their reservations in the Dakotas and surrounding regions. *See* individual listings.

— M —

Makah (Mah kaw´), "cape dwellers." Tribe of the rugged Northwest Coast, specifically the Olympic Peninsula of Washington State, where they were noted fishermen (whalers), hunter-gatherers, basket weavers, and carvers. Their reservation is in Neah Bay, Washington.

Maliseet (Mal´ uh sēēt); also **Malecite.** Allies of the Micmac and once part of the Wabenaki Confederacy (*see* Abenaki). These northeast woodland Algonquians are centered in Maine and Canada, where their bands maintain reserve lands.

Mandan (Man´ dan). Plains Indians settled along the Missouri River. They were village farmers, buffalo hunters, gatherers, and neighbors of the Arikara and Hidatsa. Today these Three Affiliated Tribes share land and similar ways of life at Fort Berthold, North Dakota.

Menominee (Muh nom´ uh nēē), "wild rice people." Great Lakes Algonquians, the Menominee were hunters, fishermen, and traders noted for their tobacco and kinnikinnick, used in their calumets (special pipes). Settlement and federal pressures, along with development of the rich resources on their lands, have forced the Menominee to the brink of decline. They continue to work for proper restitution.

Micmac (Mick´ mack), "allies." Maritime Algonquians, allies of the Maliseet, and members of the Wabenaki Confederacy (*see* Abenaki). The Micmac were woodland hunter-gatherers and fishermen noted for their fine craftsmanship. Today they live mainly on reserves in Nova Scotia, New Brunswick, and Prince Edward Island.

Mikasuki (Mick a sōō´ kēē); also **Miccosukee.** Close allies of the Seminole Indians of the South, with a reservation in Florida. These hunter-gatherers, artists, and village dwellers are developing their traditions for modern economic benefit.

Miniconjou (Mi ni con´ jou). *See* Lakota.

Mississippi Culture (Mississippian). An ancient Mound Builder culture centered along the Mississippi River and beyond, from Oklahoma to Florida. Also known as the Temple Mound Builders, they flourished from about A.D. 700 to 1150. Their great site at Cahokia (in Illinois) covered about four thousand acres, contained eighty-five mounds, and may have housed as many as forty thousand people.

Miwok (Mēē´ wok). *See* California Indians.

Mogollon Culture (Mō ´gol yon). Prehistoric Southwest farming people who lived between 300 B.C. and A.D. 1300 and cultivated the high mountain valleys, planting corn, squash, beans, cotton, sunflowers, and tobacco. They were noted for their pit houses, kivas (underground ceremonial chambers), weavings, and exquisite black-on-white pottery.

Mohawk (Mo´ hawk); also **Ganiengehaka** (Gon ie yeh´ ga), "people of the flint country." Easternmost of the six Iroquois nations and "keepers of the eastern door" for the Iroquois League, they were longhouse village farmers, warriors, hunters, traders, and statesmen. The Mohawk are noted today as "walkers of high steel" (steelworkers with very special abilities to work at great heights, as on skyscrapers and bridges), a tradition that began in 1886 with the first bridge built across the St. Lawrence River. Mohawk reserves and reservations are located in upper New York State and Canada.

Mohegan (Mō hēē´ gan), "the wolf people." Algonquian hunter-gatherers, traders, and village farmers of the eastern woodlands. Today, with federal recognition and development plans, the Mohegan live in eastern Connecticut on their own private lands and are establishing reservations, trust lands, and economic projects for their future.

Montagnais (Mon tun yay´), "mountaineers." Canadian Algonquian Indians, neighbors of the Naskapi and Cree. Hunter-gatherers and fishermen, they traveled seasonally across the vast subarctic region. Today the Montagnais live on reserves in northern Quebec and continue their traditions in the spirit of their ancestors.

Montauk (Mon tauk´). Northeast coast Algonquians of Long Island who established a confederacy of neighboring Algonquian tribes. They were whalers, fishermen, farmers, and hunter-gatherers. Their descendants live on the Shinnecock and Poospatuck reservations in southern and eastern Long Island.

Mound Builders. Prehistoric Indians of three distinct cultural groups — Adena, Hopewell, and Mississippian cultures — who lived in central and eastern North America from about 1000 B.C. to A.D. 1500. They were farmers, potters, traders, and skilled artists and craftsmen who built fabulous earth mounds and villages. These ancient peoples had sophisticated, highly organized ways of life and are considered the ancestors of many modern tribes.

— N —

Nanticoke (Nan´ ti cōke). Eastern Algonquian people of the broad Chesapeake Bay area; neighbors of the Susquahannock, Delaware, Mahican, and Powhatan Confederacy. Tribal groups are still centered in Delaware and New Jersey.

Narragansett (Nar´ ra gan´ sit), "people of the point"; also **Narraganset.** Eastern Algonquians who lived in stockaded villages in what is now Rhode Island and surrounding regions. Hunter-gatherers, fishermen, farmers, warriors, and traders, the Narragansett were early allies of the English. Although they dispersed during the historical period, the Narragansett are still centered in Rhode Island, near Charlestown, where their tribal headquarters and longhouse are located.

Natchez (Natch´ ez). Temple Mound Builders of the lower Mississippi River region who maintained well-organized villages and agricultural-hunting economies. This powerful group was dispersed as a result of early settlement conflicts and relocations. The remnants settled and intermarried among other southern tribes.

Navajo or **Navaho** (Nah´ vuh hō). *See* Diné.

Nez Perce (Nez´ Perse´ or Nay´ Per say´), "pierced-noses"; also **Nee-me-poo** or **Nimipu** (Ni mi´ pōō), "the people." Hunter-gatherers, fishermen, and horsemen of the central plateau region, centered in the Snake and Salmon river areas. Today their tribal centers are the Colville Reservation near Nespelem, Washington, and the Nez Perce Reservation near Lapwai, Idaho.

Northeast woodland Indians. Cultural group defined by scholars because of similarities in ways of life and geography. Many Iroquois and Algonquian tribes lived in the region from southern Canada to North Carolina and from the Atlantic Ocean to the Mississippi River. Much of this area was once woodland. Descendants of many of these early tribes continue to live in this region.

Northwest Coast Indians. Populated a long, narrow stretch of Pacific Ocean coastline from northern California to southern Alaska. These totem pole cultures prospered in the rich, warm, mountainous terrain of heavy rainfall and generous resources from the sea and inland rivers, where they continue to live.

— O —

Oglala Sioux (Ōg la´ la Sue´). Band of Teton Sioux (Lakota) who were skilled horsemen and buffalo hunters of the high plains. They were noted for their tipis, buffalo robes, war shields, military and medicine societies, and sacred medicine bundles. Many continue to live on reservation and trust lands in the Dakotas and elsewhere.

Ojibway (Ō jib´ way). *See* Anishinabé, Chippewa.

Okanagon (Ō ka na´ gun), "those who see to the top." Columbia Plateau people who share the Colville Reservation in Nespelem, Washington, with nine other tribes, including the Klickitat and Columbia Indians.

Omaha (Ō´ ma haw), "those going against the current." A Missouri River tribe of the Great Plains who, as village farmers, lived in earth lodges much of the year. Today they are centered on reservation lands in Nebraska near the Winnebago Indians.

Oneida (Ō nī´ da), "people of the standing stone." One of the five tribes in the original Iroquois League who were noted village farmers and longhouse people. Today they hold land in New York, Wisconsin, and Canada, where their traditions are blending with modern ways of life.

Onondaga (Onon dag´ a), "people of the hills." "Keepers of the council fire," as well as "keepers of the wampum," for the traditional Iroquois League. The central tribe in the Iroquois League, and considered the "faith keepers," the Onondaga are centered today near Nedrow, New York, where their rich traditions are blending with modern ways.

O'Odham (Ō Ōd´ am), "desert people," are the Papago (Pa´ pa gō), "bean people," and Pima (Pēē´ ma). They are considered to be descendants of the ancient Hohokam ("the vanished ones") of the arid Southwest. They were village farmers, hunter-gatherers, and peaceful artists. Today the Pima share the Salt River and Gila River reservations with the Maricopa and the Ak Chin Reservation with the Papago.

Osage (Ō´ sage). Seminomadic prairie Indians who were buffalo hunters and village farmers. Today the Osage are centered near Pawhuska, Oklahoma, where oil reserves and other economic resources enrich their lives.

Ottawa (Ott´ a wa). *See* Great Lakes tribes.

— P —

Paiute (Pī´ oot). Numerous bands of Paiute ranged widely across the rugged Great Basin region, hunting, gathering, and fishing for salmon. Their seasonal migrations followed diverse natural resources. Today the Paiute have reservations in California, Nevada, Utah, Oregon, and Arizona.

Papago (Pa´ pa gō), "bean people." Seminomadic farmers in the desert Southwest. Today there are three Papago reservations in Arizona, plus Papago lands in Mexico, in the Sonoran Desert. *See also* O'Odham.

Passamaquoddy (Pas´ sa ma kwod´ ēē), "those who pursue the pollack." Northeastern Algonquian fishermen, hunter-gatherers, and farmers of the Wabenaki Confederacy (*see* Abenaki). Their two reservations are near Calais, Maine.

Pawnee (Paw nēē´). Village traders and noted farmers of the prairies and plains, the Pawnee are relatives of the Caddo, Arikara, and Wichita. Their historic lands were in Nebraska and Kansas. Today they are centered in Pawnee, Oklahoma, near the Ponca and Oto Missouria people, and they return periodically to their homelands.

Penobscot (Pe nob´ scot), "the rocky place." Northeastern Algonquian fishermen and hunter-gatherers of the Wabenaki Confederacy (*see* Abenaki). Their reservation on Indian Island, near Old Town, Maine, also embraces numerous other islands in the Penobscot River.

Pequot (Pē´ quot), "destroyers" or "fox people." Northeastern Algonquian fishermen, hunter-gatherers, traders, and warriors of eastern Connecticut and coastal islands. This powerful tribe dominated early historic trade and intertribal and Colonial warfare. Today their tribal headquarters are on the Mashantucket Pequot Reservation in Ledyard, Connecticut, and the Paucatuck Pequot Reservation in North Stonington, Connecticut. Mashantucket has achieved federal recognition and operates successful tribal enterprises, which enrich the economies of southern New England. This is a most remarkable feat for a tribe considered to have been nearly exterminated in the early Colonial period.

Pima (Pēē´ ma), "river dwellers." Noted hunter-gatherers and village farmers of the arid Southwest considered to be descendants of the ancient Hohokam. The Pima irrigated their extensive fields and grew corn, squash, beans, tobacco, and cotton. Today the Pima and Maricopa Indians share the Salt River and Gila River reservations.

Plains Indians. Mounted horsemen, buffalo hunters, tipi dwellers — symbols of America's frontier and the heart of Indian America. More than twenty tribes lived and hunted across the immense prairies and plains of our continent's midsection. The Great Plains reach from central Canada south into Texas and from the Mississippi and Missouri rivers west to the Rocky Mountains. Each tribe had its own history, traditions, and ways of life, but they shared this broad geographic region and some similar customs.

Pomo (Pō´ mō). Hunter-gatherers, village traders, and noted medicine people in California. The Pomo continue to be some of the finest basket weavers in America. Today they live on several reservations, the largest in Mendocino County, California.

Ponca (Pon´ ka). Peaceful Plains Indians, buffalo hunters, and village farmers, the Ponca migrated west from southern Minnesota to Nebraska. Like most tribes, they suffered hunger, disease, displacement, and conflicts. Today they live on allotted land in Oklahoma and Nebraska.

Potawatomi (Pot´ a wat´ a mēē), "people of the fire." Great Lakes Algonquians who were hunter-gatherers, farmers, medicine people, and artists, with a history of hardships and complex migrations. Their migration from Indiana in 1838 was called the Trail of Death because so many died. Today the various bands have reservations in Ontario, Wisconsin, Michigan, Kansas, and Oklahoma.

Powhatan (Pow a tan´ or Pow hat´ un), "at the falls." Eastern Algonquian confederacy of the 1500s and 1600s comprising about thirty bands living in more than two hundred villages in the region that is now Virginia. Also, the name given to their powerful peace chief, father of Pocahontas. Persecution, disease, warfare, and intermarriage reduced their numbers considerably. The Powhatan continue to live in Virginia today, on the Pamunkey and Mattaponi reservations. Other bands live throughout the East as the Rappahannock, Potomac, Nansemond, and Chickahominy peoples, among others.

Pueblo Indians (Pweb´ lō), "village." Many different village dwellers of the Southwest. The Hopi, Zuni, and Rio Grande tribes — Tewa (Tiwa), Jemez (Towa), and Acoma (Keres), among others — are considered to be the descendants of the ancient Anasazi and Mogollon peoples. Their Arizona and New Mexico homelands reflect their traditional ways of life and architecture (stone and adobe terraced, multistory pueblos).

— S —

Sac (Sack), "yellow earth people"; also **Sauk.** Western Great Lakes Algonquian hunters and village farmers who were close allies of the Fox, "red earth people." Today the Sac and Fox share small reservations and trust lands in Iowa, Kansas, and Oklahoma.

Sans Arcs (Sans´ Arks´). *See* Lakota.

Sauk (Sack). *See* Sac.

Seminole (Sem´ in ole), "runaways." Tribe comprising various southeastern Algonquian tribes — Creeks and remnants of others — who were driven out of their homelands in Georgia and Alabama and sought to maintain their hunting and village farming ways of life in Florida. Many thousands were forceably removed during the Trail of Tears in 1838–39, but many hid out and fought to remain. They now have five reservations in southern Florida, as well as trust lands in Texas and Oklahoma.

Seneca (Sen´ e ca), "people of the great hill." "Keepers of the western door" for the Iroquois League. Noted hunters, village farmers, statesmen, and medicine people, they now have three reservations in western New York and additional parcels of leased land.

Shawnee (Shaw nēē´), "southerners." Algonquian people of the western Cumberland Mountains who ranged over considerable territory. Frequent rebellions and wars contributed to their decline and displacement. Today the Shawnee share trust lands in Oklahoma.

Shinnecock (Shin´ ne cock). Long Island Algonquian hunters, farmers, and fishermen who were famous for their wampum (shell beads). The Shinnecock are centered today on an extensive reservation in Southampton, Long Island, where they continue to develop tribal enterprises, especially their ethnobotany and oyster projects.

Shoshone (Show show´ nēē). Tribe living in the high, arid Great Basin region west of the Rocky Mountains, where hunting and foraging were important to their lifestyles. Today they share reservation and trust lands in Utah, Idaho, Nevada, and California.

Sioux (Sue). *See* Dakota, Lakota.

Snohomish (Snōw hōmeʹ ish). *See* Northwest Coast Indians.

— T —

Tewa (Tēēʹ wa); also **Tiwa**. *See* Pueblo Indians.

Tlingit (Klinʹ kit). Northwest Coast tribe of southern Alaska and the coastal islands of British Columbia. The Tlingit were master woodworkers, totem pole carvers, weavers, and fishermen. The salmon is still central to their economy. The Tlingit and Haida are united in the Sealaska Corporation, and each continues to develop its rich traditions and arts.

Tunica (Tuʹ ni ka). *See* Biloxi.

Tuscarora (Tuskʹ a roarʹ a), "people of the hemp." This southern Iroquoian tribe migrated north in the early 1700s to join the Iroquois League, as they sought to escape the settlement pressure and warfare of the Southeast. Today they have a reservation in northwestern New York and share reserve lands in Canada and North Carolina.

Two Kettles Sioux. *See* Lakota.

— U —

Ute (Yōōt), "land of the sun." Great Basin tribal neighbors of the Paiute and Shoshone. The Ute were nomadic hunters and gatherers. Today they are centered on three reservations in Utah and Colorado.

— W, Y, Z —

Wampanoag (Wampʹ a nōʹ ag), "people of the dawn." Coastal Algonquians of the Northeast who were noted fishermen, hunter-gatherers, village farmers, and warriors. They fought for and formed strong alliances throughout the Colonial wars. Persecution, disease, and displacement seriously eroded their land base. Today the Gay Head Wampanoag have their tribal headquarters on Martha's Vineyard, and the Mashpee Wampanoag are centered in Mashpee on Cape Cod, where their traditional sense of enterprise shapes their future.

Winnebago (Winnʹ e bayʹ gō). Great Lakes Algonquian fishermen and village farmers who share reservations with the Omaha in Nebraska and also have reservations in Wisconsin and Minnesota.

Wyandot (Wȳʹ un dotʹ). *See* Huron.

Yuchi (Yōōʹ chēē). Early farming and hunting tribe in the southeastern woodlands whose members were later absorbed into the Cherokee, Creek, and Seminole tribes.

Yuman (Yōōʹ ma), "people of the river." Southwest village farmers and hunters who lived on both sides of the Colorado River. Today they share reservation lands in Arizona, where they are developing tribal enterprises.

Yupik (Youʹ pick). Arctic people related to the Aleut, Inuit, and Inupiat, whose ancestors migrated across the Bering Strait from Siberia eight thousand to ten thousand years ago. Siberian Yupik, Pacific Yupik, and Alaskan Yupik each colonized their own unique regions and are called Eskimos. There are five separate Yupik languages.

Yurok (Yourʹ ock), "downstream people." Northern California tribe of the Klamath River territory, where they were fishermen and hunter-gatherers. Today the tribe has several small reservations (rancherias) in Humbolt County, California.

Zuni (Zōōʹ nēē), "the flesh"; also **A:shiwi** or **Áshiwi** (A shēʹ wē). Pueblo farmers and hunter-gatherers of the upper Zuni River in western New Mexico, where they originally had seven villages (pueblos). Descendants of the ancient Mogollon Culture, the Zuni are noted stonecutters, silversmiths, and jewelers. They are especially known for their festivals and dances at Zuni Pueblo, where they hold an annual fair.

Today Native Americans live every conceivable lifestyle and work at every kind of job. Many Native American men and women are tribal, business, and corporate leaders, as well as lawyers, college professors, teachers, doctors, research scientists, activists, artists, musicians, dancers, sports figures, actors, and producers. Bright success stories are reflected on many tribal reservations, yet hopelessness and grinding poverty stalk many others. Tribal leaders continue to work for greater balance and economic opportunities for their people. Many native people choose, or need, to live away from their reservations for many reasons.

A growing number of Native American people of mixed tribal descent or biracial and triracial heritage do not have specific tribal enrollment but are proud of their heritage. Many schoolchildren speak with pride about their American Indian heritage — whether they are dark-skinned, curly-haired, blond, or blue-eyed. Sometimes they know their specific ancestry; sometimes they have only heard about an Indian relative. North America is a unique multitribal, multiethnic continent that is constantly rediscovering itself. Let us celebrate these differences and use the best of each culture to enhance our American culture.

Puzzle Answers

Making Corn Grow (page 92)

acorn, scorn, corner, cornet, unicorn, tricorn, cornice, Capricorn, cornucopia, peppercorn, cornflower, cornerstone, harvest

Digging Up Artifacts (page 116)

		B	A	S	K	E	T	S		
	R	E	D		C	E	D	A	R	P	O	S	T	S
	W	H	I	T	E		P	O	T	T	E	R	Y
C	H	U	N	K	E	Y		D	I	S	K
				A	R	R	O	W	H	E	A	D
	C	O	P	P	E	R	A	N	D	B	O	N	E	F	L	U	T	E
D	I	G	G	I	N	G	S	T	I	C	K
				A	T	L	A	T	L
F	O	L	S	O	M	S	P	E	A	R	P	O	I	N	T
	C	L	O	V	I	S	S	P	E	A	R	P	O	I	N	T

Code Talker Cryptogram (page 118)

During World War Two, the Navajo Indians were among the most treasured of our fighting men. Known as the "code talkers," they could send and decipher messages in their native tongue that were undecipherable by our enemies.

The Seven Lakota Council Fires (page 123)

	1	2	3	4	5	6	7
A					T		
B				M	W		
C				I	O		
D	B		H	N		O	S
E	R	B	U	I	K	G	A
F	U	L	N	C	E	L	N
G	L	A	K	O	T	A	S
H	E	C	P	N	T	L	
I		K	A	J	L	A	A
J		F	P	O	E		R
K		E	A	U	S		C
L		E					S
M		T					

Special Message:
The Sacred Hoop of the Lakota Nation

The Akwesasne Longhouse Maze (page 120)

Acknowledgments

I am indebted to many people who have made this work possible, especially Carolyn Yoder, good friend, editor, and visionary. My gratitude also to Ted Dawes for sharing the vision, along with the entire wonderful Cobblestone family of Manuela Meier, Francelle Carapetyan, Meg Chorlian, Beth Lindstrom, Ellen Klempner-Beguin, Lisa Brown, Patricia Silvestro, Robyn Manley, Cathy Irving, Lois Kenick, Amy Brown, and Linda McNamee. Great appreciation to Peggy Cooper and the American Museum of Natural History, and to Alberto Meloni and Trudie Lamb Richmond of the Institute for American Indian Studies.

This book has been gleaned from, developed with, and inspired by many talented people. I particularly give thanks for the records, thoughts, life ways, and generosity of countless native people, to whom we are most grateful. Gratitude to Gladys Tantaquidgeon, David Richmond, Dale Carson and family, Mitzi Rawls and family, Chink Sands, Brian and Louise Miles and family, Marguerite Smith, Roddy and Josephine Smith and family, Barry Dana, Ina and Ron McNeil, Nanepashemet and the Wampanoag Indian Program at Plimoth Plantation, Nancy and Wendell Deer With Horns, Jake and Judy Swamp and family, Tom Porter and family, Ed Sarabia and family, Helen Attaquin, Gladys Widdiss, Bette Haskins, Katsi Cook and José Barriero and family, Eleanor Dove, Ella Thomas Sekatau, Joan Tavares, Slow Turtle and family, Ramona Peters, Ron and Cherrie Welburn and family, Monetta Trepp, Myra Alexander, June Hamilton and family, Mary O'Brien, and many more.

We gratefully respect the additional contributions of Cobblestone Publishing's authors and have included their bylines.

Our appreciation also to Nez Perce National Historical Park and Museum, Spalding, Idaho; The Heard Museum, Phoenix, Arizona; Museum of the Cherokee Indian, Cherokee, North Carolina; Tantaquidgeon Indian Museum, Uncasville, Connecticut; National Museum of the American Indian, New York, New York; Six Nations Indian Museum, Onchiota, New York; Iroquois Indian Museum, Howes Caverns, New York; Akwesasne Museum, Hogansburg, New York; Makah Cultural Research Center, Neah Bay, Washington; Yakima Indian Nation Museum and Cultural Center, Toppenish, Washington; Milwaukee Public Museum, Milwaukee, Wisconsin; Arrowheads/Aerospace Cultural Center and Museums, and Old Stone Fort Site and Museum, Manchester, Tennessee; Bear Butte State Park & Museum, Sturgis, South Dakota; Lenni Lenape Historical Society, Allentown, Pennsylvania; Lenape Indian Museum and Village, Stanhope, New Jersey; Moundbuilders State Memorial Museum, Newark, Ohio; Mound City Group National Monument, Chillicothe, Ohio; Serpent Mound Site & Museum, Peebles, Ohio; Mound Museum, Moundsville, West Virginia; Native American Centre for the Living Arts/Turtle Museum, Niagara Falls, New York; Black Bear Museum, Esopus, New York; Museum of the Plains Indian, Browning, Montana; Flathead Indian Museum, St. Ignatius, Montana; Pipestone Historical Museum & Site, Pipestone, Minnesota; Cahokia Mounds Historical Site & Museum, East St. Louis, Illinois; Chief John Ross House, Rossville, Georgia; Denver Museum of Natural History, Denver, Colorado; Children's Museum, Boston, Massachusetts; and the many tribal and regional resource centers, sites, and museums that have enriched our work and continue to educate us. Special appreciation to Richard West and the National Museum of the American Indian–Smithsonian.

Grateful acknowledgment of the Elders Council of the Mashantucket Pequot Indian Nation in Ledyard, Connecticut, and the Institute for American Indian Studies in Washington, Connecticut, for their vision and support.

Our gratitude also to the Native American teachers/readers on portions of this book, including the glossary: Trudie Lamb Richmond (Schaghticoke), Assistant Director of Program Planning, Institute for American Indian Studies, Washington, Connecticut; Dr. Ron Welburn (Nanticoke, Delaware, Conoy), Professor of American Literature and American Indian Studies, University of Massachusetts, Amherst; Myra Alexander (Creek), Manager of Counseling and Outreach, Native Americans in Biological Sciences, Oklahoma State University, Stillwater; Dr. Cornel Pewewardy (Comanche-Kiowa), Principal of the American Indian Magnet School and the World Cultures and Languages Magnet School in St. Paul, Minnesota.

Very personal respect, appreciation, and love to my dear family, the many elders who have taught us so much, and especially the many children we work with.

I take full responsibility for any errors or omissions in this book.

E. Barrie Kavasch is an author and illustrator of some Cherokee and Creek Indian descent. She is directly descended from Chief Powhatan, through his noted daughter Pocahontas. Kavasch is the author/illustrator of *Native Harvests: Recipes and Botanicals of the American Indians* and author/photographer of *Guide to Eastern Mushrooms, Guide to Northeastern Wild Edibles,* and *Introducing Eastern Wildflowers.* She is a trustee and research associate at the Institute for American Indian Studies in Washington, Connecticut. As a naturalist, teacher, and storyteller, Kavasch is especially proud of her Ohio, Tennessee, and Alabama roots and has deep respect for her diverse ancestry. She lives in Bridgewater, Connecticut.

Index